# Praise for
## Resilie[ncy]

"*Crisis, Compassion, and Resiliency in Student Affairs* offers insight into the often unspoken need for grit, perseverance, and self-care. The authors demonstrate how compassionate leadership in student affairs includes granting one's self grace in the midst of grief, tragedy, and uncertainty."

—BRIAN O. HEMPHILL, President, Radford University

"*Crisis, Compassion, and Resiliency in Student Affairs* centers hope and honors our noble profession, offering a path for embracing unprecedented challenges and opportunities. Our colleagues urge us to prioritize oxygen for ourselves in order to provide the compassionate leadership our students, staff, and communities need. My own journey through institutional crises and daily triage was accurately reflected; all student affairs professionals would benefit from the powerful affirmation, guide, and reminder of the import of our work."

—WENDY ENDRESS, Vice Provost for Student and Academic Life, The Evergreen State College

"Whether it is the daily critical incidents that arise, or the inevitable career-defining campus disaster, student affairs staff are consistently called upon in times of crisis. Through vivid and heartfelt accounts of campus events, *Crisis Compassion and Resiliency in Student Affairs* demonstrates the tremendous impact crisis events can have on both students and staff. The authors provide fresh insights and new perspectives on understanding traumatic events, with emphasis on how to use triage and other trauma-informed practices to support students, staff, and ourselves."

—EUGENE L. ZDZIARSKI II, Vice President for Student Affairs, DePaul University

"In *Crisis, Compassion, and Resiliency in Student Affairs*, the process of 'triage,' doing what matters most in the moment during a major campus crisis, is presented from professional and personal perspectives. The authors share their own challenges and advice on attending to the things that matter most. The book explores how to prepare for a major crisis by developing methods, training, and protocols; how to learn through reflection; and how to lead through dedication to students and staff and loyalty to the institution."

—KRISTIN S. HARPER, Executive Director, Office for Student Success, Texas A&M University

"This is one of those books that you pick up and cannot put down until you finish it. The indelible reflections and timeless wisdom shared by the authors make this an essential read for all student affairs professionals. The stories clearly illustrate the complexity of emotion we experience when responding to a wide range of campus crises, and the self-care strategies offered will help us sustain a healthier career in student affairs."

—SCOTT PESKA, Assistant Vice President of Student Services, Waubonsee Community College

"As student affairs professionals, we find ourselves called to action when there is a campus crisis. Treadwell, Russell O'Grady, and associates share their experiences with campus crises and remind us that crisis response is one of the most difficult things student affairs professionals will ever do, yet one of the most rewarding. Everyone in student affairs should read *Crisis, Compassion, and Resiliency in Student Affairs*."

—BRENT PATERSON, Assistant to the President/Chief of Staff, Illinois State University

"Only those who have truly experienced life's hard spaces with others can speak honestly about the puzzling treasure it is to serve well through crises. With compelling stories and practical wisdom, Treadwell, Russell O'Grady, and their associates invite us to re-imagine the gifts of presence in hardship. *Crisis, Compassion, and Resiliency in Student Affairs* beckons our profession to 'seize the hard day,' as it may be the most important opportunity we are given."

—FRANK SHUSHOK JR., Senior Associate Vice President for Student Affairs and Associate Professor of Higher Education, Virginia Tech; Executive Editor, *About Campus*

"Thank you for calling out my struggles with sadness as a way to find meaning and life in this work. These reflections gave me permission to tussle with my personal healing and to prioritize the listening my communities—colleagues and students—need from me. I came away from these reflections refreshed with tears and new perspectives on care for and love of my communities. I came away more human."

—KENN ELMORE, Associate Provost and Dean of Students, Boston University

# Crisis, Compassion, and Resiliency
IN STUDENT AFFAIRS

**NASPA**
Student Affairs Administrators
in Higher Education

# Crisis, Compassion, and Resiliency

## IN STUDENT AFFAIRS

*Using Triage Practices to Foster Well-Being*

KATIE L. TREADWELL,
MARIJO RUSSELL O'GRADY,
and Associates

Foreword by KEVIN KRUGER

Student Affairs Administrators
in Higher Education

Copyright © 2019 by the National Association of Student Personnel Administrators (NASPA), Inc. All rights reserved.

Published by
NASPA–Student Affairs Administrators in Higher Education
111 K Street, NE
10th Floor
Washington, DC 20002
www.naspa.org

No part of this publication may be reproduced, stored in a retrieval system, or transmitted in any form or by any means, now known or hereafter invented, including electronic, mechanical, photocopying, recording, scanning, information storage and retrieval, or otherwise, except as permitted under Section 107 of the 1976 United States Copyright Act, without the prior written permission of the Publisher.

Additional copies may be purchased by contacting the NASPA publications department at 202-265-7500 or visiting http://bookstore.naspa.org.

NASPA does not discriminate on the basis of race, color, national origin, religion, sex, age, gender identity, gender expression, affectional or sexual orientation, or disability in any of its policies, programs, and services.

**Library of Congress Cataloging-in-Publication Data**
(Prepared by The Donohue Group, Inc.)

> Names: Treadwell, Katie L., editor. | O'Grady, Marijo Russell, editor. | NASPA-Student Affairs Administrators in Higher Education, issuing body.
> Title: Crisis, compassion, and resiliency in student affairs : using triage practices to foster well-being / [edited by] Katie L. Treadwell, Marijo Russell O'Grady, and associates.
> Description: First edition. | Washington, DC : NASPA-Student Affairs Administrators in Higher Education, [2019] | Includes bibliographical references and index.
> Identifiers: ISBN 9781948213042 | ISBN 9781948213059 (ePub) | ISBN 9781948213066 (mobi)
> Subjects: LCSH: Student affairs services. | Universities and colleges--United States--Safety measures. | Universities and colleges--Security measures--United States. | Crisis intervention (Mental health services)
> Classification: LCC LB2342.9 .C75 2019 (print) | LCC LB2342.9 (ebook) | DDC 378.197--dc23

Printed and bound in the United States of America

FIRST EDITION

# Contents

Foreword — vii
*Kevin Kruger*

Introduction — xiii
*Katie L. Treadwell and Marijo Russell O'Grady*

1  Life as Triage — 1
*Marijo Russell O'Grady and Katie L. Treadwell*

2  Making Sense Out of the Senseless: A Framework for Understanding the Impact of Traumatic Events on the Lives of Student Affairs Professionals — 19
*Kevin P. Jackson*

3  All Quiet on the Campus Front . . . Not So Much? — 41
*Marijo Russell O'Grady and Laura Avitabile Wankel*

4  Collateral Beauty — 67
*Lee E. Bird*

5  Using a Trauma-Informed Framework in Student Affairs — 91
*Terry Martinez*

6  Triaging Activism, Protests, and Campus Unrest — 111
*Deb Moriarty and Santiago Solis*

7  Critical Relationships During Stormy Times — 137
*Greg Sharer*

| | | |
|---|---|---|
| 8 | Team Stewardship: Care for the Caregiver<br>*Jeffrey C. Jordan* | 157 |
| 9 | Student Affairs Administrators as Crisis Responders: The Consequences of Care<br>*Thomas Grace* | 175 |
| 10 | Faith in the Wake of Disaster<br>*Marcella Runell Hall, Rachel Alldis, and Todd M. Smith-Bergollo* | 197 |
| 11 | Learning From Tragedy<br>*Kimberly C. Thornbury* | 221 |
| 12 | A Deep Hurt and a Magnificent Hope<br>*Katie L. Treadwell* | 239 |
| | The Editors and Authors | 255 |
| | Index | 261 |

# Foreword

In my role as president of NASPA–Student Affairs Administrators in Higher Education, I have the good fortune to visit five to ten campuses each year and to meet with a wide range of senior-level student affairs administrators at a variety of NASPA meetings. If there is one common theme in the hundreds of conversations I have, it is that the work of student affairs professionals has changed dramatically over the last decade. The issues that student affairs professionals manage have become more serious, more complex, and more personally draining. I worry about our field and those who have chosen this profession as their life's work.

A reflection of a recently minted vice president for student affairs, who stated, "I've been at this for three years and I don't know how I can do this for another 20," raises a set of critical questions for student affairs. How does the student affairs profession create jobs that allow for long and satisfying careers? How does the profession sustain the effort and commitment required in the face of so many emotionally challenging experiences? How can student affairs professionals craft and shape careers that are emotionally and physically healthy for 20 to 30 years?

These questions arise from three distinct challenges facing student affairs professionals: the expanding role of student affairs around the health, safety, and well-being of students; the compelling need to focus on student success for low-income students, first-generation students, and students of color; and higher education's short- and long-term fiscal constraints.

## THREE DISTINCT CHALLENGES

The expanding role of student affairs in supporting the health, safety, and well-being of students is the most immediate and widely documented challenge. While these concerns are most acute for traditional-age college students, it is important to note that they persist through adulthood for far too many students. On virtually every campus, an ecosystem of support is required to address the wide range of mental health problems that students experience. As any student affairs professional will express, this increase in mental health issues not only directly affects clinical providers on campus, but it impacts every campus function. It is also important to note that in an educational climate that is laser-focused on student success, degree progress, and degree completion, support for students through their psychological and mental health challenges can contribute significantly to the overall campus retention strategy.

While mental health issues sometimes receive the most press coverage and attention, a broad spectrum of related well-being issues have changed the nature of student affairs work. I call this suite of issues the "big six." Student affairs plays a critical campus role in promoting mental health and suicide prevention; resolving complex sexual violence cases; advancing efforts in alcohol and other drug abuse prevention and education; responding to protests and activism; advancing social justice and inclusive campus practices; and, on many campuses, addressing the need for meaningful reform within Greek life. As we consider the purpose of this book—understanding the self-care, staff support, and planning necessary to thrive as a student affairs professional—it is important to understand the role these "big-six" issues play in the daily lives of student affairs professionals.

Another major challenge facing higher education is often framed in the context of attainment or achievement. We know that more low-income students are enrolling in higher education (National Center for Education Statistics, 2017). And we know that America, like our campuses, is becoming more racially and ethnically diverse. We also sadly must face the reality that low-income students, first-generation students, and students of color (with the exception of some parts of the Asian Pacific Islander and South Asian communities) complete higher education at about half the rate of their more privileged and largely white peers (Cahalan, Perna, Yamashita, Ruiz, & Franklin, 2016; Shapiro et al., 2017). Resolving this inequity requires re-thinking the ways in which institutions support student success on campus. The compelling needs to focus on academic pathways and advising reform and to increase coaching, mentoring, and student supports are stressing organizational structures and staff members in student success–oriented roles.

The fiscal concerns facing higher education create a challenging environment for both addressing current issues and creating future strategies. From a fiscal standpoint, higher education and student affairs are in trouble. It is widely recognized that the current fiscal models for higher education are unsustainable. A minority of institutions will only need to make minor adjustments given their elite status, but most institutions, both public and private, two-year and four-year, small and large, will deal with significant changes in the next decade. College and university chief business officers (CBOs) see this clearly. In the *2018 Survey of College and University Business Officers,* conducted by *Inside Higher Ed* and Gallup (2018), only half of CBOs feel confident that their institutions will be financially stable in the next 10 years. A decade of reductions in state appropriations to higher education, enormous pressure to control tuition and fee increases, and steady increases in the costs of providing education have all conspired to create significant financial stress at most colleges and universities. The prospect for improvement is not good, considering the subtle, yet perceptible shift in the American public's view of higher education as a private good rather than its historical place as a treasured public good. Mergers and closings, consolidation of state institutions, the increase in non-tenure track faculty, the institution of shared services, and all-too-common annual budget cuts are proverbial canaries in the coal mine. News of substantial budget restrictions, even among America's most elite colleges, are commonplace, and the solutions to guide colleges and universities forward are unclear. There is no doubt that these fiscal challenges will continue to significantly affect student affairs. The inevitable "do more with less" result of budget reductions and ongoing resource constraints comes at a cost to student affairs professionals at all levels.

The intersection of all these issues creates unprecedented uncertainty for higher education and creates a demand for solutions from families, the public, the media, and a wide range of campus stakeholders. Out of necessity, for example, the majority of campus counseling centers, intent on reducing the ratio of counselors to students, added counselors over the past five years (Tate, 2017). Where do the resources come from to support these additional positions? What is the effect on other student affairs functions? This is but one dimension of the current crisis and a good example of why *Crisis, Compassion, and Resiliency in Student Affairs* is such an important resource today.

## HOPE FOR THE FUTURE

Reading the stories shared within the following pages renews my optimism about the future of student affairs. This book reinforces the need for more lighthouses to point the way forward for the profession. We need more exemplars and role models to drive change and ensure the profession will evolve and thrive in the next decade. We are eager to hear from those student affairs leaders who have crafted personal and organizational strategies to succeed in this climate.

The history of student affairs is one of adaptation and adjustment to ever-changing student and campus ecosystems. It is, perhaps, the hallmark of the student affairs profession, and it will continue to position us well for the future.

Kevin Kruger<br>
President<br>
NASPA–Student Affair Administrators<br>
in Higher Education

## References

Cahalan, M., Perna, L., Yamashita, M., Ruiz, R., & Franklin, K. (2016). *Indicators of higher education equity in the United States: 2016 historical trend report*. Washington, DC: Pell Institute for the Study of Opportunity in Higher Education, Council for Opportunity in Education, and Alliance for Higher Education and Democracy of the University of Pennsylvania.

Inside Higher Ed & Gallup. (2018). *2018 survey of college and university business officers*. Retrieved from https://www.insidehighered.com/booklet/2018-survey-college-and-university-business-officers

National Center for Education Statistics. (2017). *The condition of education 2017* (NCES 2017-144). Retrieved from https://nces.ed.gov/pubsearch/pubsinfo.asp?pubid=2017144

Shapiro, D., Dundar, A., Huie, F., Wakhungu, P., Yuan, X., Nathan, A., & Hwang, Y. A. (2017, April). *Completing college: A national view of student attainment rates by race and ethnicity – fall 2010 cohort* (Signature Report No. 12b). Herndon, VA: National Student Clearinghouse Research Center.

Tate, E. (2017, March 29). Anxiety on the rise. *Inside Higher Ed*. Retrieved from https://www.insidehighered.com/news/2017/03/29/anxiety-and-depression-are-primary-concerns-students-seeking-counseling-services

# Introduction

### Katie L. Treadwell and Marijo Russell O'Grady

---

When Katie Treadwell began researching campus crisis leadership in 2011, Marijo Russell O'Grady was among her first phone calls. What began as two strangers meeting to discuss Russell O'Grady's experiences on 9/11 almost instantly evolved into plans for this book. Treadwell was a residence hall director at Barnard College and Russell O'Grady worked as the associate vice president and dean of students at Pace University, and like others in student affairs, as we began researching topics, we frequently turned to books, articles, and conference sessions on student crisis response to make sense of our on-the-job learning. However, we felt like something was missing. Despite our vast networks, which offered phenomenal resources, we found no guidance on the most important questions student affairs professionals ask themselves when facing crises: Am I doing enough? Did I handle the crisis correctly? What if I had identified the problem sooner? How much did the crisis change me? Why do I feel like student affairs work is getting harder? How much longer can I handle facing the everyday emotional toll of this work? The questions are endless, and the answers can often seem too elusive to pinpoint.

In creating this text, we consulted both student affairs colleagues who have guided their campuses through high-profile crises and those who manage the student emergencies that consume the attention of student affairs on a daily basis. We asked authors to share insights on their personal feelings and struggles, as well as recommendations about effective crisis leadership. The authors featured in this book represent public and private, faith-based and secular institutions. They represent a range of identities (related to race, ethnicity, professional roles, gender, sexual orientation, religion, political affiliation, and marital and parental status) and offer perspectives through their own intersectional lens. We also respect the student affairs leaders we approached to contribute to this book, but who declined to participate. Many explained that sharing their experiences of responding to major campus crises was still too painful. *Crisis, Compassion, and Resiliency in Student Affairs* does not offer easy answers or simple action steps for campus crisis response. Instead, it is intended to begin a conversation about the personal impact of leading through crisis and to create more sustainable environments for student affairs professionals to engage in this work.

Many of the authors are currently or have previously served as their institution's chief student affairs officer, dean of students, or vice president for student affairs. Some of their stories are familiar; others less so. They detail intimate recollections of their personal experiences with crises big and small, as well as practical strategies for responding to and managing them. They share essential steps for managing critical incidents and emergencies, as well as how they managed family obligations and personal wellness needs during and after the crises. Learning from experience is a hallmark of the student affairs profession, and these leaders contribute their own painful journeys to strengthen the field and help other student affairs leaders through unexpected encounters with crises.

This book is also for the more than 100,000 student affairs

professionals who serve their campuses in less senior roles: the residence hall directors, student activities coordinators, academic advisors, recreation managers, healthcare providers, student conduct professionals, violence prevention educators, and social justice advocates. These professionals also include office managers and administrative assistants, who often have the first conversations with students and parents in a crisis. Often, it is these professionals' dedication and awareness of student needs that keep crises from becoming full-scale emergencies. The book is also written for graduate assistants just beginning their journeys in student affairs and undergraduate student leaders considering their career goals. The secret to preparing for campus crises is involving all levels of staff, not only those in senior-level roles.

In chapter 1, "Life as Triage," we introduce a new way of considering the role of the student affairs leader—an approach that frames the remaining chapters. Student affairs work is, in many ways, similar to the triage approach used by medical professionals and first responders. Student affairs leaders are the first responders to the daily concerns of campus communities. The chapter also emphasizes the importance of student affairs leaders caring for themselves during crises.

In chapter 2, Kevin Jackson's model for living a triaged life and encountering crisis in student affairs pushes readers to look past the traditional view of identifying what type of crisis occurred after the fact, and instead to consider how the situation affected those individuals charged with leading through the crisis. Framed in Jackson's experience responding to the 1999 Texas A&M University bonfire collapse, "Making Sense Out of the Senseless: A Framework for Understanding the Impact of Traumatic Events on the Lives of Student Affairs Professionals" offers readers new language to define their experiences and insight into how those encounters may hold lasting implications for those involved.

Chapter 3, "All Quiet on the Campus Front . . . Not So Much?" highlights high-profile campus disasters that required a total suspension of campus operations. Russell O'Grady shares insights from her experiences with 9/11 and Hurricane Sandy, and Laura Avitabile Wankel offers a glimpse into her leadership through the Seton Hall University residence hall fire. Each was thrust into an immediate and unexpected crisis leadership role that required them to ignore their own needs to care for the campus community. They describe their emotional responses to the encounters, as well as suggestions for student affairs leaders who find themselves responsible for a campuswide crisis response.

In chapter 4, "Collateral Beauty," Lee Bird shares her unlikely encounter with two high-profile plane crashes and a vehicle that intentionally drove through a university's homecoming parade, killing several individuals. The chapter captures Bird's experiences at Oklahoma State University through a humbling and insightful look at ongoing student affairs crisis leadership. Her stories highlight the importance of building community relationships, preparing for the unexpected, and confiding in trusted friends as avenues for self-care.

In chapter 5, "Using a Trauma-Informed Framework in Student Affairs," Terry Martinez highlights the importance of the daily encounters that seldom rise to campuswide attention—the car accidents, medical emergencies, and student conduct issues that dramatically impact a single student's experience. Her applications of trauma-informed approaches to student crisis encounters offer critical reminders of considering individual perspectives when working with students. Martinez describes her realization that she needed to prioritize her own wellness, and her struggle at times to do so.

In chapter 6, Deb Moriarty and Santiago Solis share their

experiences responding to student activism, campus protests, and community unrest. As many higher education professionals know, responding to student concerns and helping their institution navigate social justice issues are among a student affairs leader's most critical—and difficult—tasks. In "Triaging Activism, Protests, and Campus Unrest," Moriarty and Solis offer timely perspectives on how they approached this task professionally and personally, as well as valuable resources and action steps all student affairs leaders can adopt when working with students.

Chapter 7, "Critical Relationships During Stormy Times," describes one institution's encounter with community unrest and the student affairs leader's role in restoring order. Greg Sharer offers invaluable advice from three critical campus partners: the institution's president, public relations director, and legal counsel. In doing so, he provides a roadmap for student affairs leaders to establish key relationships before a crisis occurs, as well as personal insights on how doing so may buoy the student affairs leader's support network in the midst of crisis.

Jeffrey Jordan shares a powerful story of encountering campus violence in chapter 8, "Team Stewardship: Care for the Caregiver." He focuses on perhaps the most critical aspect of campus crisis response—caring for the staff charged with crisis response efforts and serving students. Jordan offers personal examples and practical strategies for creating a sustainable and healthy student affairs environment, even when team members face excruciating and unprecedented tasks.

In chapter 9, Thomas Grace explores mental health implications for campus caregivers. Through "College and University Administrators as Crisis Responders: The Consequences of Care," he shares personal experiences helping a campus navigate 9/11 and other significant crises. In doing so, he introduces personal insights and meaningful research to help student affairs professionals navigate the mental health implications of their roles. Grace reminds student affairs professionals of the importance of caring for themselves while caring for others.

In chapter 10, Marcella Runell Hall, Rachel Alldis, and Todd Smith-Bergollo poignantly call readers to consider the myriad of ways students need and expect guidance through crisis, including spiritually. Their stories in "Faith in the Wake of Disaster" offer a wide range of perspectives about including spirituality resources at both secular and faith-based institutions, as well as their personal experiences helping students navigate crisis from a variety of faith and nonfaith lenses. Without prescribing a uniform approach, the authors challenge student affairs leaders to recognize the role that faith already plays in students' crisis experiences and to consider how an institution might better support this important need.

Kimberly Thornbury's story of learning through a major campus crisis encompasses nearly every aspect of professional and personal encounters with disaster. Chapter 11, "Learning From Tragedy," offers unique stories and specific strategies for helping student affairs leaders make sense of their crisis experience and move forward in a productive manner. She shares her own involvement after a tornado destroyed much of her campus and describes how focusing on learning tangible skills (like establishing a database of hundreds of damaged cars) and intangible skills (like building a strong network) helped her navigate the resulting uncertainty.

Finally, chapter 12 introduces the unique student population—one that has experienced more trauma than any previous generation—descending on our campuses and the importance of preparing student affairs leaders to meet their changing needs. "A Deep Hurt and a Magnificent Hope" discusses Katie Treadwell's personal journey to seek balance while serving students, as well as practical strategies to build hope and lead with compassion. She describes how, by focusing on post-traumatic growth, student affairs leaders can reconsider their wellness as an avenue to maximize staff leadership and student development.

Even in the absence of a crisis or critical incident on campus, student affairs is difficult work. As many of this book's authors attest, each day is all-consuming and offers little room for attending to personal wellness. Each time student affairs leaders attend an evening meeting or weekend event without the opportunity to adjust their standard work schedule, they lose valuable time to engage in the activities that make them whole. Student affairs professionals often view the ability to help students navigate crisis situations as a great honor. What might be an emergency situation for an individual student is, for student affairs professionals, often a relatively easy problem to solve. Student affairs educators have the ability to create minor miracles through emergency funding, recommendations for on-campus employment, or choosing to handle student conduct violations as teachable moments rather than opportunities for punishment. Still, the emotional impact of engaging in these activities on a daily basis accumulates over time.

Institutions and divisions of student affairs do not spend enough time talking about the mental health of student affairs professionals. Remember that the wellness strategies and resources we offer to our students, such as university counseling centers, are critical for student affairs professionals, too. For those who don't know where to turn, the National Suicide Prevention Lifeline (suicidepreventionlifeline.org, 1-800-273-TALK) provides 24/7 free and confidential support, as well as referrals to local counseling resources.

# 1

# Life as Triage

## Marijo Russell O'Grady and Katie L. Treadwell

You wake up to an e-mail informing you that 150 students filed sexual harassment and abuse charges against a campus administrator and athletics coach. Before you even get out of bed, your day is derailed.

You, on behalf of the university, are charged with informing parents and family members that the concealed carry of guns on campus is now legal in your state. Your job is to answer their questions, take note of their concerns and fear, and report back to administration. You understand why some parents tell you that you are personally responsible for their student's impending death, and yet the impact of hearing this on a regular basis makes each day at work feel a little more difficult than the previous.

You happen to answer the main office phone when a student calls, expressing significant mental health concerns and remarking that it's just not worth it anymore. Your colleagues have already left for the holiday break and you are rushing to finish your work. You are alone in the office and don't have immediate, subtle resources to enlist assistance.

Your work piles up to the point you have more tasks to complete than hours in a workday to complete them. After another full day at the office, you finally find time at home after dinner to open the next day's student conduct hearing file. After reading the violent threats the student made toward other students, you find yourself wondering why, as a young professional, you didn't know the job would involve this level of worry. You intended to become an educator, but now you often feel the need to warn your loved ones about the potential dangers you face on campus. You continue to review the disturbing conduct case, because it's your job.

You work hard, progress in the field, and achieve the next-level role in student affairs. Your portfolio of responsibilities is larger than before, but you are ready for the increased scope of institutional responsibilities. You spend all day, every day helping your staff manage crisis situations with students, going home later and later as a result.

Serving as a student affairs professional, particularly the vice president for student affairs, at any size or type of institution is a tremendous responsibility. From routine student concerns and manageable compliance issues to catastrophic incidents and rare disasters, leading student affairs efforts on a campus can be a daunting juggling task, even on an average day.

As a student affairs professional, you are the campus barometer. You track the pulse of the community, in good times and in bad. Your job is to care for the student, their network, and, perhaps, the campus community as a whole. But you don't realize that, at some point, you stopped taking care of yourself. Either as a parent who spends too much time away from home and misses too many family events, or as someone who worries about their health but can't seem to find the time to make changes to their personal life—soon every day feels like a triaged, frantic, barely-hanging-on life.

## THE MEANING OF TRIAGE

Originating as a medical strategy for urgent and emergent care, triage practices allow care providers to deliver aid to those most in need: "the sorting of and allocation of treatment to patients and especially battle and disaster victims according to a system of priorities designed to maximize the number of survivors" ("Triage," 2018, para. 1). More simply, medical triage is "the assignment of degrees of urgency to wounds or illnesses to decide the order of treatment of a large number of patients or casualties" ("Triage," n.d., para. 1). In the wake of a campus disaster, skilled medical personnel provide rapid and accurate triage services to treat wounds, make medical referrals, and prevent casualties among the victims.

Our use of the word *triage* is not meant to diminish the brave individuals—those first responders, law enforcement representatives, firefighters, doctors, and nurses—who perform medical triage at an emergency site or in the hospital. Rather, we use the triage concept to illustrate what it feels like to be the chief student affairs officer leading a campus's emergency response. Triage may also be understood in nonmedical settings, particularly when leaders assign "priority order to projects on the basis of where funds and other resources can be best used, are most needed, or are most likely to achieve success" ("Triage," 2018, para. 2). In student affairs, our work is a constant "process of determining the most important people or things from amongst a large number that require attention" ("Triage," n.d., para. 2). This work is challenging, exhausting, delicate, open to error, always simmering just beneath the surface, and rarely anticipated.

Just as in medical practices, triage decision making for student affairs requires critical thinking, cognitive abilities, intuition, and experience (Smith & Cone, 2010). These critical skills may be acquired through "thinking aloud," intentional reflection, simulations, and other opportunities to practice skills before implementing triage practices (Cioffi, 1999). But as student affairs leaders who acquire increasingly complex workloads, often lack the time or energy to engage in self-care practices, and rarely have the luxury of disconnecting from work to recharge, our capacity to accurately and effectively triage our campuses' and students' most critical needs can become faulty or even dangerous. We need the opportunity to step away and model for our students, our staff, and ourselves that it is acceptable to not be connected to a device, e-mail, or social media 24/7. As a profession, we need to be more reflective and emotionally engaged to recalibrate and sustain our capacity to serve students. We have to be able to find activities and disconnection opportunities that rejuvenate our souls and body. It is a nearly impossible undertaking, given all the pressing issues we face, and yet it is critical to continuing the work.

## THE EVOLVING NATURE OF STUDENT AFFAIRS

Student affairs is tough but rewarding work. Many professionals gravitated toward a career in student affairs after serving as undergraduate student leaders and building relationships with mentors who nudged us into a profession we did not previously know existed. We enjoyed leading students, couldn't bear to say goodbye to campus, and, if we are being completely honest, didn't have a clue what we wanted to do with our lives when we were 20 years old.

Our initial understanding of the scope of student affairs included the flashy parts—residence life, student activities, Greek life, and leadership development.

Like many traditional undergraduates, we, the authors, were deeply enmeshed in student leadership and campus life. In retrospect, we were unfamiliar with the significant and unexpected challenges that may occur in students' pursuit of higher education. Neither of us embarked on a career in student affairs fully aware of the breadth, challenge, and grief of the work we would later encounter.

When Marijo was beginning her career, the drinking age was 18. As a graduate residence hall director, she worked on a team that sponsored a campus concert complete with a hot tub and 50 beer kegs. Student affairs conversations included debates about *in loco parentis*, the role of Mothers Against Drunk Driving, and the arrival of the Reserve Officers' Training Corps (ROTC) on campus. She had her first experience with a student death as a graduate residence director and encountered another student death her first year as a professional residence director. She quickly realized that the community was following her lead, so she learned to be calm, have compassion, and think outside the box. Those experiences taught Marijo to be gritty, to think and act methodically and fast, and to see the forest and the trees. The experiences reinforced her training, her intuitive gut, and the need to communicate constantly and care for the campus community's soul. After 20 years in student affairs, Marijo thought she had seen it all, but then 9/11 happened.

As dean of students at Pace University in downtown New York City, Marijo's crisis response work culminated when she watched the first plane fly into the World Trade Center on September 11, 2001—although in some ways her crisis response work was just beginning. Her family lived just blocks from the towers, and Marijo found herself leading unbelievable campus emergency response efforts while attempting to care for her young family in a city she no longer recognized. While Marijo has since led her university through many unprecedented crises, her experiences with 9/11 defined her work in a way she could not have anticipated.

Katie's entry into student affairs began with an assigned graduate assistantship in a university counseling center in the early 2000s, at a time when the difficult issues of mental health, suicide prevention, intersectional identity development, substance abuse, and sexual assault were still not widely addressed in the field. She found herself leading campus workshops and designing learning experiences based on her insufficient knowledge of such difficult issues. Like many young professionals, she did not have the context to understand how this work created a crucial foundation for the exciting aspects of student affairs and campus learning she had anticipated. While she gravitated back toward a life of new student orientation and leadership development, Katie's trajectory in student affairs changed one cold February morning.

While Katie prepared program materials for a service–learning trip (her first professional role beyond graduate school), a routine fire alarm evolved into a campuswide active shooter situation. She sat under a steel desk for what felt like an eternity, praying, sending emotional text messages to loved ones, and listening to the sound of gunfire two floors above her windowless office. The campus officially classified the situation as a false alarm and miscommunication, and campus leaders later explained that the sound of gunfire was likely slamming doors as Campus Safety cleared the building. For a young student affairs team on a small campus, the fear was real. After serving on a handful of campus committees designed to investigate the incident and unsuccessfully managing her own undiagnosed post-traumatic stress disorder for over a year, Katie's lingering trauma of that encounter led her to pursue a research portfolio and student affairs career in understanding and learning from campus tragedy. In retrospect, dedicating her career to helping individuals and communities recover from tragedy was the only option for someone who grew up in Oklahoma City (where her father was a first responder to the 1995 federal building bombing), attended college in Waco, Texas after the Branch Davidian siege, and developed her professional identity in a post-9/11 New York City.

We, the authors, began our careers in student affairs through residence hall programs, leadership councils, and an endless string of icebreakers, but we soon discovered a deep desire to transform the way colleges and universities experience the worst of days. Of course, the good days still exist on campus—traditions, student achievements, community engagement, and students' remarkable dedication to improving lives and communities—but now daily conversations are dominated by talks of FERPA, Title IX, sexual assault and suicide prevention, mental health, alcohol and other drugs, social and racial injustice, student activism, food insecurity, implications of local and national political decisions, access and retention, outcomes, and serving students on ever-shrinking department budgets. The unprecedented priorities in higher education are vast. In addition to managing orientation programs, guiding student organizations, and ensuring that students achieve lofty learning outcomes, student affairs leaders have a deep obligation to advocate for students whose financial resources do not allow for healthy living and eating situations, counsel Deferred Action for Childhood Arrivals (DACA) and international students on the implications of political actions, create an environment that welcomes student activism while maintaining the delicate First Amendment balance, protect students who face blatant harassment, and prevent all forms of gender-based violence. As higher education funding dwindles, we take on additional routine campus obligations, adding programs to our portfolio to compensate for vacant positions on campus. But because our days are already filled managing the little moments of crisis that occur daily on a college campus, we push the routine planning, e-mail communications, and stated responsibilities of our job descriptions further into our evenings, weekends, and vacations.

As a profession, we are exhausted.

## LIVING A TRIAGED LIFE

In reflecting on her experience navigating a challenging family situation, author and speaker Glennon Doyle (2017) shared advice from a friend that may well describe the role of student affairs leaders charged with guiding their community through difficult times:

> Your family is together on an airplane right now, and there's some serious turbulence. The kids are afraid. What do we do when we're afraid on an airplane? We look at the flight attendants. If they seem scared, we panic too. If they seem calm, we stay calm. So what I'm telling you is that you are the flight attendant in this scenario, and you've been through enough turbulence to know you will all make it. Your kids are new to flying, so they're going to look to you to see whether they're okay. Your job right now is to stay calm, smile—and keep serving the freaking peanuts. (p. 4)

Student affairs leaders cannot insulate students from the pain and pressure of the outside world. Particularly in challenging political times, we are not capable of protecting students from the uncertainty, fear, and questions encircling the world—nor should we try to do so. We can, however, help them learn to navigate conversations, think critically, become advocates, and care for themselves. Our role is, as Melton (2017) described, to "point them to their pain, and say: 'Don't be afraid... you were born to do this'" (p. 5).

Student affairs is a 24/7/365 lifestyle. We often believe that we control the pulse of the campus community. It is an incredible job—we work with students, learn something new every day, and are energized by the phenomenal humans we serve. It is also an overwhelming, sometimes paralyzing, level of responsibility that we invite on a daily basis. A single wrong decision can alter your life. We encounter tragedies and personal dilemmas daily, and we devote the majority of our time to our work (in our offices, at evening and weekend events, by answering e-mails at all hours of the day). We are perpetually responding. And we should be perpetually reevaluating our processes, planning our responses, and retooling our skills. As student affairs leaders, we do not have time to properly relax and care for ourselves, and if we find unexpected moments to do so, we often do not know how.

Student affairs professionals have an incredible responsibility to care for, teach, educate, and develop the whole student, as well as an immense obligation to respond, act, report, be "on call," and be accurate for what typically feels like every moment of our waking lives. We have a duty to be on duty and to be even-keeled. It seems as though we cannot escape a defensive position of responding to concerns, cannot find ourselves in an offensive and proactive space for long enough to engage in intentional planning and prevention exercises. We keep the campus calm, respectful, consent-ful, well-behaved, and engaged, one that embraces equity and inclusion in every interaction. It is enormously stressful for us and our loved ones. But the future of higher education rests with our work toward the holistic well-being of students (and staff). Our challenge, then, becomes doing the same for ourselves.

Marijo offers this Irish blessing: May you always have foreseen and anticipated problems to solve and resolve. If only we were all so lucky. Usually, that is not the case. When there is a critical incident, the best course of action often depends on us. Things typically go haywire at 5:00 p.m. on the Friday before a holiday recess, just after the rest of campus has gone home and no one is available to help. Many of us in student affairs know that the real work—when everything "hits the fan"—often happens at 2:00 a.m. We take control of the situation, directing who leads, who follows, and who communicates. In these moments, we rely on our team's exceptional ability to handle a crisis, even though we feel enormous guilt at asking our staff to do more and work even longer hours.

Throughout our careers, we have come to understand the student affairs lifestyle and work as a type of triage. A student affairs leader's role is one of constant assessment and resulting adjustments. While few student affairs leaders are also licensed medical personnel, we encounter critical issues of student health and wellness on a daily basis. Our role is to assess, adjust, and connect students with the appropriate next step based on their area of greatest need. Our daily life is one of constant triage, regardless of whether we are "on the clock."

## Learning to Triage

In 1914, Ernest Shackleton sailed with 27 men and a stowaway from London to South Georgia Island via the Antarctic Ocean aboard a wooden vessel named Endurance (Morrell & Capparelli, 2001). His goal was to be the first to cross the Antarctic continent. After 45 days at sea, and with only one day remaining, disaster struck. The boat was caught in ice floes. For almost two years the crew camped on the ice floes, but the Endurance eventually sank. The crew steered three wooden life boats through stormy seas to the rocky, uninhabited outcropping of Elephant Island. Even today, their voyage is considered the greatest boat journey in history. Knowing his team would never survive, Shackleton attempted a 17-day, 800-mile journey in a freezing hurricane to the nearest civilization, South Georgia Island. He returned to save all of his men.

In preparing for his impossible journey across Antarctica, Shackleton picked a diverse team—a photographer, a geologist, astronomers, doctors, botanists, biologists, and seamen. The team's extensive diversity was key to its survival. In our role as student affairs leaders, we employ many of the same lessons that Shackleton demonstrated through his journey (described in Morrell and Capparelli's 2001 book on Shackleton's leadership):

- Never lose sight of the ultimate goal, but focus anxiety on short-term objectives. Your team may not be able to envision a day when you aren't still in the midst of the crisis. Help them see what to do next.
- Set a personal example with visible, memorable symbols and behavior. (For instance, each semester, Marijo's campus memorializes the events of September 11, 2001, with a welcome-back event for students.)
- Instill optimism and self-confidence, but stay grounded in reality. Grieve with your students and staff members and help them find hope.
- Take care of yourself. Maintain your stamina and let go of guilt.
- Reinforce the team message constantly. We are one. We live or die together.
- Minimize status differences. Insist on courtesy and mutual respect.
- Master conflict. Deal with anger in small doses and engage

dissidents. This is particularly critical when working with parents and family members after a campus crisis.
- Lighten up. Find something to celebrate and laugh about. Encourage reflection on your team's accomplishments during the crisis response.
- Be willing to take big risks.
- Appreciate the diversity that people bring to the table.

Similarly, in *Adrift: 76 Days Lost at Sea*, Steven Callahan (2002) described constructing his own raft, which capsized in the ocean six days after his departure. He faced insurmountable challenges for food and shelter, watching helplessly as five or six boats passed his raft during the 76 days. Callahan fought the elements, becoming both the hunter and the hunted. But he survived. In a subsequent edition of the book, Callahan (2002) described meeting a 10-year-old boy who posed a thoughtful question:

> I complained about the lack of wire in the fishing kit, but I described a light on the top of the raft powered by a battery in the water. 'Weren't they connected by a piece of wire?' he asked innocently. Duh. Sometimes it takes the wisdom of a ten-year-old to show us how stupid we can be. (p. xiii)

In a moment of crisis, fresh eyes are critical to the endurance of the journey. Diverse viewpoints create an opportunity for inclusion and success, not to mention survival. Particularly in difficult moments, each team member plays an important role for the leader. Their gifts create the greater good. Through our teams, we experience great tenacity, courage, compassion, ingenuity, and creativity.

We are all in the student affairs boat together. The work is hard. Sometimes, mistakes are our best teachers. We become more competent through the experience. Student affairs leaders must come to the table with knowledge, practical skill, understanding of policy, and political savvy. Knowing what battles to choose and when, as well as how to gain status as the "go-to person," are important skills to foster. Being seen solving problems is essential. Building confidants and relationships takes hard work, knowing when to speak and when to listen, and understanding the political dynamics of the discussion at hand. Every organization and each institution presents a unique set of challenges and opportunities to those within it. While having a set of academic and/or professional knowledge is important, perhaps even more valuable is having the organizational savvy to recognize and navigate political turmoil, create one's niche within the organization, manage supervisory relationships, deal with changing priorities, and build networks that allow a student affairs leader to thrive professionally.

In developing student affairs triage skills and planning for crises on campus, responsibility charting may provide a useful framework. Responsibility charting identifies "where one role ends and another begins" (Galbraith, Downey, & Kates, 2002, p. 89). It may be useful when "there are major decisions that involve multiple roles and where gaining clarity is important" (Galbraith et al., 2002, p. 89). In responsibility charting, leaders create a grid of all major decisions and roles, and assign codes at each intersection—who has responsibility, accountability, and veto power, versus who needs to be consulted or informed (Galbraith et al., 2002). Widespread tactical intervention and campus crisis response requires assigning the right tasks to the right people based on their unique skills and talents. Managing a crisis response, however large or small, is something that student affairs officers seem readily able to handle with care, compassion, poise, justice, and savvy, having built dependable networks and partnerships among other facets of the institution. Even on a daily basis, there is a tremendous—though not publicly recognized—responsibility to make the right decision every single time.

The responsibility of being the person in charge centers first on knowing your job, the parameters of your role, the university, and yourself—and knowing them well. Second, sadly, it centers on a constant state of exhaustion and mental fatigue. We never have time to mindfully think, intentionally plan, and carefully chart a path as we triage our way through each day. Finally—and, honestly, most scarily—is the fear of goofing up (mostly because you are exhausted) or making a bad/wrong/poor (as the media will label it) decision. Most of us are at-will employees. Some student affairs leaders get housing and/or other campus benefits. Making the wrong decision can create a domino effect of unexpected life-changing experiences. The sheer liability of our choices and the consequences of our decision making can create waves on campus, loss of life, loss of our jobs, and even lawsuits. (And so, as standard professional practice, we recommend obtaining professional liability insurance through your professional association to protect yourself in these situations.) We don't have a manual at our bedside or legal counsel in the middle of the night when we are making decisions. But 99% of the time, we as student affairs leaders make the right, best, and just decision. It is in our DNA, our gut, and our head as we mentally review procedure manuals and checklists. The job comes with immense pressure every day. At the end of the day, you are the liability insurance for your institution. And it can be scary.

Over the years, Marijo has been approached by several visiting parents asking if all of us deans for students have the same personality and energy. She jokingly answers "yes" but believes it to be true. Student affairs leaders are all on, and all in, all the time. We are the negotiator, the energetic warm personality, the crisis responder, and the security blanket for students, parents, faculty, and staff. We are the face of crisis for our communities; most often, our presence brings a de-escalation effect and a sigh of relief. During a typical day, we often are presented with many little or big crises. We are good on our feet, know the policies and boundaries, and offer a voice of reason and justice. It is an awesome and incredibly stressful responsibility. There are many facets of a crisis that must be dealt with, each immediately and in its own specific way, and we must remain grounded in reality but focused on possibilities. While no emergency manual or crisis protocol will ever fully prepare a campus to encounter disaster, student affairs leaders may utilize organizational planning and systems thinking approaches offered by Bolman and Deal (2013) to prepare themselves and their campus for a crisis:

- Identify the relevant relationships (determine who needs to be led and how).
- Assess who might resist cooperation, why, and how strongly (determine where the leadership challenges will be).
- Develop, wherever possible, relationships with those people to facilitate the communication, education, or negotiation processes needed to deal with resistance.
- When the previous step fails, carefully select and implement more subtle or forceful methods, as needed.
- Get to know people, find common interests not based in position titles, invent options for mutual gain (committee work, task forces, professional development), and bargain for win-win situations.
- Build consensus.
- Recognize whether you are following the rules that are understood and accepted by all players.

Student affairs leaders must take a wide-angle view of what needs to be done in the immediate moment, the next hour, the following day(s), and so on. If the crisis has a large impact, it will be key for student affairs leaders to work with the president, provost, legal counsel, university relations, and other critical campus partners. Crises never happen when we expect, and we never have the emergency response plans in our hands when we need them. All we can do is focus on restoring community safety, creating a compassionate environment, and guiding our campus toward doing the right thing at each step of the journey.

## Redefining the Work

Crisis events are stressful and emotionally and physically taxing, often require 24-hour hands-on leadership, typically happen in the middle of the night, and often produce guilt about time spent engaged in work and not with family. As crisis responders, student affairs leaders possess a 100-miles-per-hour brain and operate with a 24/7/365 tether to our electronic devices. It is a lifestyle, not a job.

If we are to survive as individuals and thrive as a profession, we must redefine the student affairs vocation and lifestyle to include a better understanding of balance or centeredness in our lives. We often feel hypocritical in telling others to take time away, disconnect, engage in self-care, develop emotional resiliency, and put family first. These acts are nearly impossible, because student affairs leaders are "on" all the time. We have an intrinsic need to control crises and routine campus functions, which inevitably spills into our personal lives. Our families and loved ones cope with the realities of our work: bartering on-call responsibilities during holidays, balancing family vacations with unplanned campus incidents, or struggling to schedule an afternoon away from the office. We feel that if we go off campus or take a day off, something will happen. It takes a concentrated (and often unsuccessful) effort to be present at home given the unending demands for a student affairs leader's attention.

For a student affairs professional, each day takes all of you: all of your attention, your energy, and your mind. As Renee Piquette Dowdy (2013) wrote in *What Breaks You*, "It breaks you when you are torn too many times from the things that make you well. And I can say from experience it takes an incredibly strong person to dig deep and hold to those things when institutionally there are not conditions created to support you" (p. 2). Impossible as it seems, student affairs leaders must prioritize time to recharge and refuel to push through the busy days and the catastrophic incidents that require total devotion to the job. It is important to involve members of the student affairs leadership team, communicate with them often, keep them in the circle to help manage the crises, provide other points of view for consideration, and ensure time away for self-care to sustain the team's capacity to lead with stamina over the long haul. This is particularly true when you can't see the end in sight.

The chapters that follow offer intimate glimpses into the personal experience of serving as a senior student affairs leader during a major campus crisis. The stories are deeply humbling and personal, tragic and beautiful. While many of the events that follow are well-known examples of student affairs crisis response, the student affairs leaders involved offer new insights into their harrowing personal journeys to manage a campus tragedy, restore a sense of peace, and navigate their own grief along the way. Their tales offer lessons learned and opportunities for student affairs professionals at all levels to consider their own actions should the unthinkable occur. While their experiences are vastly different, each of the stories expresses an undeniable duty to bring meaning to chaos, one captured in Rilke's (1934) *Letters to a Young Poet*:

> Perhaps everything terrible is in its deepest being something helpless that wants help from us. So you must not be fright-

ened . . . if a sadness rises up before you larger than any you have ever seen; if a restiveness, like light and cloud-shadows, passes over your hands and over all you do. You must think that something is happening with you, that life has not forgotten you, that it holds you in its hand; it will not let you fall. . . . It is always what I have already said: always the wish that you may find patience enough in yourself to endure, and simplicity enough to believe; that you may acquire more and more confidence in that which is difficult, and in your solitude with others. And for the rest, let life happen to you. (pp. 52–55)

# References

Bolman, L. E., & Deal, T. E. (2013). *Reframing organizations: Artistry, choice and leadership* (5th ed.). Hoboken, NJ: John Wiley & Sons.

Callahan, S. (2002). *Adrift: 76 days lost at sea*. Boston, MA: Mariner Books.

Cioffi, J. (1999). Triage decision making: Educational strategies. *Accident and Emergency Nursing, 7*(2), 106–111. Retrieved from https://www.sciencedirect.com/science/article/pii/S0965230299800319?via%3Dihub

Dowdy, R. P. (2013). *What breaks you*. Retrieved from NASPA–Student Affairs Administrators in Higher Education website: https://www.naspa.org/constituent-groups/posts/what-breaks-you

Doyle, G. (2017). *The most valuable thing a parent can do for their kids*. Retrieved from http://www.oprah.com/inspiration/glennon-doyle-melton-parenting-children-of-divorce

Galbraith, J., Downey, D., & Kates, A. (2002). *Designing dynamic organizations: A hands-on guide for leaders at all levels*. New York, NY: AMACOM.

Morrell, M., & Capparelli, S. (2001). *Shackleton's way: Leadership lessons from the great Antarctic explorer*. London, UK: Nicholas Brealey.

Rilke, R. M. (1934). *Letters to a young poet* (M. D. Herter Norton, Trans.). New York, NY: W. W. Norton.

Smith, A., & Cone, K. J. (2010, January). Triage decision-making skills: A necessity for all nurses. *Journal for Nurses in Staff Development, 26*(1), E14–E19. Retrieved from https://insights.ovid.com/pubmed?pmid=20098163

Triage. (n.d.). Oxford University Press. Retrieved from https://en.oxforddictionaries.com/definition/triage

Triage. (2018). In *Merriam-Webster*. Retrieved from https://www.merriam-webster.com/dictionary/triage

# 2

# Making Sense Out of the Senseless

## A Framework for Understanding the Impact of Traumatic Events on the Lives of Student Affairs Professionals

### KEVIN P. JACKSON

I must admit that I thought long and hard about contributing this chapter to the book *Crisis, Compassion, and Resiliency in Student Affairs*. My initial response in and of itself underscores the need for just such a book. That is, I hesitated not out of a concern that I lacked wisdom or experiences to share; quite the opposite, I was less inclined to "go there" in sharing what I do know about the subject—knowledge gained from lived-life experiences so painful that it has taken me quite some time to be able to write about them without being swept back into them. I became intimately familiar with this concept in my own journey through crisis, compassion, and resiliency as a student affairs professional over the past 35 years. My hope is that in your career you will not face the type of tragedy that befell Texas A&M University in 1999, when I served there as a member of the Division of Student Affairs. Nor will you come face-to-face with death and injury so overwhelming that it alters forever how you see yourself, the profession, and the world around you. Nor will you find yourself tossed about in a legal process that seeks to expose every action you have ever taken—or perhaps more important, not taken—in an attempt to determine the extent to which you and others may have been associated with, or even worse, responsible for some aspect of the devastating event. That is my hope, yet the reality is if you stay in this profession long enough, you will face tragedy—hopefully not like the Bonfire collapse—but very real and painful human experiences nevertheless. Such experiences can take many forms—a succession of student suicides, an automobile accident involving multiple student fatalities, an active shooter on campus, a natural disaster with devastating consequences to your community, or, in my case, a student-led event that went terribly wrong. Therefore, because of this reality, we need to explore a topic that is complex and deeply personal—our life as triage or, put another way, how we increase our ability to function effectively and remain whole in times of overwhelming despair and suffering.

Tragedy affects people in different ways. The literature on the subject identifies a host of physical, cognitive, emotional, and behavioral reactions associated with trauma and its aftermath. These range from an inability to concentrate to prolonged sadness, insomnia to hypervigilance, feelings of guilt and shame to uncontrollable bouts of crying—all, if left unchecked, can result in deeper issues of anxiety and depression (American Psychological Association, 2004; Substance Abuse and Mental Health Services Administration, 2014).

Research also indicates that "trauma can affect one's beliefs about the future via loss of hope, limited expectations about life, fear that life will end abruptly or early, or anticipation that normal life events won't occur (e.g., access to education, ability to have a significant and committed relationship, good opportunities for work)" (Substance Abuse and Mental Health Services Administration, 2014, p. 60). What remains less identifiable are the dynamics, both real and perceived, that contribute to the severity of the impact a tragic event and its aftermath may have on us, especially when we are operating within our professional capacities. Furthermore, little is known about what we can do as student affairs professionals to understand more fully and work to prevent the negative effects of tragic events both on our lives and on the lives of our staff, our students, and our loved ones.

My own lived experiences and observations indicate there is a critical intersection between how we perceive our own agency within the experience, whether accurately or not, regarding our proximity to, response during, and sense of association with or alleged

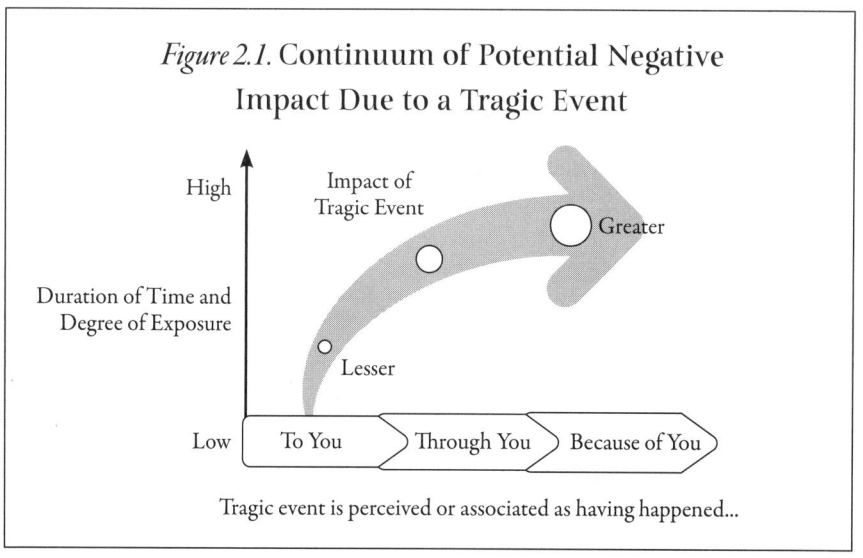

Figure 2.1. Continuum of Potential Negative Impact Due to a Tragic Event

responsibility for preventing the event and its subsequent outcomes. That is, I have concluded the potential negative impact of a tragic event on one's professional life—and, in turn, personal life—intensifies along a continuum wherein you perceive that the tragic event happens to you, through you, and/or in some way, whether rational or not, because of you. Any overlap creates additional complexity and pain in an already deeply challenging situation, as do duration of time and degree of exposure. Figure 2.1 illustrates this concept.

For me, working from this continuum of potential negative impact encompasses more accurately the reality of what one encounters when dealing with traumatic situations in student affairs, and I hope it provides a framework from which the affected professional can begin to sort through and seek help to process the flood of emotions a tragic event and its aftermath can trigger. As is consistent with the literature on this subject, avoidance strategies, which we seem to master early in our careers, are not advisable and can lead to long-term negative consequences on one's physical, psychological, and spiritual health. Our propensity to deflect or disassociate with our feelings perpetuates a destructive cycle in that "initially, the avoidance works, but over time, anxiety increases and the perception that the situation is unbearable or dangerous increases as well, leading to a greater need to avoid" (Substance Abuse and Mental Health Services Administration, 2014, p. 73). Avoidance may have tremendous detrimental effects on one's ability to be effective in their professional and personal roles (National Center for Post-Traumatic Stress Disorder, n.d.; Substance Abuse and Mental Health Services Administration, 2014). Consequently, I offer this chapter with the humility that comes from having tried and failed to cope with tragedy on my own, and the recognition that no one of us has the answer to living life as triage, but together we can start a national dialogue that will better equip all of us to do so.

As we begin, I must provide a disclaimer. Much of what I will share with you is based on my remembrance of an event so painful that I spent much of my life after the experience attempting to push it to the farthest recesses of my mind and keep it there. Of course, it would not stay, so I sought differing ways to understand it. Some provided greater insight than others. None was sufficient. It was a difficult and sometimes self-imposed journey of solitude, although many people have been there for me along the way. As I share my story, I attempt to recall facts that occurred some time ago and describe feelings that are, at times, beyond my ability to comprehend, much less capture through words. I am also mindful that numerous individuals were affected much more than I was by this tragedy, and I would never want to do anything that would add to their hurt. To that end, I will do my best to share my experiences accurately and sensitively, and hopefully help those sojourners in our profession better understand how to lead themselves and others from a space of compassion and resilience during times of tragedy.

## Memories That Never Go Away

I remember vividly the morning of November 18, 1999—the phone ringing just before 3:00 a.m., the answering machine clicking on before I could reach my home phone, the somber voice of my vice president for student affairs saying: "Kevin, the Bonfire stack has collapsed. Students have died. Others are trapped. I need you to go to the site right away." I stood motionless in my living room, unable to grasp what I had just heard. *Bonfire stack has collapsed. Students are dead. Others are trapped.* The sentences made no sense, yet a deep sense of dread washed over me. My wife touched my shoulder and said, "Kevin, you have to go. They need you."

## THEY NEED YOU

As student affairs professionals, we are drawn to our work primarily because we desire to help others learn, grow, and develop. Much of our identity centers on the notion that we can and do make a difference in people's lives, especially college students who are on their journey to adulthood. For me, I became acquainted with the profession through a series of student groups I joined and later became a leader of while in college. The most profound set of experiences occurred during my senior year, when I helped facilitate a leadership training organization. Through this experience, I learned much about myself, others, and the world around me. I also was under the tutelage of a student organization advisor who would forever shape the trajectory of my life. It was a simple question she asked me as a college senior: "Kevin, have you ever thought about a career in student affairs?" To which I replied: "This is a career?"

Fortunately, she was a gracious soul who overlooked my naïve response, taking the time to explain what she did and how she had become involved in the profession. This conversation nudged me onto the path of further exploration and led eventually to my first position in higher education, serving as a residence hall director. From my first day of assuming the role of a student affairs professional, I was enamored with the idea of working with kindred spirits—those who sought the high ideals of the education, maturation, and preparation of college students. It is an exciting and dynamic environment, one that still speaks deeply to me, and others, as we help shape the future by engaging with bright and motivated young men and women in the enterprise of intellectual curiosity, interpersonal growth, and spiritual formation. I have also learned it is an environment that comes with unexpected twists and turns when the positive, life-changing experiences we intend to provide become, on occasion, deeply wounding, life-altering events.

## LIFE-ALTERING EVENTS

Early in my professional career, I experienced situations involving student injury and, on occasion, student death. Interestingly enough, I do not recall discussing this topic in my graduate preparation courses nor gaining insight into how to address such situations in my early professional development work. These tragic events typically happened "to me"—by which I mean the injury or accident occurred, I was notified, and I assisted through some form of university-led response. One such experience occurred during my first year as the advisor to a winter carnival sponsored by a university in Colorado, where I worked at the time. The annual event drew hundreds of students to the ski slopes for a weekend of fun and fellowship. Tragedy befell the event when a student died from hitting a tree while snow skiing off the trail. The student fatality deeply affected our community. My role was to inform the winter carnival committee members of the death and to assist them in gaining access to counseling and other supportive services as needed. Later, we spent a good bit of time discussing how we might mitigate an accident of this nature from occurring in the future and established an educational program to inform student participants of the dangers of skiing out of bounds. The death of a student during an event I advised was troubling, as was witnessing the reaction of others I worked closely with; yet as disturbing as it was, I found some solace in the fact that I had no control and little influence over the factors that led to the accident.

Some years later and during my time at Texas A&M University, I experienced a tragic event I would describe as happening "through me."

The tragedy involved an automobile accident I came upon right after it occurred. Students had been participating in a weekend activity cutting trees for an annual event called Bonfire. I was the primary advisor to the group that sponsored the event. This incident involved students in a pickup truck riding back from the off-campus location of the event. Two students were in the truck's cab and several others were in the truck's bed. The driver reportedly became drowsy, drifted off the road, and overcorrected, causing the truck to roll on its side and flip over several times. The force of the rollover ejected the students from the truck's bed. One died and others were badly injured. The students in the truck's cab sustained less serious injuries but still required medical attention. I arrived at the emergency room shortly after the injured students and was able to check on them. While doing so, a father of one of the injured students arrived. He was visibly distraught, understandably so. When I introduced myself to him, his concern for his son's injuries shifted to anger and he began to blame the accident on the university, believing that if the school did not support the activity his son would not be in the hospital. In his heightened state of anger, he grabbed me by the front of my shirt and shoved me toward a wall. Fortunately, another staff member was in the emergency room and intervened on my behalf.

As one might imagine, the whole experience was quite unnerving—seeing the scene of the wreck, learning a student had died, being in the emergency room with the injured students, feeling the despair and wrath of the father projected onto me. In the weeks and months that followed, I served as the key contact person between the university and the students and their families. As such, I attended the funeral of the student who died, checked on the injured students, referred family members with questions about medical insurance coverage to appropriate offices and followed up to make sure they got answers, and advised student leaders on how we might improve the safety of students traveling to and from the off-campus site. I was, in many ways, an emissary working on behalf of the university with the injured parties, attempting to assist, as best I could, in the healing process. While doing so, I was working with student leaders to make changes to the activity based on what we had learned about the cause of the accident. These changes included setting a later start time, banning students from riding in truck beds, coordinating buses to transport students, and establishing a rest stop between the cut site and campus.

In calling on my earlier experience with the ski accident to help me navigate this tragic event, I initially overlooked a significant difference between the two. In this case, the nexus between the accident and my professional role and personal experience was closer, more intimate. That is, I came upon the accident and saw the aftermath of the wreck—etching a vivid image in my mind of what occurred. I interacted with injured students and an upset parent at the emergency room—experiencing in a deeply personal way the pain, fear, and anger of those present. I represented the university in offering assistance to the family of the deceased student and the families of the injured students—interactions that spanned several months and continued to associate me, at least to the families, as a person representing a deeply painful experience in their lives. It also created ongoing exposure to this traumatic set of experiences for me as I served in this role. Although I could sense a personal emotional toll, it seemed to me at the time that this was part of my job. I just needed to deal with any feelings of sadness, anxiousness, or concern in the best way I could, which typically began with logic and ended in avoidance. It simply did not occur to me that I might need assistance in processing the initial and ongoing experiences, so I pushed through and "soldiered on."

As this type of tragedy unfolds, you find yourself involved in and called on to take action based on your official capacity, while at the same time being confronted by and sorting through your own feelings of sadness, pain, sorrow, and grief. You sense, and rightly so, that how you respond has repercussions for not only the students you serve but their families and loved ones as well as the university you represent and possibly your own job. As such, you feel a stronger association with the tragedy—a feeling that may be reinforced by the reactions of others—and a sense of responsibility to make things as right as you can. To this end, you tend to push your thoughts and feelings aside to focus on meeting the needs of those impacted. To do otherwise would be self-serving and weak; at least, that is what the inner voice in your subconscious mind tells you. This approach, although initially efficient, can lead to a pattern of overlooking your own inner work, which, left unchecked, becomes problematic. The challenge is that you typically do not identify the depth and breadth of impact that a traumatic event has when it happens "through you" until you begin to see noticeable effects on some aspect of your work or personal life, and even then you may attribute such manifestations to feeling tired, being overworked, or needing to toughen up.

The third way a student affairs professional responds to, and/or may perceive to be involved in, a tragic event resides within a domain I describe as happening "because of you." It is the most difficult one to navigate and, unfortunately, is becoming more prevalent owing to the nature of our litigious and blame-associated society. This domain can contain characteristics that overlap with the happens "to you" and happens "through you" classifications, yet it has a distinct difference—there is an added dimension that attempts to associate and/or is perceived to associate the tragedy with something you did or did not do in your official capacity as a university employee. The full effect of this element is especially difficult to understand and come to grips with because it strikes at the very core of who we are in the work that we seek to do. Our work is predicated on the desire to help students improve their lives, to become more fully the person they have been created to be. Therefore, coming face-to-face with the thought or allegation that you, as a student affairs professional, may have overlooked something that could have prevented—or, worse yet, may have unwittingly allowed—an event that resulted in student injury or death, is reprehensible. It can create numerous intense psychological challenges that pervade the multiple complexities before you, including the care of the injured parties, the support of your staff, the response of the university, the relationship with your family and loved ones, and your own well-being. This was my experience with the tragedy known as the Bonfire collapse, which killed 12 students and injured 27.

## The Collapse

Texas Aggie Bonfire was considered by many to be the most cherished of all Aggie traditions—an annual event that spanned 90 years and symbolized Texas A&M's burning desire to beat the University of Texas in football. By the late 1990s, over 5,000 students joined in each year to build an approximately 60-foot-tall structure, called Stack, in the shape of a four-tier wedding cake design, made from several thousand trees cut, trimmed, and transported to the A&M campus from a nearby landowner's property.

At the time of the collapse, I was serving as a special assistant to the vice president for student affairs, a position I accepted after working for more than a decade as the senior associate director of the Memorial Student Center (MSC). As the senior associate director of the MSC, I served as the advisor to Bonfire from 1995 to 1997 and hired the advisor that served in this capacity at the time of the collapse. I had been in the vice president's office for less than one year when the accident occurred.

After hearing the message from my vice president on the morning of November 18, 1999, I dressed and went immediately to campus where Stack had been constructed. I was totally unprepared for what I saw. One large section of the four-tier structure lay on its side in a twisted compilation of logs and baling wire, which was used to secure the logs to each other. My initial impression was that a bomb had gone off and blown out the side of Stack. Later, I would learn that the combined force of the weight of the upper tiers, along with logs being inserted from the upper tiers into the lower tiers, created such stress that the wiring method used to hold the logs together on the lowest tier gave way, resulting in a sudden and catastrophic failure of the base structure. Without a solid base structure to rest on, sections of the upper tiers broke loose, creating a chain reaction that sent an entire side of Stack crashing to the ground. The students who were working on Stack at the time of the collapse had little warning of what was happening. Some were thrown away from the falling Stack; others were buried within its massive logs. In a matter of seconds, the deafening roar of falling logs ceased and an eerie silence fell upon the site.

I arrived to a thick blanket of dust that hung in the air and mixed with smoke from the smaller watch fires that lined the perimeter of Stack to provide students working throughout the night with a place to warm themselves. I tried to orient myself in the darkness but the haze distorted the red, blue, and white strobes of the first responder vehicles' emergency lights. As I made my way toward the partially collapsed Stack, I remember vividly the look of shock in the eyes of those who witnessed the event—a mixture of horror and disbelief as they came toward me uncertain of what to do or where to go. Next, I saw two students lying on the ground, covered partially with a tarp—it took me a moment to realize they were dead. Words cannot describe the despair and heartache that welled up inside me; simply stated, I was overwhelmed completely by what I saw, heard, and felt. My mind was locked in a seemingly endless loop of taking in information, but I was unable to process any of it. The situation was unfathomable. The only coherent thought I could muster was that I had to pull myself together and help in whatever way I could. Numerous ambulances were arriving on the scene to transport injured students to two area hospitals. Several other student affairs colleagues were arriving as well. We gathered quickly and determined that we needed to identify which students had been working on Stack when it collapsed, account for them, and then determine who was missing. I volunteered to go to one of the hospitals. Another colleague went to the other. We agreed to call periodically to provide reports on students transported to the respective facilities. The remaining staff helped organize the response around the Stack site.

I spent the next 48 hours with minimal sleep, working first to identify missing students among those taken to the hospital and then returning to campus to assist in the communication center set up to respond to the thousands of phone calls that poured in. Although my memory of what transpired over the ensuing weeks is disjointed, I do remember a crushing sense of despair as the Aggie family, the surrounding community, and the state mourned the multiple student deaths and injuries. We held memorials, candlelight prayer vigils, and a benefit concert and established an endowment to help defray the cost of medical expenses. At every turn, deeply moving acts of care and compassion emerged—including the University of Texas changing its annual campus event before the A&M vs. Texas football game from a pep rally to a candlelight vigil, lighting its iconic tower maroon, A&M's school color. I also remember the relentless nature of the news media as reporters sought to beat their competition to the latest story or breaking news lead. Articles and live reports speculating on reasons for the collapse were plentiful, as were speculative reports on responsibility. Bright yellow "crime scene" tape cordoned off the areas around the collapsed Stack and only authorized personnel were allowed to enter. Although described as routine, the use of crime scene tape by local law enforcement agencies had a chilling effect on those of us who worked with Bonfire.

After the initial response and time of mourning, we entered a heightened period of remembrance of the fallen, ongoing care for their families and loved ones, and continued support for the injured. During this time, I helped lead a group of student, faculty, and staff volunteers to collect, document, and store items from the impromptu shrines that arose around the Stack site—hundreds of pictures, poems, drawings, crosses, and letters that had been left as expressions of grief, despair, love, and hope. In addition, several A&M class rings—an Aggie's most prized possession—were left at the base of the flagpole in front of the main entrance to campus as a show of support for the families and loved ones of the deceased and injured. This experience added to my already growing sense of despair, burying the heartache of the tragedy even more deeply into my conscious and subconscious mind. And, if this was not painful enough, the questions of how and why this tragic event happened moved front and center on everyone's mind, but most especially in the media.

To answer these and other questions, the university established an independent Bonfire commission to investigate and produce a report detailing the cause of the tragedy. I was interviewed, along with other staff, faculty, and students who had worked with Bonfire. Eventually, the university issued a report that described the technical reasons for the collapse while noting that cultural myopia contributed to an inability to recognize warning signs that could have signaled that Stack's structural integrity was not as sturdy as perceived. Being present at the public event during which the commission presented its report deepened the sense that more could have been done to avert this tragedy from occurring. Once the commission completed its work, the university established a task force to determine if Bonfire could be built in a safe manner while remaining student-led and staff-advised. I served on the task force, and over the course of the next year we determined this would not be possible. Shortly after the task force completed its responsibilities, several university administrators were named in lawsuits associated with the Bonfire collapse—myself included. The legal proceedings lasted several years and fueled numerous media stories, subpoenas, accusations, depositions, attempted mediations, and other interactions aimed at determining who, if anyone, was responsible for the tragic event. In the end, the lawsuits would settle without going to trial, but the painful experiences associated with the process, especially the depositions, took a significant toll on everyone involved and left me with a deep-seated sense of unease about working in a profession that relied heavily on the decision making and action taking of primarily 18- to 22-year-olds.

The Bonfire collapse and subsequent events profoundly shaped the lives of everyone they touched—some more severely than others. I was forever changed. In many ways, the experience caused me to grow up and mature in the profession. I was called on to perform roles I would not have sought on my own nor been exposed to under normal circumstances. In other ways, I struggled immensely in both my professional and my personal life. I was fortunate to have a strong support network—a loving family, strong church community, and supportive colleagues—in place prior to and in the years following the tragedy. While my network was of immense help, the sheer magnitude of what occurred, along with the crushing weight of carrying a sense of shame and guilt, as irrational as it was, left an indelible mark on me—a mark so painful that I would eventually seek help for understanding and coping with it.

This journey began when midway through the first year of the collapse, the university brought in a counselor to help staff members process our feelings of pain and grief. I sat in on a few group sessions, and through this experience I began to learn more about trauma and its effects on those who experience it. Yet I was still operating under the false assumption that I was different, stronger if you will, and would be able to work my way through the waves of despair and heartache that roiled inside of me. I was wrong.

It was not until the end of the second year following the collapse, exhausted and no longer finding joy in my work, that I began to talk more openly about my struggles and look more deeply into the research on trauma, its effects, and ways to find healing. This led to the realization that I needed someone with whom I could process my thoughts and feelings on a regular basis. It resulted in my decision to see a counselor, and his diagnosis that I, like many impacted by the Bonfire collapse, were experiencing symptoms of post-traumatic stress disorder. Counseling helped prepare me for what would be a long and at times arduous journey to feeling whole again.

In retrospect, I think I could have dealt more effectively with some of what I carried if I had been able to identify and seek assistance in addressing it earlier. Yet as I look back, none of us who experienced this traumatic event and its aftermath seemed to be able to articulate what we were feeling. And, although seeking professional assistance was suggested on more than one occasion, we, or at least I, could not "go there" early on owing to my compulsion to "be there for others." This overriding tendency to "be there for others" should surprise no one in our profession. It is, as I stated earlier, one of the compelling reasons we do what we do. Under more normal conditions of our work, it provides us with strength of purpose during the long days and nights of the academic year and serves as true north when we face complex campus issues. Yet, under extreme conditions, such as those posed by a tragic event, it can, if left unchecked, become an impediment to long-term effectiveness and lead staff, including ourselves, to leave the profession. Consequently, and almost paradoxically, what we must learn is that in order to take good care of others, we must take good care of ourselves.

## Taking Good Care

The idea that, as student affairs professionals, we should be better at taking good care of ourselves and our staff when dealing with tragedy has been an uneasy companion of mine since the Bonfire collapse. In fact, it ultimately led me to remain in the profession after a particularly difficult set of "dark night of the soul" experiences that occurred as I tried to navigate the manifestations of what later would be explained to me as post-traumatic stress. The desire to somehow draw on what I learned from this tragic experience and its aftermath to help others ultimately trumped the internal conflict that wanted me to believe walking away—protecting myself, if you will—was the only safe choice. I am glad I stayed. And, although the continuation of the journey has not been without peril, the joy of working alongside college students and those who are passionate about the ideals of higher education has exceeded significantly the darker moments. Realizing this, I felt it was time to share what I know about working through tragedy with the hope that in some way small or large this insight can help student affairs professionals take better care of themselves and their staff when faced with the unthinkable.

I have learned that a tragedy, by its very nature, is a deeply painful and widely impactful occurrence. It typically defies reason and creates strong inner turmoil that, if left unchecked, can lead to long-term psychological and physiological harm. In higher education, tragic events seem more prevalent or, at least, are reported more frequently than in previous decades. Whether it be an active shooter on campus resulting in multiple casualties, an automobile accident with mass student fatalities, a hazing-related death of a student, or a student-led event that results in serious injury or death—when these types of events occur, student affairs staff typically carry a primary responsibility for responding to and working through the tragedy. That said, little has been written about how to recognize and describe the varying degrees of impact a tragic event can have on a student affairs staff member as they work in their professional capacity. Furthermore, there is a dearth of information available on how to take better care of ourselves and each other when faced with and working through tragedies in our professional capacities.

Drawing on my own journey experiencing and working through tragic events, I have described in this chapter a framework to help the reader better understand and respond to the dynamics that interact to intensify the impact of a tragic event on their professional life, which in turn takes a toll on their personal life. Furthermore, I hope that such knowledge will assist us in taking better care of those we serve alongside in this noble yet, at times, extremely challenging profession of student affairs. Based on years of reflecting on and working through my lived-life experiences with tragic events, I identified a pattern between how we perceive our own sense of agency within the tragedy and its potential impact on our professional and personal lives. This pattern, as illustrated in the first part of the chapter, is comprised of three domains along a continuum of lesser to greater probability of impact.

The domains involve a tragic event that you perceive or associate as having happened to you, through you, or because of you. Because tragic events tend to defy reason—that is, one cannot explain or rationalize what has occurred—how one perceives what has happened and/or their association with it can be difficult to understand. Therefore, recognizing how proximity to the event affects perception and association is important. By being there and experiencing the tragedy firsthand, the association becomes even stronger and the impressions more deeply embedded. Yet proximity is not just physical; it is psychological as well. That is, one can feel proximate because of work responsibilities, resulting in a closer association with a tragedy and its aftermath and a more intense sense of responsibility by the nature of their professional position. Consequently, one can perceive, or others may allege, that there was a duty to prevent the tragic event from occurring, creating the perception that the incident happened possibly because of something the person did or did not do. Understandably, this is the most challenging domain to work through and has the highest potential for negative impact on a student affairs professional.

Duration and frequency of exposure to the elements within each domain can intensify the potential negative influence of the experience, as can any perceived overlap of the domains. By working from this mental framework, student affairs professionals can be better equipped to triage a traumatic set of experiences and not only handle the work at hand with compassion but also develop strategies for resiliency by taking steps to mitigate the potentially negative psychological and physiological impact these deeply disturbing events can produce. Furthermore, the descriptors along the model's continuum can be used to identify and talk about how you and your staff members perceive the situation. The model provides a common language from which to work as well as a basis from which to encourage yourself and others to explore options for seeking assistance. In essence, it gives permission to "go there," whether individually or collectively, and deal with the pressures and issues brought on by extraordinarily painful events that certainly strain, if not exceed, our professional knowledge, skills, and abilities.

The model helped me frame and bring greater clarity to what I was experiencing years after the Bonfire collapse. It also empowered me to seek the assistance I needed to work through lingering negative emotions and seek a path to reconciliation and restoration. It also helped me years later to lead both myself and a division of student life through a tragic event that occurred involving a university-sponsored program under the division's oversight. Although the circumstances of the incident were very different than the Bonfire collapse, the event was traumatic on a number of levels because multiple guests suffered injuries, some serious, while thousands of attendees looked on. In drawing on the model, I made sure that in addition to attending to the needs of the injured parties both at the time of the accident and in the days, weeks, and months afterward, I also worked closely with staff who were involved in the incident and provided support to those who were injured. Further, I sought ways to keep myself mentally and physically healthy throughout the process. In doing so, I was able to lead from not only a position of compassion but also one of resilience.

For far too long, many of us have soldiered on as student affairs professionals in the face of profoundly difficult times, placing the needs of others ahead of our own psychological and physiological health. Our intentions have been honorable, our methods flawed. It is time for us to better equip ourselves to recognize the types of traumatic situations we and our staff face and to respond in ways that preserve our ability to lead well, both professionally and personally, in the immediacy of the situation as well as over the long haul. I hope this chapter will encourage you to do so and provide you with a framework from which to develop specific strategies to take good care of yourself and others.

> *"Her harmony came not through the complete absence of chaos, but in the realization that she was resilient enough to come back stronger from anything that she could endure."*
>
> —Lee, 2017

## References

American Psychological Association. (2004, January 16). The effects of trauma do not have to last a lifetime. Retrieved from https://www.apa.org/research/action/ptsd.aspx

Lee, B. (2017, September 8). Untitled poetry [Instagram post]. Retrieved from https://www.instagram.com/p/BYzbBISB7Mw/?hl=en&taken-by=beccaleepoetry

National Center for Post-Traumatic Stress Disorder. (n.d.). Avoidance. Retrieved from https://www.ptsd.va.gov/understand/what/avoidance.asp

Substance Abuse and Mental Health Services Administration. (2014). *SAMHSA's concept of trauma and guidance for a trauma-informed approach* (HHS Publication No. [SMA] 14-4884). Retrieved from https://store.samhsa.gov/shin/content/SMA14-4884/SMA14-4884.pdf

# 3

# All Quiet on the Campus Front . . . Not So Much?

## Marijo Russell O'Grady and Laura Avitabile Wankel

Student affairs leaders give it our all, 24/7—no time for self-care; always concerned about our community; constantly planning, retooling, training, and hoping we're prepared for the unimaginable. We also need to report up—to the president, provost, legal counsel, and university relations—and channel information to external and internal partners and stakeholders. It can feel like we have post-traumatic stress disorder every day. Some days we want our responsibilities to end when the day does, but that isn't a reality for student affairs leaders.

Tragic events on campus differ in scope from those that impact the surrounding community and the nation, yet each requires the expertise of your community, your own resources and skills, the skills of your team, and the nimbleness of your institution. Planning, preparedness, and training are key, but so are personal strength, a sense of right and wrong, compassion, communication, resilience, a solid team, and campus partners (both external and internal).

In Marijo's first two jobs in student affairs, she was called on to manage unfortunate student accidents. When she was a graduate assistant, one of her residents was stabbed and killed at a nearby off-campus bar. In her first professional position as a residence director, a student from her residence hall died while playing baseball in a floor-versus-floor challenge off campus. It was a rainy day, and the batter's grip on the swinging bat loosened. The bat struck a floormate in the back of the head, killing him instantly. Thirty years later, Marijo met up with one of her resident assistants from that time, who remarked, "You were only four or five years older than us, and yet, you knew exactly what to do—with the police, the family, the students, and the resident assistants."

During her 30-plus years of professional experience, Marijo has overseen or led a crisis team for tragic accidents; suicides; residence hall fires; three hurricanes (Gloria, Irene, Sandy); sexual assaults; two murdered students (off campus); protests; a loose boa constrictor; drug busts; power outages; a shooting; a woman driving through a path of students and others in a public park; a cyanide incident; a suspected active shooter; hate crimes; mental health crises; federal agents on her campus; and more. Yet the most significant event and, in hindsight, learning experience was when she managed the response to the World Trade Center tragedy on September 11, 2001. Marijo worked and lived with her spouse and 1-year-old son only a few blocks from the towers. She says it can be hard to talk about even today: some days she is fine, other days she tears up as she speaks. "You unconsciously, neatly, pack your suitcase of baggage that you can't address in the moment so that you can be composed and lead well; you compartmentalize to lead and self-protect. Then later, you neatly repack your suitcase of baggage and move forward," she says.

Laura's career in student affairs has spanned close to 40 years, with 20 spent as a senior student affairs officer. Like most senior student affairs officers, she devoted many years to preparing and moving up through the ranks, serving in operational and leadership roles in residential life and housing, campus activities, college union management, judicial affairs, and so on. All practitioners must learn to "think ahead" as well as to react quickly and effectively manage ambiguity and challenges under many constraints and unique settings. While in these roles, we have the unusual vantage point of dealing with the very best and the very worst of what occurs on our university campuses. Many of us see, as Clark Kerr observed in 1963, our institutions as small cities. They are discrete ecosystems filled with hopes, dreams, possibilities, and sometimes bureaucracy, sadness, and despair. Each campus creates a unique context that shapes the student experience in its own image. Campus communities also frequently demonstrate their character and resilience when a crisis strikes. While the many campus micro-communities may at times exhibit strained and even adversarial relationships with each other, they remarkably emerge to find common ground when the larger community has been deeply hurt or harmed in some way.

Unfortunately, witnessing and managing crises have always been an integral part of life as a student affairs practitioner. Student affairs and senior university leadership work certainly present the opportunity to learn and grow daily—to discover the ability to dig deep even when it is hard to imagine there is anything left. Laura had one such experience: a devastating fire that struck the residence halls at Seton Hall University on January 19, 2000. Although many aspects of this experience are a blur for her, many things made an indelible impression on her heart, mind, and soul.

Usually crises on campus are "just" a campus community issue or concern, but 9/11 and Hurricane Sandy—and issues surrounding them—are still in the news today: national security and terrorism, funding for physical and mental health first responders and others affected by the disasters, the level of security required when traveling on planes, funding to rebuild communities, and so forth. The events described in this chapter were the impetus for several campus, local, city, and national practices. For example, the events Laura managed at the Seton Hall University fire catalyzed changes that resulted in the installation of fire suppression systems in residence halls across the nation.

Here we share glimpses into our experiences as a chief student affairs officer through the Seton Hall University residence hall fire, the September 11 terrorist attacks, and Hurricane Sandy. Use them as case studies, tabletop drills, and opportunities to reflect on student affairs crisis leadership and staff development.

## SETON HALL FIRE, JANUARY 19, 2000 – LAURA

It was a cold January day when my phone rang at 4:35 a.m. Of course, it was not that unusual for a call to come in the middle of the night, but this time my associate vice president was on the line, and he sounded unusually distressed: "There's a fire in Boland Hall. It's bad. You need to come." Boland Hall is a first-year student residence hall with approximately 700 students residing in two separate wings that adjoin on each floor. I drove the 23 miles from my home to the dorm in record time while contacting other key university leaders to alert them to the unfolding challenge ahead.

When I arrived, the flashing lights from firetrucks, police cars, and ambulances created an eerie backdrop to the pre-dawn chaos before me. Firefighters, police, students, and staff were running in various directions; smoke was pouring from the building; individuals were being carried out on stretchers. Students in their nightclothes were tearful and dazed as they looked for friends and roommates while clutching their blankets, stuffed animals, and jackets. We quickly opened the student center to create a gathering place for students to get out of the frigid air and into some shelter. It would be the beginning of a very long and difficult semester.

The early hours were overwhelming as emergency responders, residential life employees, and other university faculty and staff frantically attempted to do something to be helpful. The number of individuals exiting the building, combined with the dark and the cold, made it very difficult to truly comprehend what was happening, who was being transported, who was okay, and who needed help. Several individuals were being treated at the scene, while ambulance after ambulance carried students to multiple area hospitals. It was hard to even imagine where all these ambulances and firetrucks were coming from; clearly, there was a significant mutual aid response from surrounding towns.

Seton Hall University is in South Orange, New Jersey, a small suburban town 14 miles outside of Manhattan. It is one of the country's oldest and leading Catholic universities, serving more than 10,000 undergraduate and graduate students. In addition to the normal mix of faculty, staff, and students, Seton Hall also has a significant priest presence on campus. This faith community played a critical role in our recovery from this tragedy.

The New York City media descended on us immediately from all directions. As we were trying to figure out who was where and what exactly had happened, reporters with microphones and cameras started broadcasting immediately, looking to get the scoop for the early morning drive-in news. Then, as we were primarily focused on attending to our students, the media infiltrated our student center, which was serving as a triage area. Corralling the media into a controlled environment, away from students, became a priority in order to protect students' privacy in their most vulnerable moments. Many reporters were aggressive, intrusive, and without empathy. Once New York media started broadcasting, we were deluged with frantic family members calling and showing up in search of news about their students, along with many sensation seekers with nothing but curiosity to offer.

As dawn started to break, we learned that we had 3 fatalities and that about 58 students had been transported to multiple hospitals. Who exactly was where was still unknown. The emergency response from the state, county, and local authorities was overwhelming. The executive team convened to plan our journey forward—and what a journey it was. Simply gathering the facts and identifying the deceased and injured (and where they all were) was daunting. The scope and diversity of issues and necessary tasks was well beyond the Division of Student Affairs: This was a major institutional event, and it required a full institutional response.

Naturally, our students and their well-being was the single most important thing to us all. This common sense of purpose drove us to quickly mobilize necessary support without the negotiation typically accompanying requests for support—now was clearly not a time for "business as usual." After I said that we needed a way for students to reach their loved ones, my colleague, the vice president for finance and technology, immediately had a phone bank up and running in the student center. As an executive team, we naturally gravitated to our areas of expertise and collaboratively started to distribute the general categories of responsibility (e.g., student support, public relations and media management, internal communications). We never could have planned or staffed to the diversity and sheer volume of people and activities that needed our attention.

Yet somehow, we mobilized a massive effort that was well beyond the sum of our individual parts.

Because this event occurred before 9/11, the entire field of campus crisis management was considerably less sophisticated than it is today. In fact, when it was time to respond to 9/11, we were much more prepared than many others. I learned an extraordinary amount from working with the county emergency manager, who convened situation meetings that included all university responders and emergency first responders from EMS, police, fire, state police, local government, facilities specialists, and others. Our initial task was to meet hourly and report new information from our sector of responsibility, including the identification of critical needs. These group sessions were incredibly valuable in helping us to create meaningful structure and organization for a situation steeped in chaos and confusion.

Almost instantly when the news broke, we started to receive an outpouring of offers from volunteers who wanted to do something, anything, to help. On one level, this was a wonderful expression of humanity and concern, and yet on another, it was one more thing to manage. Being able to distinguish between what is needed and helpful and what is not is time consuming, and it requires considerable diplomacy as well as situational and institutional knowledge.

Managing those who wanted to help exposed a significant leadership challenge that I had never contemplated. So many things needed to be done that required a certain level of experience, background, and knowledge, and these things simply exceeded the available experience across my team. Student affairs units (housing, counseling, security, etc.) represent a cross-section of experience in terms of both years and scope of work. This is a strength, not a problem, under normal working conditions; however, that is not the case when dealing with a large-scale crisis. Although many people were willing to take on any task, not every task could be taken on by anybody. Simply put, we needed five people with the background of the vice president for student affairs, the director of residence life, or director of counseling to advance many of the agendas and make certain decisions.

The one thing that helped mitigate this concern was the phenomenal outreach and tangible support we received from so many good student affairs colleagues in New Jersey and across the nation. Deans, vice presidents, counselors, and other professionals came to our campus to help where they could. Some filled aforementioned gaps, including identifying alternative suitable housing for hundreds of students, working with junior staff to organize projects and approaches, helping student and professional staff debrief and process what they had experienced, and bringing qualified counselors to help us respond to our students' emotional needs. The experience and presence that these colleagues brought to the campus had an incredibly positive impact on the tasks at hand and our staff morale. I will be forever grateful to them for their care and concern in our time of need.

I also received hundreds of e-mails from colleagues across the nation—some I knew, many I did not—who simply wanted to express their condolences and well wishes, offering to help. Many of these e-mails were read in the very early morning hours of the days following the fire, when I was attempting to sleep in my office but usually found myself glued to my computer. These messages touched my heart and provided solace when I needed it most. The powerful bond that connects the student affairs profession was most evident during these moments. The most surprising and moving e-mail I received, however, was not from a colleague; rather, it was from a former student from whom I had not heard in many years. In fact, I had suspended this student for lighting a poster on fire in a residence hall at another institution many years before. His message said, "I saw what happened in the news, and I knew you were there. I had to send a note to express how sorry I am that you are dealing with this, but even more so, to thank you for preventing me from causing a similar situation so many years ago. I could never have lived with myself, and I am so appreciative for what you did." Never again would I question the impact that we can have on individuals, even when it is least expected.

While our team grappled with the logistics of housing and feeding students, destroyed personal belongings, and a significantly damaged building (three floors of which would remain offline for the duration of the spring semester), we also attended to the psychological and emotional needs of students and staff alike. This could not be a one-size-fits-all approach, as the circumstances of our students and staff differed greatly. Some had merely been inconvenienced by needing to leave the building on a cold January morning; others had lost their friends and personal possessions, sustained injuries, and seen things they would never forget. A stratified approach that best leveraged our available resources of personnel and that would optimally meet students' needs became another significant leadership challenge.

Relocating students' belongings to an offsite warehouse and shuttling students and their families to review the possessions and file insurance claims was a logistical and emotional nightmare. So many administrators and faculty were working well outside the normal scope of their roles. It was not uncommon to see information technology or business office staff comforting and assisting students and their families as they sifted through their belongings. Faculty and academic administrators were convening groups of students who simply needed to talk. People stepped up wherever they could to create solutions and support. Many individuals discovered a new range of skills and formed some very interesting work teams that would never have come together under normal conditions. Another positive by-product was that a new level of understanding, respect, and appreciation for the insights, contributions, and work of the student affairs team emerged.

As we gained some distance from the initial event, we identified ways that work efforts could be segmented and redefined both hourly and daily. In order to ensure that the individuals most impacted by the fire were not lost in the confusion, we designated an area that was staffed by the career center team. All personnel in that area had student affairs backgrounds and possessed the requisite skills to work closely with students in a caring way. These students required a tremendous amount of support and, in some cases, basic needs, such as clothing. Each student was assigned a case worker who was responsible for ensuring that the student had a personal connection with one individual who would serve as their advocate and concierge. Their case worker would facilitate and ensure their linkage to the help and support they needed, thus eliminating all unnecessary bureaucracy or delay in connecting the most vulnerable students with the appropriate support. Many of the career center staff developed lifelong bonds with those students, but we avoided layers of bureaucracy and red tape, enabling us to customize, personalize, and expedite our response.

Dealing with the mental health needs of the campus community was daunting. Everyone needed to process what had happened. Although some of it could be addressed in group listening sessions, much could not. Students were not the only ones who needed help: Residential life staff, particularly those who worked in Boland Hall and had immediately responded to the tragedy, needed to restore equilibrium to their lives. They had seen and done so much that they were forever changed. They acted as heroes do, selflessly giving and placing themselves in harm's way to help others escape and survive.

My first meeting with those folks was a difficult and powerful moment. Words escaped me—I did not know what exactly to say that could adequately acknowledge what they had done and offer comfort and reassurance that we would all heal and move forward. Staff members knew they had not failed; nevertheless, they had a strong sense of responsibility for their residents and were deeply troubled by the tragedy. In those first moments, the best I could do, as I looked into their exhausted and dazed eyes, was to repeat what our president had said to our executive team when we first came together earlier that morning: "We will start our meeting with the Lord's Prayer and be mindful that in it we ask for today's bread, not tomorrow's bread, or next week's or next year's bread; we ask only for today's bread. We will move forward each day, asking for that day's bread." The power of faith was never more palpable to me than it was during those initial moments.

Another clear leadership challenge was getting staff to step back and get some rest. People were functioning on pure adrenaline. Staff members found it very difficult to take care of themselves without feeling guilty that they were somehow derelict if they tried to sleep, eat a proper meal, or leave campus. Helping and in most cases directing them to take care of themselves became increasingly more important as the days and tasks dragged endlessly on. Knowing when to step back and leave others in charge was an important lesson for all of us to learn.

As a Catholic university, faith was integral to our mission and a significant aspect of our healing journey. Faith and spirituality allowed the community to reflect, bond, find hope, and, for some, even find peace. The campus priest community, some 50 men strong, spent innumerable hours tending to the hospitalized students and their families, listening and praying with those who sought their counsel, and organizing services to celebrate the lives of those lost to the tragedy. Regardless of our beliefs or religious affiliations, or lack thereof, it was possible to focus on our common humanity and move forward. All members of the campus community, regardless of their affiliation (e.g., priest, administrator, faculty, student, security officer), discovered new ways to connect to each other's humanity. An unbreakable sense of common purpose and a community spirit of hope and healing emerged.

As I reflect on those days with the benefit of time and considerable distance, many lessons and memories are indelibly etched in my consciousness. Although the days were long and hard, the community was resilient. The capacity of all those people to have found ways to give their time, talent, spirit, and energy to others for the sake of making them whole again attests to the indomitable goodness that resides in all of us. The complexity of managing a crisis and its aftermath cannot be fully appreciated until you do it. Handling logistics, communications, and staff well-being all converge, demanding time and attention that often exceed resources. The unfortunate evolution of our profession has made crisis management a well-planned, elaborate, and practiced part of our work.

Although communication has always been a challenge, it is even more problematic today. Individuals expect—and often are able—to get live video coverage of everything. Social media outlets will often carry news of an event even before it is reported through mainstream channels. Managing and accurately communicating the message is far more difficult than it has ever been. While I do not have solutions to the many aspects of crisis management, I do know that putting thorough and practiced plans in place, developing strong collaborations with campus and local emergency responders, and having a caring, motivated, dedicated, and flexible team of good colleagues will always ensure the best possible outcome to a difficult situation.

## September 11, 2001, Pace University, New York City – Marijo

*At 8:46 a.m. on September 11, 2001, the North Tower of the World Trade Center was struck by American Airlines Flight 11 and collapsed at 10:28 a.m. The South Tower was hit at 9:03 a.m. by United Airlines Flight 175 and collapsed at 10:05 a.m. The 47-floor 7 World Trade Center collapsed at 5:20 p.m.*

It was an incredibly beautiful, clear-blue-sky day, the first Tuesday of the semester and the first day of my UNV 101 class. I was in the office early as usual, taking advantage of the quiet time to complete tasks. My office faced New York City's City Hall, just a few blocks up from the World Trade Center. Around 8:45 a.m., I was on the phone with my supervisor when he asked, "What is that noise?" I replied, "Oh, a loud low-flying plane just flew by." I had just seen the first plane fly by the Woolworth Building. I heard the plane hit the North Tower from my office, and yet I replied, "I don't know. I see lots of people running. I think it is a bomb. I will call you back." My brain could not compute what I had just seen—it was too unbelievable. A bomb felt more believable as I saw crowds running up toward City Hall, both sides of Broadway, and toward the Brooklyn Bridge. I saw thousands of people running and walking over the bridge. They were covered in gray and tan ash.

I slammed the phone receiver down, descended nine floors to the street, and saw the tower on fire. I found students, neighbors, and workers crying and bloodied; some stood paralyzed with horror. We watched with mouths agape as people jumped from the burning towers. Many people were running toward Pace. I told people to get inside and went to my office. The cell phones were jammed with everyone calling around the world. Using my office landline, I called the babysitter and told her to "stay inside, don't open windows or use air conditioning. It smells like gasoline outside. Stay in place with the toddler." I know she wanted to walk out and take him to her home in Brooklyn, but the situation was too uncertain. My last words to her were, "*Stay* until one of us gets there." I called my husband, my parents, and my in-laws and relayed the same message to each of them: "We are good. We will be in touch."

Springing into action, I rushed to the security base—a pre-established campus command center—and began distributing breathing masks and bottled water. We asked the campus community to gather in the large assembly areas—the gymnasium, theater, cafeteria, large lecture halls, and student union—for safety and used mass communication (at that time, bullhorns and the public address system). We sent staff to residence halls, even halls we leased close to the disaster. Staff told students to shelter in place until they were told otherwise. We were trying to contain over 8,000 students and determine who was accounted for and who was not. If students had to leave the building, we required them to say where they were going and give contact information. We gathered emergency supplies—food, water, batteries, flashlights, and more—and began to seek alternative shelter options for students who could not return to their residence hall rooms. Many injured individuals went to the hospital across the street (which was not affiliated with Pace), and people with minor injuries came to campus. We sent staff to nearby hospitals and to outer boroughs, where the ferries were landing with evacuees.

A rumor began in the gymnasium that there was a gas leak, so the crowd there began to panic and push. We addressed the group and informed them that there was no leak, instructing them to shelter in place. I reflect now that this must have been about 9:03 a.m., when the second plane struck the South Tower. The facilities teams immediately shut down all the in-take and exhaust fans and valves so we would not contaminate our facilities or our air. I remember looking out of our outdoor courtyard area in the main building after both towers fell. I don't recall if it was 10:00 a.m., noon, or the afternoon, but I could not even see my hand in front of my face. No buildings. No cars. It looked like a bomb had hit. All that remained was covered with a khaki-colored ash, and an acrid smell of fire, gas, diesel, plastics, and other contaminates filled the air. I felt like I had fiberglass insulation in my eyes, nose, and throat.

Students in nearby residence halls had an unobstructed view of the events of 9/11; faculty and staff had not yet arrived on campus or were stuck in transit. In the moment, to be candid, we had no clue where our community members were located. A board of trustees meeting was scheduled for that morning, since we had recently renovated our World Trade Institute on the 55th floor of the North Tower. Thankfully, the renovations were not complete, so the trustees met at the midtown center. The university formed a second command center in midtown and later on the Westchester campus.

The next day, with help from the NYPD, the mayor's office, and the Office of Emergency Management, we were able to get city buses to transport our community members out of Lower Manhattan to the Brooklyn-leased residence hall and the Westchester campus, both of which were supplied with food, water, clothes, books, sleeping bags, cash, and counseling by the afternoon. Tuesday night into Wednesday morning we were able to get a back-up generator, since our city partners also thought it would be needed for the hospital across the street and the Pace community.

Later we learned that there were no injured people—only dead. It was heartbreaking to see emergency personnel come to the university covered in ash looking for food, a safe place to sleep, and water. On Thursday, we were able to set up hotlines for parents, pushing communications through word of mouth, instant messenger, and walkie-talkies until systems were restored, having gone down for several days. Staffing hotlines was difficult because we were not always able to tell parents where their children were. Later, the admissions office became a National Guard hospital and the student union a morgue. We put dark paper on all the glass windows and cleared the room of chairs, leaving just tables. It felt grim.

The university connected with the Borough of Manhattan Community College (which lost an academic building in the disaster) and other area universities to share resources (e.g., generators, residence halls, classrooms, trailers). After every space of every building was cleaned and provided with large HEPA air filters, Pace reopened its doors—10 days after the attack.

During the crisis, Pace's president called the emergency response team together frequently each day to plan, brainstorm, chart our next move, and identify how to get the university up, open, and healed. The team relied on business and academic continuity back-up plans; foremost, the team's priority was community safety and the physical and mental well-being of students, faculty, and staff. The president resided in the main residence hall that academic year to show the campus community that it was safe to return.

I can say affirmatively that counseling is necessary for large- or small-impact events/crises. It is not to be underestimated. It is key—at the moment of crisis, throughout the management of the situation, and, in this case, many months thereafter—to rely on counseling consultants for the community. Alternative classroom content delivery (e.g., video, research papers, independent projects, online discussions), space delivery (e.g., using online and group classes), and extended semester calendar templates were useful. In hindsight, maintaining printed contact information for students, staff members, and executives, as well as phone numbers to hospitals, contract vendors, food service, facilities management, and emergency supply providers are all helpful when you have no electricity and no communication system. Phone service, e-mail, and even ATM access were impossible for a time. A well-trained staff is essential when the unexpected happens—training faculty and staff on their roles before a crisis occurs is critical. Remembrances and community services are also important ways for the campus community to heal and unite. Diverse people and religions came together, focusing on healing rather than on the terrorists' mission. Sadly, Pace University lost 47 members of the campus community and/or alumni on September 11, 2001. We arranged for 75 four-year scholarships for students whose families were the most directly affected.

On a personal note, it was a difficult time. Sometime late that Tuesday afternoon or early evening, my husband managed to walk home from 14th Street, navigating all the police barricades and telling officers that he was trying to get home to his son and babysitter. We finally met up at home and were told to evacuate the apartment building. We were told simply to "go to the river." We packed a "go" bag of clothes, water, and personal documents and began to leave the apartment. My toddler turned to me and said, "City gone, Mommy," because you could see nothing out of our windows—just gray ash, no buildings. After carrying a suitcase and a toddler in his stroller down 16 flights of stairs, we decided to return to Pace. Try keeping a breathing mask on a toddler while frantically lugging suitcases—we looked like a mess, we were covered in ash, and, it goes without saying, we were pretty freaked out. We set up in an empty residence hall room and stayed there until we could leave (the following Saturday, September 15). Throughout those days and nights, I assisted students who didn't know where to go.

I returned to work at Pace's midtown center on 45th Street on Monday, September 17, and classrooms reopened on September 25, 2001. The combination of having to respond to a national and a campus crisis that also directly affected my family and forced me to evacuate my home was a double whammy in terms of trauma and its after effects. When my family returned to our apartment, my son said, "City back, Mommy sad." This statement broke my heart, and I realized that I, too, was not quite myself.

I am glad that I sought counseling to help me sort out my feelings about my role in that day and the guilt of not being able to directly protect my family. It helps immensely to get yourself on the right track, to recalibrate—the "check-up from the neck up." Today, I live across the street from the Freedom Tower and see the site from my bedroom window; it is a regular reminder of pain and sadness, but also gratitude.

Notable projects came out of this experience, beyond our annual remembrance events. Pace student Joshua Good (2001) shot video of the attacks from his residence hall window, choosing not to release the footage until 15 years after that day and graciously granting me permission to reference his work here. On the 10th anniversary, Pace University (2011a) produced *Pace Remembers 9/11,* a video of those of us who were on site that fateful day. Additionally, Pace University produced a 9/11 oral history project, some contributors offered writing and others shot video (Pace University, 2011b).

## Hurricane Sandy, October 22 through November 7, 2012 – Marijo

The second large-impact crisis event of my career was Hurricane Sandy, also known as Super Storm Sandy, in 2012. In 2011, my family evacuated to Pace for Hurricane Irene, which turned out to be nothing more than a rain and wind storm. So, my spouse refused to evacuate for Sandy, despite us living in the evacuation zone in Lower Manhattan on the Hudson River. We stockpiled batteries, flashlights, food, water, power cords, and such at home and, of course, at the university.

Our decision to ignore the mayor's request to evacuate the city became a blessing. We were unable to reach the hotel I had reserved ("just in case"), because transit was shut down. Our apartment building ended up being one of very few that did not lose power. When I came home from managing a crisis each day, I found neighbors and friends in my home 10 at a time for showers, charging stations, the news on television, and my ability to whip up hot food. I was exhausted but, again, grateful.

On campus, the residence halls were full. At first, students were happy to have no class, but later they became bored without full electricity. When the mayor began closing the city and all mass transit, Pace encouraged any individual who had a safe place to go to leave campus and to inform us where they were headed. In hindsight, students who left for New Jersey and Connecticut probably fared worse, as those areas lost electricity for a longer time.

Security, residence life staff, and I gathered all residents into the residence halls that had back-up generators. Because the main building (which contains a freshman residence hall) runs on natural gas, we had it better than did others in Lower Manhattan. The university contacted Borough of Manhattan Community College, New York University, and other local institutions for shared resources; however, each one had "Sandy" issues to contend with. We offered charging stations to power phones and portable lamps. We also provided hot food (scheduled buffet meals and an evening snack, not full service), and a Halloween movie night. (I'm not sure, to this day, how the RAs jury-rigged a movie.) Eventually, we needed to transport residents by university bus from residence halls three and four blocks away to the main building, as those halls were running out of diesel. Cots were set up in the gymnasium and theater lobby. Hot food continued for about four days, until we realized we could not sustain campus operations another week to 10 days. The Pace daily status report stated: "NY campus—no electricity, no steam, no elevators, no apparent major damage to any property on emergency generator power at Pace Plaza [meaning only life safety power on generator]. On generator power at 55 John St., 106 Fulton evacuated and closed, 41 Park Row closed; Brooklyn Residence did not lose power. No internal phone service between NY and Westchester, cell phone service spotty, food available for students." With no public transportation available, we housed cafeteria workers, facilities staff, and security personnel who were critical to maintaining an open campus, along with students and anyone who needed help. We announced that students could stay but the status was as such.

We encouraged students to perform community service in the neighborhood, to both alleviate their boredom and address the large need in terms of the elderly and flooded downtown communities. An article in *The Chronicle of Higher Education* (Peterkin, 2012) cited the service our students performed during the crisis. We reopened the downtown campus doors on November 7, 2012, and began to set up wide-scale relief efforts for community members affected by the storm.

In their graduation video, several members of the class of 2016 commented on how Hurricane Sandy was the best bonding experience the university ever planned. You must find humor where you can. Some days you can't make this up.

## Leading and Building Partnerships in Times of Crisis

In a crisis, communication and contact with staff and campus partners is challenging and requires a different way to lead. During 9/11, Marijo recalls working with others in a more directive style (e.g., use these exits, remain in the gym, wear a mask), but after everyone left campus and only the people at the Command Center remained (i.e., the president, the president's chief of staff, the director of security, director of counseling, and herself), communication became more collaborative. Marijo had very little contact with the outside world until her cell phone started working the following Sunday, and she saw people other than her family only after she relocated to the midtown center on the following Monday. They all just cried as soon as they saw each other. All official communications were sent via the president's office and university relations. During Hurricane Sandy, the community was all together—students, staff, faculty, and dining and security workers—and Marijo was on conference calls with the executive team, again in the command center.

Any crisis of magnitude needs a communication plan during and after the event, typically led by the president, legal counsel, and university relations, with the vice president for student affairs (VPSA) as a partner, not necessarily the leader—even though the VPSA often has the best information, usually having been present at the crisis scene. Written and in-person communication and e-alerts are valuable. Crisis response and communication protocols are what a good, ethical community does, but they also allay fears. We continually reinforced and communicated available resources for the community; the most salient was counseling.

In crisis situations, Marijo has found it works to break down position authority and lead where everyone is more equal, but with specific roles/tasks/skills, with the delegation and decisions resting with the VPSA (and the president/executive team). Set up communication centers and plans (directors to communicate to their staff/units, to and for students/parents), so the information trickles down. Communication must be frequent and transparent.

The VPSA is often seen as the de-escalator, the comforting person, the heart and warmth of the campus. It is impossible for a VPSA to attend every residence life, counseling, campus activities, or diversity affairs staff meeting to directly provide information and a "comforting touch." The leader must take charge, see the forest for the trees (and sometimes see the forest and the trees at the same time), and offer plans of action and networks for support. Therefore, VPSAs should give staff opportunities to participate in the decision-making and solutions processes.

Diffuse tensions at all cost. Student affairs leaders tend to rely on humor, if appropriate, or a hug, again, if appropriate. What should be a given is having a close-knit, well-trained team that knows when to lead and when to follow; these individuals must be able to follow instructions and think on their feet. Generally, a VPSA's mind is in SWOT (strengths, weaknesses, opportunities and threats) mode, but an eye must be kept to other essential business—that is, the emotional well-being of staff. It is critical for staff to take care of themselves for both their individual well-being and to ensure that they are functional for the duration of the emergency. It is also helpful to utilize responsibility charting (Galbraith, Downey, & Kates, 2002) as a way for everyone to know whose responsibility is whose and what actions should take place next. It is best to do tabletop drills or case studies with staff, but make sure to also include security staffers and others so that each team is allowed to talk through, practice, and get comfortable with emergency and continuity planning (Department of Homeland Security, 2018; National Association of College and University Business Officers, 2018). Leaders must train and retrain staff, assessing and fine-tuning the process for a positive and safe student experience. Pace even developed a brochure and web page that is still in use: "Proper Planning Promotes Preparedness" (https://www.pace.edu/security-emergency-management/emergency-procedures). In particular, it emphasizes the need to be ready with a stocked "go" bag and printed copies of important phone numbers.

A VPSA must build a solid team and, in crisis, use each individual's strengths. Building a network of internal and external "dependables"—people who have operational (food, oil, water, beds) and physical (able bodies) resources—who can be relied on for a quick response is key. This can be likened to building, in concentric circles, collaborations or partnerships across service areas or disciplines on campus. These circles of relationships overlap, eventually forging a sense of trust to enact or to "call on" teams of volunteers, thinkers, and doers.

Caring for staff in times of crisis requires shifting one's mindset away from SWOT mode. Often, to keep busy and not think about an experience, we quickly start to plan future committees, a policy review, or a revision of emergency procedures. While one side of the brain is working on the emergency and the immediate next steps, the other side is working on how best to care for staff. The things that come to mind first are debriefing and giving people time off, but everyone experiences crises in very different ways. Some individuals retreat, physically and emotionally, while some gather around other people; some remain calm and others break down. Offer resources and create understanding, time, and space for people to process the experience and move forward.

The day-to-day work experience in student affairs can often feel like a triaged life. Each day a phone call, e-mail, or visit from a student or a faculty member drops little "bombs," or messes, for us to fix. We juggle administrative responsibilities as well as daily student crises—illnesses, deaths, absences during finals, disruptive behaviors, angry parents—which can set off a string of reactions and missed meetings. Often, we find that we are good at managing these kinds of issues, because most often they are not life-threatening situations (although the students might disagree).

Though student affairs leaders are able to triage responses every day, we often fail to practice self-care. Balance and boundaries are important. It is vitally important to take time off, use vacation time, and step away from the cell phone. It can be difficult, but each person has to find their own way to refuel. Having friends outside of higher education can offer new perspective and allow you to laugh differently, sometimes more wholeheartedly. Student affairs work requires that we prepare our minds and bodies for the daily demands and be at the ready for emergencies, big and small. Always remember that "rest and self-care are so important. When you take time to replenish your spirit, it allows you to serve others from the overflow. You cannot serve from an empty vessel" (Brownn, 2013, p. 1).

It is also important to have trusted colleagues with whom you can vent, create and vet solutions, and develop tactics. Build partnerships with other senior student affairs officers nearby for resource sharing and for an ear to talk out what is happening. This provides a space to talk freely and obtain an outside point of view, and it will calm your brain. Develop strong relationships with the president's office and chief of staff, so you can alert them of any coming storms and be seen as a problem solver—someone useful to have around day to day but even more so in a crisis.

Eleanor Roosevelt's (1960) words in *You Learn by Living* ring true for our work: "You gain strength, courage, and confidence by every experience in which you really stop to look fear in the face. You are able to say to yourself, 'I lived through this horror. I can take the next thing which comes along. . . .' You must do the thing you think you cannot do" (pp. 29–30).

# References

Brownn, E. (2013). My spiritual sabbatical [Blog post]. Retrieved from https://eleanorbrownn.wordpress.com/2013/09/04/rest-and-self-care-are-so-important-when-you-take-time-to-replenish-your-spirit-it-allows-you-to-serve-others-from-the-overflow-you-cannot-serve-from-an-empty-vessel

Department of Homeland Security. (2018). *The national seminar and tabletop exercise series for institutions of higher education (NTTX)*. Retrieved from https://www.dhs.gov/nttx

Galbraith, J., Downey, D., & Kates, A. (2002). Designing dynamic organizations: A hands-on guide for leaders at all levels. New York, NY: American Management Association.

Good, J. (2001). *New September 11, 2001 raw video* [Video file]. Retrieved from https://www.youtube.com/watch?v=siYkDNbeRZk&feature=youtu.be

Kerr, C. (1963). *The uses of the university*. Cambridge, MA: Harvard University Press.

National Association of College and University Business Officers. (2018). *Risk management and campus security*. Retrieved from https://www.nacubo.org/Topics/Other-Business-Areas/Risk-Management-and-Campus-Security

Pace University. (2011a). *Pace remembers 9/11* [Video file]. Retrieved from https://www.youtube.com/watch?v=tHgJLz3AD_E

Pace University. (2011b). *Pace University: 9/11 oral history project*. Retrieved from http://webpage.pace.edu/911oralhistoryproject

Peterkin, C. (2012, November 8). A week after Hurricane Sandy, students step up their relief work. *The Chronicle of Higher Education*. Retrieved from https://www.chronicle.com/article/A-Week-After-Hurricane-Sandy/135686

Roosevelt, E. (1960). *You learn by living: Eleven keys for a more fulfilling life*. New York, NY: Harper Perennial.

# 4

# Collateral Beauty

## Lee E. Bird

Tragedy is a difficult but good teacher. Writing this chapter as I look toward retirement allowed me the chance to reflect on the many tragedies our campus has faced. The images that surround the incidents are indelible, as are the lessons: Do the right thing; focus on the victims and the people who love them, not the cost of doing so; keep your promises; look for the good; say "thank you" as often as possible and let people know that their acts of kindness and sacrifice matter; and be a good neighbor—when other campuses are in crisis, reach out to those on the front lines.

The opportunity to help others is what has kept me in student affairs for more than 40 years—I worked 23 years as the senior student affairs officer at three different campuses and the past 17 years at Oklahoma State University (OSU). I have found that managing student and campus crises is regrettably commonplace. Students face family issues as well as those related to loss, personal identity, finances, relationships, academic skills, and life direction, among other things. Sometimes we can perform "minor miracles," such as providing money for food or to pay down a bill, fixing a car or a computer, helping a student connect to a faculty member or a business contact, or offering alternatives to a vexing personal problem. Major campus crises require similar skills—such as care and concern, as well as problem solving—but these skills are not necessarily subject to the same "muscle memory" as those used in our daily professional lives. Major crises are unique. Not every problem has a solution, and we may feel helpless or overwhelmed by both the challenges and the opportunities that crises create. At OSU, where I serve as vice president for student affairs, we have had more than our fair share of crises.

Five years before I accepted my current position, I was deeply moved by how the state of Oklahoma dealt with the bombing of the Alfred P. Murrah Federal Building in downtown Oklahoma City, just an hour south of the OSU campus in Stillwater. The blast killed 168 people, many of whom were children, and injured over 600 more. I remember where I was when the news showed the devastation to the Murrah building and other structures in a 16-block radius. The tragedy occurred on April 19, 1995; on April 19, 2000, the Oklahoma City National Memorial was dedicated. Soon after, an on-site museum opened to visitors—it was one of my first stops when I moved to Oklahoma.

At the memorial I learned about the "Oklahoma standard," a level of care and community service characterized by kindness and sacrifice in the face of adversity. Inside the memorial was a quote by a member of one of the eleven urban search and rescue teams that had been activated by the Federal Emergency Management Agency. Dennis Compton of the Arizona Task Force said, "We went to Oklahoma City to assist with a horrible situation that centered around death and destruction, but we went home with a life lesson on how a community should react to adversity" (Warner, 2015, p. 1). This statement, which appears on a plaque at the Oklahoma City Memorial Museum, acknowledges that in a time of great crisis and loss, lessons can be learned about beauty and community. Wally Amos of Famous Amos Cookies once said, "When you're going through hell, don't stop to take pictures" (Thomas, 1996, p. 43sf). This becomes our challenge: looking for and remembering beauty, rather than destruction, whenever possible. Some lives have been lost; others have been changed forever. Families must cope with the loss of a loved one—a child, a spouse, a parent, a sibling, a dear friend—and, try as we may, we can't change that reality, but we can offer help getting through the crisis to the reality of a "new normal." Little did I know that within just a few months of my arriving in Oklahoma, OSU would face a significant crisis.

## 2001 Plane Crash

At 5:37 p.m. on January 27, 2001, a plane carrying 10 members of the OSU basketball family (two athletes, six operations and media personnel, and two pilots) crashed in a snowy field near Strasberg, Colorado, following a game against the University of Colorado. I received the news of the crash shortly before 9:00 p.m. that night. My director of counseling learned of the suspected crash from a neighbor who was a highway patrol officer, and called me to let me know what she had heard. The 9:00 p.m. newsbreak confirmed the crash, and we drove to campus and discussed where we could do the most good.

I had been at OSU for only six months at this point. I was still figuring out the strengths of each of my direct reports. Over the course of the weeks that followed the crash, I would come to fully appreciate them for the strength and care my staff showed.

We arrived at the basketball office by 9:13 p.m. to talk with players, coaching staff, the athletic director, the vice president for business and finance, and OSU President Jim Halligan. Coach Eddie Sutton, who had traveled from the game in Colorado on a separate plane, was desperately trying to reach family members of those killed in the crash before the nightly news aired at 10:00 p.m. The anguish of this task was clear in the voices and faces of the administrators gathered around Coach Sutton. Outside that office, players questioned why, others cried, some prayed. All were in shock and devastated by the loss of teammates and colleagues. Counseling staff members began calling in, asking where they were needed, and they were assigned to the residence halls where the deceased players lived and to those with a high concentration of student athletes. Food service opened in select halls almost by magic, but the cash registers remained off. After Coach Sutton, our athletic director, and President Halligan left to go to our small airport for a news conference, Suzanne Burks, director of counseling, met with her counselors in the halls.

Around midnight, we received a call that senior administrators, public information officers, the counseling director, and athletic staff would meet at 2:00 a.m. at a local business away from campus, as statewide media outlets had begun to swarm campus. The purpose of the meeting was to plan next steps, including serving families, planning a memorial service, and performing many other tasks. Athletic colleagues were clearly emotional and dealing with their own profound sense of loss. The meeting ended at 4:00 a.m., with several key decisions having been made:

- A lead team—composed of a campus police officer; the assistant vice president for business and finance, who had survived two plane crashes during the Vietnam War; and an attorney who worked for the athletic department—were to

travel to Colorado later that morning so they could be the eyes and ears of the family members who lost loved ones, help answer questions, and ensure the safe return of the deceased and their personal effects.
- A campus memorial service would be held three days later in Gallagher-Iba, our basketball arena, which was not completely finished from a major renovation. We discussed arranging for music and speakers and helping to transport family members from airports in Oklahoma City and Tulsa to the campus in Stillwater. Family members and their guests would be provided travel and lodging.
- Our president's instructions were clear: *no one* was to offer guesses on the cause of the plane crash, publicly or privately. We didn't know the cause and were not qualified to offer an opinion.
- Each family was assigned a representative from each of the following campus units: University Counseling Services, Human Resources, and Athletics. Any family question or need could be addressed to these representatives, day or night. (The bonds created between campus staff and the families have remained strong for 15-plus years.)
- Burks and I would meet with families who lived nearby as soon as possible.

By 10:00 a.m. Sunday, Burks and I were in a car preparing to meet with Stillwater families in their homes. Careful notes were taken at each home regarding immediate needs, names of extended family, and trusted friends. At every home, we left our business cards with instructions to call us day or night if we could be of any help before or after the memorial service.

As we moved from house to house, I received a call from a neighbor who would have a meal prepared for us whenever we had time to eat. This gracious offer and delicious meal remains one of my fondest memories—roast beef served quietly before a crackling fire. No questions, no TV, just a calm moment in a raging sea of emotion. This offer was repeated each night throughout the week. It was a gift from the heart of a good neighbor and friend, Sandy Barth, who saw this as her way to help. This, I would learn, is part of the Oklahoma standard.

Every staff member immediately sought ways to assist and care for our campus community. One purchased black and orange ribbon (our school colors) at every store she could find between Dallas and Stillwater. She and many student volunteers made over 15,000 ribbons to be worn by our campus community. Each person had unique relationships and assets that we would need to tap in the days ahead, such as finding capable student drivers, appropriate vehicles to use, student volunteers to help with parking, and a source for orange teddy bears with angel wings to give to each family member. My staff took the initiative to say, "What can I do to help?" Their communication with each other and with me was excellent, allowing us to perform necessary tasks quickly. Equally important, when someone said, "I can do that," we trusted it would be done and it was. Staff not on the front lines made sure that those who were had what they needed.

## *The Memorial Service*

The service held Wednesday afternoon was beautiful. Everything—the seating arrangements, the large photographs of the deceased placed on stage, and the musical performances—came together. The service was both deeply personal and representative of the larger campus culture. Fourteen thousand people crowded the newly dusted arena. Lunch for the families was provided before the service, and each family was escorted into the arena by its counselor. OSU athletic teams, including the basketball team, were seated on the arena floor. As the first family entered from the practice gym where lunch was served, everyone—without being asked—stood in silence as every honored guest took a seat. "One More Day" by Diamond Rio played as guests filed in. This became an indelible memory from that day, as did a sentiment expressed by President Halligan: "We are trying to encircle you with our love." Truer words were never spoken. During the service, he also remarked, "We will remember," and we have. He promised a memorial at the crash site and at Gallagher-Iba as well as free OSU tuition for the children of those who perished—several of the men on board had babies and small children—and we have kept those promises. In the days that followed the campus memorial service, we attended individual funerals in Oklahoma City and Stillwater. They provided an even more personal glimpse into the lives and the potential of those who were lost in the horrible crash.

As the campus service ended, the cold weather broke. I slept better that night but knew full well that the hard part lay ahead of us: help 10 families begin the healing process and tend to the needs of a hurting campus and community.

The following week, I discussed having an outside facilitator conduct a formal critical-incident stress debriefing exercise. I had previously participated in such training, as had many of my counseling staff members. This may be why they passed on this opportunity: They knew the symptoms to look for (trouble sleeping, disorientation, memory issues, uptick in alcohol use, anger, anxiety, muscle soreness, etc.) and felt comfortable talking to each other and their loved ones to avert some of the problems associated with acute crisis. Instead, they opted for a dinner at my house. The counseling staff prepared and distributed wonderful information sheets that could be rapidly and widely shared with faculty, staff, students, and community members. For many of our students, this was their first death experience, and they wanted more information on, and in some cases help with, processing their feelings.

## The Colorado Memorial

At the campus memorial service, President Halligan had promised that a memorial would be built at the crash site. Over the months that followed, family members and university officials made plans, the university purchased the crash site property, and construction began.

The Colorado Memorial was dedicated on August 25, 2001. Once again, travel and lodging arrangements were made for family members and guests. Never was there a discussion of cost. Our administration did the right thing at every turn to serve the grieving families; they were our focus and priority. Campus personnel were handpicked to serve specific roles before and during the dedication. I was honored to serve on a three-person counseling team. We arrived early to meet with emergency medical services (EMS) personnel in Strasberg and to see the crash site and memorial. Several months before the dedication, a lead team traveled to Colorado to walk the site and remove items such as bolts, paper, salt and pepper packets, and other debris. National Transportation Safety Board (NTSB) members had previously searched the area. I was shown a picture of this NTSB team from that day: 10 sunbeams pierced the clouds over the workers. The photo gave me goosebumps. I don't believe in coincidence.

The day before the dedication in Colorado, the counseling team met with family members who wanted to view the crash site and memorial before the official service. We walked and talked with them. August 24 was hot, and all of us were parched and sunburned at the end of the day. A large trough for ice and water was ordered. Later that evening, we joined family members for a dinner at the hotel to discuss service logistics. The next morning was cold and rainy as we boarded two buses for the nearly 45-minute ride to the memorial.

Police and highway patrol blocked entrances to the freeway as we passed. When we finally arrived, EMS, sheriff department personnel, highway patrol officers, and others formed two columns, flanking us as we made our way from the bus to the temporary seating area. Area police and EMS workers quickly searched their vehicles and called neighbors and friends for blankets to keep the family members dry and warm. When the service ended, the rain stopped and the clouds parted. Family and their friends were allowed to walk from the memorial to the crash site (about a quarter mile). Music selected by members of the campus support team played on the loudspeaker to disrupt the feed to media listening devices. At the site, family members could talk to NTSB members and emergency personnel who had responded to the crash.

Following the dedication, we boarded the buses and joined the EMS and NTSB personnel for a lunch provided by the local elementary school staff, an expression of love and care that touched our hearts. Later that night, OSU staff (counseling, logistics, marketing) were treated to dinner at a steakhouse owned by an OSU alum. We talked and relaxed together. The intense stress that we had experienced began to subside—that is, until the hotel's fire alarm went off overnight and we were forced to wait in the parking lot for several hours. It turned out there was no fire: Someone had set off a fire extinguisher and the dust had activated the alarm. We laughed about not being able to catch a break. I gave up and tried to sleep in the lobby of a neighboring hotel until the firetrucks cleared out.

## The Gallagher-Iba Arena Memorial

A few months after the Colorado memorial dedication, the Gallagher-Iba memorial was dedicated before a basketball game against the University of Colorado; it was January 2002, one year after the plane crash. The monument is simple and beautiful with a bronze statue called the *Kneeling Cowboy*. The names and images of those lost were etched in marble walls behind the statue, and two marble benches were placed there for contemplation. Our colleagues and new friends from Colorado joined us at this final memorial service. I don't remember who won the game. It didn't really matter. Both the Colorado and the Gallagher-Iba memorial were funded by donations. At the close of the dedication, President Halligan gave to each family a commemorative plaque featuring a likeness of the *Kneeling Cowboy* and made from the same marble used in both memorials. A week or so later, those of us involved in the memorial dedications and care teams received a similar gift from him at a luncheon he hosted.

A 5K and 10K run named "Remember the 10" was launched a few years later by a community member to help fund scholarships and provide specialized grief training for our counseling staff. Here again, someone used his interests and talents—in this case, as a running enthusiast and event coordinator—to help something good grow from something tragic. The night before the run each year, family members and university officials attend a dinner hosted by the university. Most of the families are represented. It is a time not only for reflection but also for catching up and looking ahead.

The children of the deceased are now grown, and family members have done their best to move forward with their lives. Like them, we will remember that day—always.

## Lightning Strikes Twice: The Second Plane Crash
### November 18, 2012

While visiting my mom in hospice care in Phoenix, I received a call from Burks letting me know that the plane carrying our women's basketball coach and assistant coach had gone down 45 miles west of Little Rock, Arkansas. I couldn't believe it: How could this happen to our campus again? The pilot, Olin Branstetter, and his wife, also an experienced pilot, perished along with Coach Kurt Budke and Coach Miranda Serna. I took an early flight home. Once again, Gallagher-Iba was transformed for another campus memorial service. The pilots were honored along with the coaches. Students hosted a candlelight remembrance in our Student Union and purchased four large, orange, lighted wreaths to be placed on our iconic Chi Omega clock in the center of campus. I attended the funeral services for the Branstetters and the service for Coach Serna, which was held in New Mexico over the Thanksgiving weekend.

## THE HOMECOMING TRAGEDY
## OCTOBER 24, 2015

A third tragedy took place the morning of our homecoming football game. The OSU homecoming parade is a long-standing town and gown tradition in the Stillwater community. Campus clubs and organizations, city services agencies, bands, politicians, and others participate each year. The parade goes down Main Street, with viewers lining both sides of the route. On parade day 2015, my office staff was selling spaces in a parking lot to benefit the United Way and did not participate in the parade. Typically, I would have participated with fellow volunteers for the American Red Cross.

Mitch Kilcrease, assistant vice president for student affairs and student union director, who was helping at the lot, received the initial call from a staff member at the parade. A driver ran a barricade near the end of the route. The caller heard that several people had been killed and many others were seriously injured. We didn't know at the time if this was a terrorist act, a drunk driver, or something else, but we knew it was going to be devastating for our community.

Our media communications staff, having just learned about the tragedy, had the wherewithal to ask all their contacts on social media to go silent, including all communication about the game, the homecoming events, beating the opposition, and so on. Everyone complied. As new information about the tragedy emerged, it was shared thoughtfully.

I decided to go directly to our local hospital, calling Burks on the way. Our small hospital would soon be overwhelmed with people, and I believed I could be of the most help there. In Arizona, I was a volunteer emergency medical technician for 14 years, and when I moved to Minnesota, I volunteered for more than seven years as a patient advocate in the St. Cloud Hospital Emergency Trauma Center. I also served on the Stillwater Medical Center (SMC) Foundation Board and knew many of the emergency room (ER) staff from prior emergencies involving students. Throughout these many roles, I had seen and experienced many horrible things (shootings, stabbings, serious accidents, acute illness, overdoses, etc.).

When I arrived at SMC, I was greeted by three people I had never seen before. Two introduced themselves as physicians from the hospital at the University of Oklahoma (our rivals) and the third was a chaplain, also from Oklahoma City. They were headed to the game when they heard about the tragedy and decided to volunteer their services at SMC. They helped perform triage at the walk-in emergency doors, allowing medical center staff to receive patients arriving by rescue helicopter and ambulance.

The car that ran the barricade struck an unmanned police motorcycle and ran over several people before coming to a stop near a light pole. The crash occurred between the float carrying children from our Campus Child Learning Lab, which had just passed through the intersection, and the last two parade entries: the OSU ROTC (Reserve Officers' Training Corps) unit and a Stillwater Fire Department truck, complete with gear and very capable firefighters. The firefighters drove straight into the chaos and immediately began triage: sorting the injured, providing first aid, covering the bodies of the dead, and OSU ROTC members helped protect the scene. The tales of heroism and sacrifice that day were remarkable. We heard amazing stories from people at the scene and those who came to the hospital.

Volunteers and professionals worked side by side to provide care to the wounded. The most seriously injured were taken by helicopter to trauma hospitals in Tulsa and Oklahoma City, each 60 to 70 miles away. Hall of Fame Street, just two blocks from campus, became a helipad; ROTC members, medics, and firefighters ran gurneys to and from the waiting helicopters. The helicopters landed and took off eight times. Some moderately injured were taken by ambulance and private vehicles to the hospital. Taylor Collins, still partially costumed to portray OSU mascot Pistol Pete, got his truck and helped deliver two injured children to the hospital for care.

In our hospital was controlled chaos. Friends and family were trying to unite with loved ones. An additional waiting area was created in a large room adjacent to the emergency room. Although the ER was nearing capacity, there was no yelling or racing around by staff. Having practiced mass casualty exercises, these professionals moved deliberately to care for the injured and to connect victims to family members and friends. The magnitude of the tragedy became clearer as counts revealed that 3 were dead at the scene and nearly 50 additional people received minor to life-threatening injuries.

Two additional counselors and the campus psychiatrist, on her last day in Stillwater before joining another university, arrived at the hospital, and we spread out to answer questions, reunite families, and comfort those around us. The hospital staff credentialed us to work, allowing us access throughout the ER and on the floors. I assisted several family members of the injured and dead. Some I knew from campus; some were strangers. I worked with, among others, the boyfriend of Nakita Nakal, who was killed at the scene, and Hedley, a young girl with significant facial injuries and a possible brain injury. She had been thrown to safety by Leo Schmitz, who suffered massive head and leg injuries. Leo was airlifted to the University of Oklahoma Medical Center in Oklahoma City. His wife received care for a cut on her leg at SMC before she, her son, and her daughter-in-law left for the hospital in Oklahoma City. Their vehicle key was in Leo's pocket when he was struck by the car, and it was bent at a 90-degree angle. I offered to find someone in the hospital who could straighten the key, and so I became known to the family as the "key lady." Leo was in intensive care for months at OU Medical Center and would later lose his leg. I reached out to his family at the hospital while I was in town for a meeting. They were taking a break, but I left a note for them with one of the nurses. I signed it "Key Lady" so they would know who I was. It worked, and we have connected several times since the tragedy. Leo had grabbed Hedley, who was watching the parade in front of him, and threw her backward. She had facial and other injuries, but she lived because of his selfless, quick action. The two of them are quite a pair, and they and their family members are now good friends.

Nash Lucas, a red-haired 2-year-old, was surrounded by doctors and nurses trying to stabilize him and prepare him to travel by helicopter to Children's Hospital in Oklahoma City. Nash's mother (an OSU student and employee) sustained injuries in the crash and was seen in the ER while they worked on her son. Nash, our little redhead, would perish from his injuries shortly after arriving at Children's Hospital. The death of children is emotionally unforgiving. Children should not die before their parents. The parents of the two young people killed (ages 2 and 23) will spend a lifetime thinking about what could have been: friends, school, sports, weddings, and more. Their grieving process will likely be longer and more difficult than others. Those of us who care for these individuals must take the long view and remember as they do all the milestones ahead.

At around noon, food from local restaurants was arriving at the ER. People in our tight community wanted to help. The exhausted staff took turns having a much-needed break. Tears and hugs abounded in the breakroom. Eventually the ER cleared. Many patients were treated and released, while some headed to surgery or to hospital rooms upstairs.

The decision to play the football game was made earlier in the day. The team hid their usual bravado and took a knee for a moment of silence before the game. Names of the dead were released that evening, and the community began the long grieving process yet again. At the football game, we hugged more and talked more, trying to convince ourselves that we were resilient and could survive another tragedy.

My Campus Life staff coordinated a candlelight vigil for the day after the tragedy at 9:00 p.m. Area ministers led prayers and provided acoustic music outside the Student Union. We welcomed approximately 500 students, staff, and community members to the vigil. I honestly did not want to go—I was physically exhausted and didn't know if I could effectively comfort anyone else—but I was so glad I did. The 20 or so hugs I received from colleagues and students were very therapeutic. I enjoyed the music and could meditate as a participant, not a leader. I even got a wag, lick, and hug from one of the therapy dogs on hand at the event. This program bolstered me to face work the next day.

OSU has a robust pet therapy program started by our campus's first lady, Ann Hargis. Several dogs (marked with "Therapy

Dog–Pet Me" on their orange jackets) attended the vigil with their human handlers, seeking out students and staff most in need. The dogs (nearly 50 in the program) and their handlers also went to offices most affected by the tragedy and to areas where students typically congregate: the Student Union, library, Greek housing, and residence halls. These dogs were always a welcome sight, and their healing powers were well used over the next few weeks.

I attended three memorial services in a 24-hour period the week of the tragedy. Nash's was the second—and the hardest. What a cute little boy he was. He loved John Deere tractors. A man reached out through the OSU Cowboy social media network to offer a free casket made to look like a John Deere tractor (bright green) for Nash. Administrators, staff, and students from our parking and transportation department and others were offered a ride to the funeral in one of our bright orange buses, a courtesy extended because Nash's mom worked part-time for OSU's parking and transportation department. There was talk of a possible protest at the funeral by members of the Westboro Baptist Church; thankfully, it did not occur, but local law enforcement made a plan just in case and greeted us when we arrived at the church.

We found a Buddhist priest to help celebrate the life of Nakita. She was an Indian student who attended a college 60 miles away but spent a great deal of time at ours. Her boyfriend, an OSU graduate student, was surrounded by a loving group of Indian students and faculty. They had crowded the ER waiting area to provide what comfort they could. He was unable to see her body and bravely used her phone (provided by the police) to call her mother in India. Although he did not address her in English, it was clear to all of us in the room what was being shared. The worst news a parent could hear was delivered from half a world away. It broke our hearts.

The final memorial was for Bonnie and Marvin Stone. Marvin

was a well-respected agricultural engineering research professor who retired from OSU several years before but was a regular on campus. His wife, Bonnie, was a beloved woman who worked at Institutional Research. She was known campuswide as a hard worker and a giving person. Her colleagues shared stories of her work and life with Marvin. They had an incredible marriage and life together, and their loss was profoundly felt across campus.

University Counseling Services and Human Resources made counselors available to our campus community for several days after the tragedy. I commandeered the career services area to make room for several vetted community counselors, our employee assistance counselor, and some of our campus counselors to provide short-term counseling; it was offered to any faculty, staff, or community member. Therapy dogs were available in the waiting area almost all day. Ministers were there as well. Free food and water was provided nearby for anyone to take. Other mental health efforts were created to assist our larger community. Faculty and graduate students in our counseling and psychological training clinics collaborated with elementary school teachers to help them support children who witnessed the incident. I worked with the Oklahoma Homeland Security Mental Health Unit to provide counseling and support at a nearby church for those who might not feel comfortable navigating campus and parking issues. This service, while advertised in our local paper and on the radio, was underutilized, but we felt it was important to offer.

## *Saying Thank You: The Homecoming Tragedy*

In the week following the memorials, our campus hosted a thank-you dinner and program for all first responders, helicopter medical teams, and hospital staff. The dinner helped provide a sense of closure as family members and survivors had the opportunity to meet the people who had helped them that day. Caregivers saw those they cared for healed, or healing. Tears and hugs filled the room even as we continued to grieve for those lost and those recovering in hospitals across the state. Joy won that night.

As part of our campus thank-you to our community heroes, our media staff developed a video, which was shown that night and later posted on the Internet. The following message was shared in the video:

> *You celebrated with us. . . .*
> *You marched to honor us*
> *Then you rushed to our aid*
> *And we thank you.*
> *You treated our wounds*
> *You started the healing process for all of us.*
> *You are professionals—the best of the best.*
> *And we can't thank you enough.*
> *For those of you who have prayed with us and for us*
> *We thank you.*
> *To all the universities who have held us in your hearts*
> *We may compete on the field,*
> *But off the field we were brothers and sisters united together*
> *We love you and we thank you.*
> *These days are dark.*
> *But let the orange sunset on that fateful night remind all of us that there are better days ahead.*
> *You have shown us strength.*
> *You have given us strength and hope, thank you.*
> (West Films, 2015)

The words were read by students and by OSU's president and first lady. Members of our campus community were given the opportunity to be part of that effort. Several hundred of us gathered on a campus lawn with a drone flying above us as we, too, said thank you. The message was heartfelt.

Just before Thanksgiving 2015, Stillwater Medical Center forgave all bills for those injured that day. Several patients were still in the hospital recovering. I have never been prouder of our hospital. Just days after the tragedy, the SMC Foundation Board (on which I served) started #StillwaterStrong to raise funds for those injured or killed. We raised nearly $500,000, and every penny was distributed to the family members of the deceased, to the seriously injured, and to those treated and released from the hospital that day.

## Homecoming 2016: One-Year Anniversary

The streets were crowded as the parade started. Our campus horse, Bullet, and its rider led the parade. Behind them, to honor those lost the year before, sheriff's deputies led three riderless horses and a riderless pony (representing Nash) with boots placed backward in the stirrups. Rescue volunteers and first responders (representatives of campus and city police, the Red Cross, city emergency management staff, rescue helicopter pilots, ROTC members, and others) were the grand marshals. Parade onlookers stood and clapped loudly to thank them.

Before writing this chapter, I asked Mumbe, my colleague whose children and husband were injured at the parade, if she would be willing to meet with me over coffee and reflect on the events of that day. She told me her story and how thankful she was that her children and husband survived. She shared with me that two weeks before the tragedy, she was riding in the car with her family and randomly selected a Bible verse for them to memorize. Mumbe opened the Bible to 2 Thessalonians 3:3: "But the Lord is faithful; he will strengthen you and guard you from the evil one."

Mumbe recalled that it sounded like a bomb went off when the driver's car hit the unmanned police motorcycle and parade goers.

People were injured by the car and debris from the police motorcycle. She and her son were standing a little back from the street and her husband and daughter were together some distance away. She never heard the brakes applied. Some onlookers and the police said that the car was traveling at nearly 60 miles per hour and that it sped up as it entered the crowded space.

Mumbe remembers the blood of those who had been killed instantly. She remembers how quickly the fire department laid out colored tarps, necessary for organizing the wounded for care and transport. Mumbe looked across the street to see her friend Erin and her son. Mumbe looked around and saw her husband, Clement, holding what appeared to be their lifeless daughter in his arms. She kept recalling the verse they had learned in the car—"But the Lord is faithful; he will strengthen you and guard you from the evil one." She kept saying to herself, "God is faithful." She remembers seeing the ROTC cadets, volunteers, and EMS staff working. Brian Nance, the man who stopped to help her son, saw that she was distressed about her injured daughter and said, "Go, I've got this." EMS workers laid Mumbe's daughter on the ground and began their assessment. She said the drive with Erin to OU Children's Hospital was difficult, but she remembers saying over and over, "God is faithful." Mumbe's daughter had blood at the base of her brain, but it was determined that she would not need surgery to correct the problem. Mumbe remembers the therapy dogs stopping by their hospital room and a visit from the OSU president and first lady. The president went to hospitals in Tulsa, Oklahoma City, and Stillwater the day after the crash. Mumbe's daughter was released from the hospital after several days; Mumbe's son and husband were treated and released from SMC the same day as the crash.

Mumbe said that their children's room had a bunk bed but neither child could use it for some time due to their injuries. She and her husband opted to put all the mattresses in one room, where they all slept. Mumbe admitted continuing this arrangement longer than medically necessary because of the comfort it brought all of them. She said she might create the same arrangement the next Christmas Eve, so they could all be together and reframe that memory. Mumbe was thankful that at the thank-you dinner she had the opportunity to meet several of the people who took care of her kids, but did not know the person she first encountered caring for her son.

Brian Nance, a friend from my church, was the other person I asked to interview. Brian commented on how thankful he was that the float carrying Learning Lab kids was missed and that both the ROTC and fire department were so close to the intersection where the car ran the barricade. He is haunted by what he saw and experienced that day, and has depended on his wife and family for support. Brian said he wished he knew the name of the person he helped so he could have some closure. Brian described Mumbe's son to a tee. I shared this information with Mumbe, and they have connected. Coincidence? I don't think so.

Brian told me that our campus mascot Pistol Pete (Taylor Collins) recognized him at the parade on the first anniversary and stopped to give him a huge hug. These two men had performed first aid and had loaded Mumbe's son, her husband, and another injured child into Taylor's truck for the short ride to the hospital. Their connection was a touching reminder of a very difficult day and the memories they shared. Both men did what they could to offer aid and support to those in need. They were two of the many heroes that day, but neither would use such terminology.

## Final Thoughts

Since volunteering at the St. Cloud Hospital Emergency/Trauma Center and having worked as a counselor, I have generally been able to compartmentalize my emotions rather successfully. Talking to friends about what is going on in my work and volunteer life is the best stress reducer I have found.

One person to whom I have turned for support over the past 25 years was a fellow university administrator and writing and speaking partner, Mary Beth Mackin. In 2006, we published a book on the First Amendment with another colleague, Saunie Schuster. Mary Beth knew crisis. As a noted national trainer in Critical Incident Stress Debriefing, she had witnessed tragedy up close in her work with fire, police, and EMS staff in Wisconsin. She was the first person to reach out to be sure I was safe on that dreadful homecoming day and the person I turned to, to debrief and be sure I didn't forget anything in our response to the incident. She understood the stress, sadness, and exhaustion that accompanies tragedies of this nature and was there always to reassure, comfort, and calm. I tried my best to do the same for her. We talked almost every night following each of the major campus crises I mentioned here. She had also been there for the death of my cousin on 9/11 and the death of my parents, and for many other major events in my life. Several days after the homecoming incident, Mary Beth confided in me that she had developed a training scenario that was eerily similar to our tragedy: It was complex, and it involved both campus and city resources. Her training scenario involved a drunk driver breaking through a barricade killing and injuring several people at a homecoming parade. She had just used this training scenario with police and fire personnel in Tennessee. On October 30, at 3:14 a.m., she sent me this text: "I am so proud of you and the work you are doing. Please take care of yourself. Love you. M.B." That message sustained me.

Eight days later, my dear friend died suddenly from an undetected heart ailment. Now it was my turn to receive "the call," help with arrangements, make several death notifications to our association colleagues, and deliver the eulogy at her campus memorial service. The events of the previous two weeks sunk in, in ways I couldn't imagine. Even though I had other caring friends who did their best to help me get through the dark days, I felt very lost and alone. The grieving process that I had talked often about with others became real and visceral. Every waking moment for the next several weeks, I thought about our long and wonderful friendship, our retirement plans that would not happen. A tightening in my chest wouldn't let me catch my breath fully and was a constant companion for days. I was reminded that life and death issues are consuming, and all of the people that lost loved ones were likely in that same difficult place. My empathy for those grieving their losses was off the charts: I hurt for them and myself.

I pray our campus will never suffer another tragedy, but I am thankful that I live in a community where everyone does what they can to help in a crisis; that generosity gives me a sense of peace, strength, and hope. This is what I have learned from these tragedies:

- Experience is a good but often painful teacher; those experiences taught me that I am more capable and more resilient than I thought I was.
- We should accept the kindness of others, and make sure to pay that kindness forward when we can.
- Calls, notes, and offers of help from colleagues in our small world of higher education are so important. In dark, challenging moments, such gestures remind us that someone has our back.
- Knowing that people care, believing in the power of prayer, and living and working in a place that exemplifies community are immeasurable gifts.

## References

Thomas, D. (1996, June 12). Cookie founder doles out advice. *Omaha World-Herald,* p. 43sf.

Warner, E. (2015, February 9). Bombing anniversary offers chance to reflect at museum. *The Edmond Sun.* Retrieved from http://www.edmondsun.com/multimedia/photos/featured/bombing-anniversary-offers-chance-to-reflect-at-museum/article_0f34c958-b095-11e4-abb9-9724e9db5619.html

West Films. (2015, November 11). *Stillwater strong–Thank you* [Video file]. Retrieved from https://www.youtube.com/watch?v=q-Fil3CywLg

# 5

# Using a Trauma-Informed Framework in Student Affairs

## Terry Martinez

The average day in the life of a student affairs professional is fairly predictable: hourly meetings, unmanageable inboxes and never-ending e-mails, incident reports, budget reports, status reports, meals with students, and evening programs. What we cannot predict, however, is when we will be pulled to address an individual student crisis or situation that will take over our routines, or when a broader issue will suddenly demand our attention and force us to pivot. These circumstances—such as a student illness, acute mental health challenges, or other emergencies—call for us to work with students and often their family members, our student affairs partners, faculty members, and close friends in collaborative ways not merely to get through the crisis but also to help ensure ongoing student success. This chapter will explore how student affairs practitioners can utilize a holistic framework to support students who may be dealing with myriad issues; such a framework addresses various aspects of their lives, to help them rebuild a sense of control and power so that they may continue to focus on academic achievement and degree completion.

Over the past 30 years, I have been directly involved in managing countless crises—from large-scale, very public matters that have appeared in newspapers and on television to issues that had a less visible impact. I will discuss the latter here, but regardless of the size of the matter, all of these issues affect those experiencing and those managing them.

When I was a new professional in residence, I was often the first to hear of a situation as it was unfolding. The terms *on the ground* and *in the trenches* are often used to describe the work of a new professional. We are often the first ones to gather information and assess a situation quickly so that decisions on how best to respond can be made and appropriate follow-up managed. Over time, my role has changed from the initial source of contact, as a hall director, to the person ultimately responsible for ensuring that effective systems, processes, and protocols are in place and appropriate resources are allocated so that workers on the front lines are supported in the moments they need it most. As the dean of students at two large private research institutions, my role was to serve as the conduit for communication for various constituents, including senior officers, mid-level managers, and students.

On the first night of orientation one year, a student tragically took her life. She plunged 13 stories to her death shortly after checking in, setting up her room, and participating in the first round of introductions and icebreakers. In the immediate aftermath, my role as dean was to ensure that the transition to college for the other students and their excitement about this next step in their lives of independence were not marred or interrupted. At the same time, I needed to address the fears and sadness of those who were left wondering what they could have done to prevent such a tragedy; gather and share information with our partners in the public relations office, counseling center, campus safety, and other offices; ensure that our student leaders and residential staff received the information necessary for beginning a new academic year; and follow up with staff members who were most directly affected by the student's death. All the while, I was keenly aware of the stories of the student's death, her activities in high school, her background and smiling images of her appearing in major news outlets across New York City and beyond. I was managing up, down, and across—and waiting patiently before I could take a moment to care for myself.

In my current role as vice president and dean of students, my job in managing crisis situations is ultimately to be the face for my division and the institution on student-related matters. This means I shoulder the ownership for whether our students are perceived as being well served or poorly treated, even though I do not directly manage the myriad issues that need tending. For example, during a recent outbreak of norovirus on campus where nearly 100 students contracted the virus, my role as the division head was simply to support those staff members who were managing various aspects of the outbreak, essentially standing back and letting the capable others do their jobs. The health center staff was working with students and the Department of Health. The associate dean was coordinating efforts with our Facilities Management staff for the cleaning and maintaining of our facilities, ensuring our food service operations were appropriately adjusted, and sharing information with our Communications Office to keep our various constituents regularly updated. My role was to stay abreast of the situation, consult as necessary, and ensure adequate resources were available to support the effort.

In writing this chapter, I gave thought to the overwhelming

number of crises that I—we—deal with every year. I am always amazed at how many we encounter. I end each year with such gratitude for my colleagues, who have shared these experiences with me, and for the opportunity to shape students' lives—often in profound ways—in moments when they need us most. Working with students as they learn and grow is why many of us entered this field; helping them manage through crisis is where we have arrived. A framework to approach both of these responsibilities is useful.

Many crises demand intense and focused attention, such as the examples described in the other chapters, but this chapter will focus on the smaller, ongoing issues that we face every day—our daily grind. Dealing with intense situations each day can leave anyone exhausted and drained. As student affairs leaders, we must recognize the importance of self-care to maintain empathy while we tend to our myriad responsibilities and priorities. This was a lesson I realized far too late in my own career. Much is known about the impact of stress on our bodies if it is not managed appropriately; moving from crisis to crisis without a plan for recovery affects us, our staff members, and ultimately, our work with students. It is just as important to develop a healthy routine as it is to plan our goals for a new academic year.

## A Useful Framework

There are many ways to deal with a student who may be facing a crisis. A trauma-informed framework is used by mental health professionals who deal with clients who have experienced traumatic childhood events such as ongoing physical or emotional abuse, violence in the household, or living with an alcoholic. It employs a person-centered response to treatment; that is, it focuses on improving an individual's all-around wellness rather than on simply treating the symptoms of mental illness. The framework recognizes that clients are vulnerable and that past trauma can influence other, current areas of their lives: relationships, social life, self-esteem, ability to think clearly, and ability to process feelings, among others. Adapting a trauma-informed framework to our work as student affairs professionals, particularly those not engaged in a therapeutic or counseling relationship, allows us to consider various other aspects of a student's life that might affect a student who is navigating crisis. In such a holistic approach, it is equally important for us to consider friends, family, academics, and finances, not just the presenting issue—particularly as we come up with solutions that may have long-lasting implications. This approach encompasses emotional and physical safety, the meaningful sharing of power and decision making, allowing students to give input and take ownership in the options available in the process, and recognition of individual strengths that are identified, built on, and validated (Harris & Fallot, 2001). Our roles in crises, regardless of their duration, are not intended to be therapeutic in nature; rather, we are called on to address the crisis, move toward resolution, and minimize the impact on others. A trauma-informed framework in our work, however, would allow a student affairs professional to keep the student at the core of the interactions when supporting them through a crisis and to use other factors to inform each individual case.

This framework directs us to employ a 360-degree analysis of a student's assets (personal strengths, financial capacity), potential partners and champions, prior ability to problem-solve, and resiliency. We must seek to understand a student's lived experiences both inside and outside of the classroom and to identify if there are aspects of a student's life that might serve as additional barriers to moving the student through crisis. This investigation provides us with information on where we can push a student further or when we should be careful to extend additional support.

The framework similarly allows us to offer solutions that may be efficacious and can demonstrate an institution's support for each student as an individual. Higher education is a culture dominated by necessary institutional policies, protocols, and consistency, and that is important; however, individualized support infuses our protocols with humanity and empathy. It is a balance of consistency and tailored measures that can bring about a coherent solution.

In each case that follows, I escribe ways in which a student needed to navigate a crisis and how the use of a holistic framework guided the course of action during the initial presentation and throughout the entirety of the interaction.

## *Case Study: Carolyn*

"There is a student and her mother here to see you. They don't have an appointment but say it's urgent and they look pretty upset." This was how my next appointment was announced to me, in hushed tones. I immediately scanned my memory to see if I knew her name, if she had a bad roommate situation, or if she wanted an exception to some policy, but couldn't recall any particular incident.

I could feel the tension and concern as the student and her mother settled into seats in my office but immediately detected that it wasn't anger; rather, it was sadness or fear, or perhaps a combination of the two. "Carolyn has been diagnosed with leukemia. This is new information to us, and we are trying to process everything and weigh our options. She will begin treatment immediately." Both of them talked for a bit, processing out loud the need for normalcy, routine, and continuity while at the same time acknowledging that adjustments or accommodations could and should be made. The goal—they emphasized more than once—was to complete senior year if possible. Carolyn wanted to graduate with her friends, and it would be important for her to focus on this goal. And so, this became a goal for all three of us. I assured them of this partnership and was certain that we could identify a team on campus to support her: the resident assistant (RA) and her academic advisor, who would check in on her; the food service manager, who would ensure that meals were delivered on the days she received treatment at the nearby cancer treatment center; the faculty members who, without hesitation, would provide needed extensions (and, in some cases, alternate assignments when a class presentation was just not possible); and the conference services office, which offered her parents a room at no cost when they needed to support her through treatment. These were only a few of the groups that would work together over the next seven months to ensure that Carolyn crossed that stage and celebrated with her friends.

A holistic approach in this situation meant that, together, the team made sure that the student felt she was in control of the decisions being made. Faculty members allowed Carolyn to determine, based on where she was in the treatment during the semester, whether she could participate in the ways outlined in their syllabi. At no point did they eliminate expectations for rigor or learning. Instead, they allowed Carolyn the opportunity to demonstrate what she had learned in alternate yet equally meaningful ways. They were creative in their approach and let her decide how much she could push herself each day.

Her academic advisor checked in with her weekly, in the event she needed tutors, extensions on papers, a different location for an exam, or other accommodation. Her advisor coordinated such efforts, reducing the need for Carolyn to go back and forth with each faculty member.

Student affairs leaders also provided support for her closest friends, who were dealing with anxiety and concern for her. We recognized early on that some of Carolyn's friends were hypervigilant about her well-being—sometimes in unhelpful or unhealthy ways that had a negative impact on their own well-being. We facilitated a conversation with Carolyn and her friends so that they could all openly discuss their concerns and fears, and Carolyn shared her frustrations with feeling as if her well-intentioned friends were coddling her. Two of her friends had recently lost close relatives to cancer, and Carolyn's illness brought that grief back to the surface; campus counseling services provided emotional support to help these students navigate their grief.

Our approach allowed Carolyn the space to recognize her inability to function on days when she was unable to get out of bed, but also to participate fully in cocurricular endeavors when she felt strong enough to do so. For her, I believe, this represented living her life to the fullest and moved her to her goal of graduating with her friends. We supported her and her network of friends and faculty members, and we provided relief for her parents, who appreciated knowing that she had a team in place to check in on her and allow her as much routine as possible. Through a holistic campus approach, Carolyn felt empowered to manage her illness while continuing to pursue her academic degree.

## *Case Study: Adam*

Three different faculty members e-mailed my office to express concern that Adam had missed class for three weeks and had not turned in assignments. In our follow-up conversations, we learned that even when Adam did show up, he was withdrawn and did not participate; even his appearance seemed to have deteriorated over the course of the semester. Although he had submitted some assignments, he was on the precipice of falling far enough behind that he might not pass. He was not the same person that these professors knew him to be; he was no longer himself.

Adam and I decided to meet, and I was surprised when he arrived on time. He had a disheveled appearance and seemed lethargic as I began the standard probing to help determine if he was depressed, suicidal, or addicted. He was, in my opinion, quite simply tired. After what seemed like endless moments of silence and assurances, he tearfully and exhaustedly shared that he had been having trouble sleeping and lacked motivation because of an unmanageable home situation. He related that he had not slept more than a few hours a night for months. He then proceeded with details of a worsening home life that began when his father passed away when he was 12. His mother was left to care for Adam and his two younger siblings alone. Her mental health and caretaking ability quickly faded, and she eventually faced debilitating depression. After some time, she was unable to work or function, and ultimately the family moved in with relatives. When she emerged from her depression, she began a new life with a new partner who didn't meet with Adam's approval. Adam expressed concerned about this man's temper and the environment for his younger siblings, but he assured me there had been no physical violence. Adam traveled the two hours home frequently, mostly on weekends, but had not gone home to stay the past two summers and felt unsure about where he would live that summer. He had just lost his campus job and would soon be facing eviction from his off-campus apartment over nonpayment of rent. He was unsure of where he would get his next meal.

Adam had just over a month to figure out living arrangements and to map out how he might salvage the remainder of the semester. We focused on his academic workload for a bit and came to realize that with enough focus and commitment, he could salvage the balance of the semester with passing grades—albeit not the ones he was hoping for. Our plan moving forward included his voice, an opportunity to build on his strengths, and focus and attention on his physical and emotional safety. Adam was a willing participant, and it seemed he simply needed someone to help him map out a manageable plan—rather than the catastrophic scenarios he continued to play through his mind.

He qualified for emergency funds that would allow him to maintain his housing until he could get back on his feet. We worked with his advisor and realized that he could drop a course and still stay on track toward his degree, but he also worked with his advisor to determine whether he was in the right major, as his passion for the hard sciences was not what it once was. I connected him with the student employment office to find a job that better met the needs of his schedule and would not require him to miss classes. Finally, and most important, Adam agreed to meet with someone in the counseling center. He realized the grief that continued to weigh on him. In our conversation, I learned that Adam's campus friends did not know about his home life or his struggles, although his roommates were aware of his financial difficulties. He felt too embarrassed to share with them and compartmentalized his home experience from his college one. It was clear that he was quite resilient: He had overcome a lot to get to this moment, and with enough focus he would be able to continue his journey.

Adam and I had checked in periodically for the remainder of the semester, and he seemed to be thinking more clearly, dealing with difficult feelings, and addressing his issues of low self-esteem. He knew his home life wasn't what he had hoped for, but he was now better able to focus on the things he could control at that moment. He had come to the realization that he couldn't help his siblings in the future if he failed out of school. Most important, Adam began sleeping with more regularity and was able to manage academic and life tasks, which he had previously avoided.

At each step, Adam came up with solutions, considered viable factors for each option, and ultimately decided what his next steps would be. We had worked together to deal with the immediate crisis of finances and were quickly able to get him back on his academic path, salvaging what could have been a disastrous semester. We had discussed his incredible capacity to deal with difficult situations in the past and his need to tap into that ability again. Providing Adam with some resources and allowing him to take charge of his situation enabled him to regain control of what was, for a time, a seemingly uncontrollable situation that was affecting his academic life—and his future potential.

## Case Study: Jake

Our campus safety office was informed of a student who had been found passed out on the steps of a campus building and had been transported to the hospital for intoxication. My student affairs team contacted his parents, who saw this behavior as a familiar pattern for Jake. In doing so, we learned that this graduate student had a history of alcohol abuse and had previously taken time off to enter a rehabilitation center, but he left treatment against the advice of the program and his parents. He had moved back into his off-campus apartment and, by all accounts, was having a successful semester. We learned that he had been working on his research closely with his advisor, who reported that Jake had not demonstrated any concerning behavior, had met his deadlines, and was otherwise functioning effectively. Jake's advisor was surprised to learn of this relapse.

Several days later we met with Jake and his parents, who expressed an equal amount of frustration, concern, and embarrassment. Our goal for this meeting was to assess Jake's ability to function and determine how we could best support this family, which seemed to have fluctuated between crisis and relief for several years. Jake indicated that this incident was an anomaly—that it was only recently that he had begun drinking again—and he had convinced himself that he was in control of his drinking.

Employing the trauma-informed framework—which enables individuals to be self-determinant in moving forward—in this case was rather difficult, because this particular student did not feel he was in crisis, was unwilling to share in decision making, and, at least at that moment, did not consider himself in physical danger. Our meeting ended with an agreement that Jake would reach out for help should he find himself slipping into previous patterns of self-destruction. Over the next three months, Jake would have more frequent incidents of dangerous drinking behavior that would result in a trip to and then release from the hospital. Each time, his parents would come back to support him and leave after familiar (and consistently unfulfilled) promises to reach out if he needed assistance. All the while, he continued to meet his academic obligations and was not disruptive to other students or to faculty. Jake was clearly a functioning alcoholic.

One evening in a drunken state, Jake found himself in an unsafe neighborhood and was badly beaten and robbed. While recovering from his physical wounds, he finally shared his vulnerability and was willing to allow his parents to make some immediate decisions for him. He no longer felt physically or emotionally safe, and he articulated the need for someone other than himself to make decisions in his best interest. Once again, his parents opted to admit him into an intensive residential rehabilitation center, and he would take a hiatus for the remainder of the semester.

This case was particularly challenging, since Jake was an adult who had been on his own for a few years. When he initially came to our attention, an important and primary need was for his physical safety, but more importantly, was his desire to own the decisions about his life. He expressed a strong need to ensure that he was driving the decisions and sought to gain more independence from his parents. Remaining in school was imperative to him, since he had found recent academic success and had built healthy relationships with his peers; maintaining success and stability in both of those areas were important markers for Jake.

Of course, all of this shifted for him. He eventually had no control over his drinking and did not feel empowered to make his own choices. Admitting his need to rely on his parents to make decisions for him was devastating to him. The strengths he believed to possess during his previous recovery period diminished. His addiction stripped him of his validated independence and sense of self, but he could articulate where he needed the support and could take pride in the successes he achieved during his sobriety.

## *Case Study: Raj and Teddy*

Each Monday morning, I was accustomed to reading the campus safety reports from the weekend. One such report detailed an incident in which a student, Raj, was in an elevator with a female friend after a night out. A drunk football player, Teddy, got into the elevator with them and began making comments of a sexual nature to the young woman. Raj asked the student to stop. Teddy continued to harass the young woman and began taunting and threatening Raj, who stated firmly that he did not want a confrontation; Raj simply wanted Teddy to stop bothering his friend. Teddy became enraged, shoved Raj against the elevator wall, and began yelling racial slurs and screaming "What are you going to do?" repeatedly. He then punched Raj in the face, breaking his glasses. Teddy exited the elevator on the next floor. Raj suffered a severe injury to his eye and was taken to the emergency room. He did not want to press charges.

I met with Raj, a slight young man with a quiet demeanor. His eye was still a little swollen and bloodshot, and he seemed embarrassed by the entire situation. We spoke about the incident and potential outcomes. Raj insisted that he did not want any action taken against Teddy, but he wanted to move from his building to another so that he would not run into him on a regular basis. I informed Raj that it was he who could decide whether to contact the police to file a report and press assault charges; however, the institution was choosing to take action against Teddy through its own judicial processes and Teddy would, minimally, receive a sanction of suspension. We discussed what such an institutional process would look like, including placing a no-contact order between the students, but Raj firmly and consistently insisted that he wanted no part in that process.

As I probed a bit more, Raj shared that he was aware Teddy was a star player on the college's football team and had been witness to several drunken (and what I would describe as bullying) behaviors in the past. Raj insisted that he just wanted to be left alone and wanted no part in our process. When we discussed parental notification, Raj again insisted that he did not want us to do this. I asked him to reconsider, because it was likely that his parents would receive the bill from his hospital visit and notice his injury when he went home for fall break in just a few days. Raj reconsidered and called his father that evening. His father was incredibly upset and wanted to meet with me the next day to discuss our process moving forward.

Raj's father was a mild-mannered, soft-spoken man who wanted to understand what a process would look like and how, more important than anything else, we would protect his son from retaliation. He shared with me that Raj was bullied when he was younger and that it had a considerable impact on him: Raj had withdrawn from all activities, felt isolated, and experienced depression. His father did not want this to happen again. He tearfully shared how incredibly happy Raj was at the institution and how Raj simply wanted to go about his studies and enjoy his time with his small group of close friends. What both men feared most was any retaliation, ongoing taunting, or ostracism.

In the meantime, our student conduct office contacted Teddy, issued a no-contact order, and let him know that he would be going through a judicial process. He and his coach appeared in my office the next day, and Teddy issued a remorseful apology to me and offered to do the same with Raj. The coach had already contacted a substance abuse counselor and Teddy and his parents had agreed to ongoing treatment once the season wrapped in two weeks. He knew he had substance abuse issues for some time and had been delaying any treatment until after graduation. We informed Teddy that, his desire for treatment aside, a physical assault on another student warranted an immediate suspension until we could facilitate the hearing process, which could take place after Thanksgiving.

Teddy was concerned about missing classes and wanted to remain on track for graduation, so we asked his professors if he could perform independent student assignments during his time away. Each faculty member allowed it because Teddy was an exceptional student; in fact, it was likely that Teddy would receive academic distinction in his major at graduation. The most difficult issue for Teddy (and his coach) to deal with was his not playing the last two games of the season. The institution received numerous e-mails and phone calls about this decision from alumni and parents who implored us to treat Teddy with kindness and compassion and to allow him to finish his outstanding college football career. Teddy was ultimately suspended by the hearing board and his graduation delayed.

Using a trauma-informed framework with Raj was particularly helpful. His case is a good example of how past situations can have a direct impact on an individual's present. His previous experience with bullying and the resulting fear, isolation, and depression influenced how he wanted to proceed in his case with Teddy. His father's involvement and role as an advocate helped bring Raj's past to light and likely prevented another retreat into isolation. Having a small group of connected and supportive peers helped Raj to see that he didn't have to retreat socially and that he could continue to participate in the activities he enjoyed. He could see how he can use the past as a reference but not fall into the same debilitating patterns.

Working with Teddy was a bit more challenging. He presented a great deal of self-awareness and confidence, and I believed he genuinely wanted to address his substance abuse issues. He was remorseful, embarrassed, and accountable for his actions. Still, I was challenged in dealing with him because he had physically injured another student whom I wanted to protect. I had to manage the competing priorities of holding him accountable and wanting to treat both students with dignity and humanity. Teddy was someone who had competed at a high level, both athletically and academically, all through high school and college. He was charming, and his friendly demeanor made it easy for him to avoid consequences and, more important, confront his substance abuse issues. He saw this moment as one that could change his life and really wanted to tackle it with as much fervor and desire to succeed as he did with the other areas of his life.

## Applying a Trauma-Informed Framework in Student Affairs

In each of the cases, several factors contributed to how we managed the variety of crises, from handling the immediacy of the situation to planning for next steps. Each instance called on campus partners to work openly together and commit to work in the best interest of the student. Each case was approached with a recognized need for an individualized plan and with the student actively participating in decision making. Students had a voice, were treated with respect, and contributed to the overall plan. The institution demonstrated respect for each student, provided information regarding options, and recognized that offering the opportunity to make choices made a real difference.

Our work as student affairs professionals is developmental, and in each of our interactions we should consider where a student might be developmentally as an immediate and determinant factor in how we deal with the student. As mentioned earlier, a trauma-informed framework in a student affairs setting is not intended to be therapeutic; we should leave that work to those who are trained to be therapists. What this framework does provide, however, is a broader lens through which we can view a student's past and current assets, and an insistence that we allow a student to have a say in the choices made. It is an opportunity for us to ask, "What has happened in this student's past to get us to this moment? How can we use the student's ability to navigate any previous challenges to help the student get through this moment?" We inquire, "Where are the student's strengths, weaknesses, and resources, and how do we tap into them?" When we seek answers that provide a fuller picture of a student's circumstance, we can preserve each student's individuality and do our work with a bit more humanity and dignity. Working with students as partners in managing their crises and in identifying their strengths and resources lets them tap into their own resourcefulness and break down a crisis into more manageable tasks.

## Final Thoughts

Because student affairs professionals deal with ever-changing and unexpected student issues daily, we constantly pivot from one matter to the next. As a result, we must learn how to compartmentalize various situations in order to keep our energy levels and our levels of care consistent. Each of the situations described in this chapter didn't unfold with ease or quickness in one meeting, of course. In between, and sometimes immediately following each meeting, were routine student meetings and issues that demanded the same care and attention as did the crises. To put the burden and complexities of one case aside momentarily allows us to ensure that the student in front of us is the priority. This constant switching and reprioritizing, however, can be mentally exhausting and can lead to burnout. Important for us then is to find the appropriate partners on campus with whom we can debrief these situations in ways that allow us to have closure or mental resolution for each case. Talking through with partners can provide space for clarity before the next case to come before us. Our partners in crisis can help us to reflect on the case, brainstorm solutions, and create potential pathways forward. Such reflection also offers emotional decompression.

We must tend to our own well-being, which can so easily be deferred maintenance for convenience of time. Practicing the balanced lifestyle we expect of our students should be how we manage our own lives, particularly since our roles do not fall into the 9-to-5 structure of a typical workday. Coffee with friends, midafternoon walks, or daydreaming about a vacation might provide us with just enough of a respite. Taking inventory of ourselves provides an opportunity to gauge, rest, recharge our energy, and face the next challenge with a renewed commitment.

Prioritizing my own well-being is something I have learned to do much too late in my career. I wish I had had more mentors to model this behavior or more supervisors who had provided me with the time to care for myself. All too often I felt as if the semester just needed to roll on until the next available break in the calendar, but then I somehow became ill with a horrible cold or flu. It was only then that I was forced to slow down and recover. If not illness, then complete exhaustion settled in, and I would come crashing into the end of the semester with a need for isolation and sleep. It was obviously my own body forcing me to pause and heal.

Today I have reframed how I use my time. In prioritizing my daily tasks, I no longer add exercising, personal errands, or down time after the day is filled with my work commitments or constrain them to the weekend hours. I see my days as ones that begin when I rise at 5:30 a.m. and end when I go to bed at 10:30 p.m. While these days are long indeed, they are now a contiguous series of the things that need to be done for work and for life rather than bifurcated to weekday responsibilities and weekend errands. It is not unusual for me to make time during my day to grocery shop, take the dog for a long walk, or be home for two hours or so, usually reading for work purposes, before heading back to work for evening events or meetings with students. This also means that I don't mind taking a few hours on Saturday morning to wrap up work from the previous week or prepare for the next. This balance allows me to feel ready for those moments when big crises require my attention for longer periods of time.

As a supervisor who wants staff members who are engaged, committed, and passionate about their work, I am equally concerned that they do not experience burnout. Modeling a healthy approach encourages others to follow. An important role of a supervisor is to create constructive change and maintain a supportive environment. As leaders, we can build a supportive work environment that promotes employee health and well-being. Staff members are more likely to take time to care for themselves if they see a leader who does the same. My hope is that you, too, will consider reframing your time so that you can sustain the energy and passion necessary to work with students in caring and rewarding ways.

## Reference

Harris, M., & Fallot, R. D. (Eds.). (2001). *Using trauma theory to design service systems* (New Directions for Mental Health Services, No. 89). San Francisco, CA: Jossey-Bass.

# 6

# Triaging Activism, Protests, and Campus Unrest

## DEB MORIARTY AND SANTIAGO SOLIS

Activism, protests, and unrest have long been an integral part of student life on college campuses throughout the United States. Although the concerns expressed by student activists have varied from campus to campus, over the years one thing has remained constant: the passion, determination, and sense of urgency student activists inject into their cause. In recent years, many college students from across the nation have organized to end systemic and structural racism. Student activists have demanded institutional commitment, including strong diversity action plans, specific interventions with clear objectives, and accountability with full transparency. Some college administrators have resisted, while others have responded more favorably, feeling compelled to provide greater diversity and to develop more inclusive environments conducive to learning for all students.

Prior to 2004, Towson University (TU; a large, public, four-year institution) had a reputation as a commuter school and an institution where students went home every weekend. TU is located approximately two miles from the city of Baltimore and nine miles from the center of the city. Upon starting her position as vice president for student affairs (VPSA) in 2004, Deb Moriarty's charge was to create a vibrant campus life and strong sense of community for all students. Time and resources were invested into identifying and including students in leadership roles, and working with them to define their ideal campus community and to identify steps for building on that vision. Students felt empowered by this level of agency to create their ideal campus and welcomed the support provided to shift the campus climate and narrative. The TU campus has grown from approximately 17,500 students in 2004 to over 23,000 in 2018.

In her long career as a student affairs administrator, Deb experienced student activism first as a new professional at the University of California, Los Angeles, in the early 1980s, and then midcareer while working with highly engaged students at the University of Michigan. Throughout her career, she has used her working knowledge of the First Amendment to help students understand why stereotypically themed events (e.g., a fraternity that wanted to host a Cinco de Mayo event with costumes that were offensive to the Mexican culture) are insensitive and offensive.

Like Deb, Santiago, who serves as an associate vice president of student affairs at TU, first encountered student activism in the 1980s, but as an undergraduate student at the University of California, Berkeley, experiencing firsthand the power of students organizing and boycotting classes to pressure the administration into hiring more faculty of color. Three decades later, he once again witnessed students organizing for the same reason, at TU. As part of the TU administration, he was confronted by a group of students challenging him to support their list of demands. For Santiago, supporting social justice means teaching students to self-advocate, question the status quo, and challenge unjust systems that marginalize and oppress, in order to create a more inclusive campus environment.

## Student Activism Returns to Campus

After seven years of building relationships with students and empowering their leadership at TU, the climate for campus activism emerged in the fall of 2011 for the first time since the late 1960s and early 1970s. That fall, a student submitted a request to create a new student organization named Youth for Western Civilization (YWC). The purpose of YWC was to "organize a right wing youth movement that will turn the tide on campuses across America . . . [and] combat the leftist status quo on immigration, multiculturalism, and traditional curriculums" (Dionisopoulos, 2011, paras. 8–10).

Based on the mission statement submitted by YWC, the Student Government Association (SGA) was reluctant to approve this group. However, the Division of Student Affairs staff worked with SGA leaders to address their concerns by reviewing the process to recognize student organizations. Student government was advised that it was clear that the group met the criteria and could not be denied based on the viewpoint it was promoting. This resulted in a heated debate at an SGA meeting and marked the beginning of a challenging and complex journey of navigating free speech while supporting the needs of many marginalized students. The Division of Student Affairs staff found it imperative to work with the staff trying to accommodate all students while also struggling with their own feelings and beliefs that were in opposition to YWC's purpose.

YWC brought anti-LGBTQIA+, anti-Muslim, anti-immigration, and other ideals to campus that were contrary to TU's values of inclusion and diversity. YWC's actions (e.g., chalking campus with their messages, hosting a controversial speaker who identifies as a "race realist") ignited members of the campus community to protest loudly and reaffirm their presence.

After much campuswide discussion, demonstrations, teach-ins, and the establishment of a Diversity Task Force by the university's president, YWC's time on campus was short-lived: Amid the controversy the group was creating, the group's faculty advisor resigned from the position, leaving YWC out of compliance with the requirements to be a recognized student organization. From this precipitating incident, and as highly visible incidents of racial injustice made the national news with alarming frequency, on-campus activism continued to grow. The deaths of Trayvon Martin (2012), Michael Brown (2014), Eric Garner (2014), Walter Scott (2015), and Freddie Gray Jr. (2015) created a national dialogue that carried over into the campus community. The Baltimore uprising in the spring of 2014 and the University of Missouri's student protests in fall 2015 also prompted student activism at TU, culminating in a "takeover" of an SGA meeting and the president's office in fall 2015.

Our prior work creating strong, supportive, and empowering relationships with student leaders was helpful with the appearance of YWC. However, we learned lessons from the "takeover" experience and have continued working to best support our students and create a welcoming and inclusive environment. The remainder of this chapter will outline some of the work we did leading up to the incident, as well as lessons learned and our ongoing commitment to the well-being of our students and staff.

## KNOW YOUR STUDENTS

Under Deb's leadership, a student affairs priority has been getting to know all student leaders, using the broadest definition of the word *leader*. Rather than focusing simply on positional leaders in student organizations, the Division of Student Affairs identified students involved in all types of mentoring roles (e.g., resident advisors, orientation leaders, student ambassadors, a wide variety of peer mentors) and treated them the same as position leaders. We created a Council of Student Leaders (CSL) that meets monthly to discuss issues impacting students, encourages networking and collaboration among student organizations, and allows us space and time to get to know these leaders and to hear their hopes and concerns about the campus community. The CSL comprises representatives in leadership roles from about 40 of the largest and most representative student organizations on campus (e.g., SGA, Residence Government, the Black Student Union, Greek Life).

Student involvement in exploring and creating a vision for campus life has been critical. Highlighting to the campus community and the administration the important role that students play as mentors and role models to new students has also been significant. In addition to working with the CSL, we established a campus-based LeaderShape Institute (a weeklong retreat that emphasizes ethical leadership and the development of relationships that might not otherwise be formed), hold meetings with student organizations at the beginning of each year, and attend student events. We also have established monthly meetings with the SGA president and VPSA, as well as the president of the University Residence Government. As a result of this work, students have become increasingly engaged in open and honest dialogue with us and each other. It is much easier to engage students in complex and difficult discussions because they are already used to providing feedback, suggestions, and even harsh criticism to us.

However, simply getting to know students is not enough; it is important to empower them to take on leadership roles and take ownership of creating the campus and student life they want. TU's students are its best champions. Students with leadership responsibilities are often the first point of contact for new students navigating the institution. Therefore, it is important that student leaders know and are comfortable with the values and expectations of the institution.

Starting with new student orientation, we set clear expectations based on TU's mission and values regarding diversity, inclusion, and equity. We make this a priority in our training of peer leaders and ask them to initiate discussion of these topics with new students. Around 2006, we created a "Tiger Pledge" that outlines TU's values and expectations—for example, "I will . . . treat others with civility and respect." This pledge is introduced during the "Welcome to Towson" program and recited by students at New Student Convocation. Reinforcing such expectations frequently, including through summer mailings, social media messages, welcome week activities, and residence hall meetings, affirms TU's community values. It is important to reiterate to students that they have a great deal of agency and power in creating the campus climate they want. At graduation, TU students have a commencement pledge that parallels the Tiger Pledge they learn during orientation—for example, "I will . . . take responsibility for the social and environmental consequences of my decisions."

We must work to include students in decision making across the institution. Often, no one even considers including the student voice until someone from student affairs points out the importance of this perspective. At TU, SGA is responsible for appointing students to serve on the majority of university committees (including those of the University Senate). Previously, SGA collected a list of students interested in being involved with student government and then appointed them to a committee based on their availability during the meeting time. We now work with SGA to help them think about students' areas of interests in order to appoint them to committees that best match their interests. This ensures students who serve on university committees are invested in representing the student voice related to the issues on which their committee focuses. While we do not get involved in SGA's process of making those individual appointments, we help them to re-envision how they set their students up for success as committee members. We encourage student government appointees to report committee work to the student governing body.

In addition to meeting with students regularly, for the past 10 years, many student affairs staff members have served as facilitators for TU's LeaderShape Institute. This has accelerated our ability to develop strong and meaningful relationships with first- and second-year students, many of whom go on to serve in leadership roles across campus. When challenges and complexities arise based on a particular issue, for example a free speech issue, student mentors/leaders provide thoughtful and valuable ideas and solutions.

As a result of these various interactions with students, they know that they can trust us, and although we might not always agree, we are committed to being forthcoming with each other.

Some key takeaways from TU's intentional actions to be inclusive of the student voice include the following:

- Make it common practice to involve students in any decision-making process.
- Work with your staff to identify opportunities to meet and interact with students.

- Be present at student leader retreats and training programs to reinforce your commitment to their success as leaders and to continue to share your vision of students' role in creating an inclusive and welcoming community.
- Ensure that training for all student leaders includes sessions on cultural competency and identity development.
- Help your colleagues develop the skills needed to engage students in conversations about cultural competency and identity development.

## COMMUNICATE, COMMUNICATE, COMMUNICATE!

Ongoing efficient and effective communication with your supervisor, colleagues, and staff will prevent unexpected and unpleasant surprises. Students are often way out in front of any situation due to their use of social media. For example, the administration learned of offensive chalking on campus from students posting pictures and their reactions on social media. It is essential to be nimble.

As issues begin to emerge, share updates with your supervisor and your colleagues at the cabinet level from the beginning. Issues that rise to the level of "crisis" should not be the sole responsibility of student affairs. In fact, our observation over the past 10 years has been that student activism, free speech, and crisis management are no longer largely the concern of the VPSA and staff in the Division of Student Affairs. In today's climate, many of your colleagues will have a role in attending to emerging issues. Legal counsel, communications, equity and inclusion, alumni and development, and the provost will all have a response that views the issue from a different set of lenses and perspectives. This can be both helpful and frustrating to navigate. Know what is expected in terms of sharing information with your colleagues. It is important to clarify who is responsible for what so that you are not stepping on each other's toes. Seeking guidance, feedback, and support from your colleagues will make them more likely to "have your back" during emergencies and challenging situations.

Be prepared for media attention and work with the communications team to develop a plan of action—including creating talking points and identifying a designated spokesperson(s) to field questions and represent the campus. Talking points should be agreed on by members of the president's council working most closely with the situation. The spokesperson can be either someone from the communications department or a student affairs leader, although each president will have different expectations about who assumes this role. If you are the designated spokesperson, ask for coaching or training on working with the media. You can also ask someone from communications to be present when you are interviewed and signal if you are going too far in responding to questions.

A note on administrative changes: From the time that YWC emerged on our campus to today, we have had three presidents (and two interim presidents), each of whom has brought their own style, philosophy, and experience to TU. Success as a senior-level student affairs officer is dependent on one's ability to adapt to these significant leadership changes. Getting to know a new president and understanding their style and expectations does not happen overnight; however, with time and patience, a solid working relationship can be established with a new leader.

Preparing a president for working with students is a big part of a VPSA's responsibilities. It was helpful to create a small binder of materials introducing the Division of Student Affairs, the leadership team and its responsibilities, and key programs and initiatives. For TU's current president, it was important to bring her up to speed on campus activism and the activities of the students who called themselves #OccupyTowson.

## Embrace Student Advocacy

Student affairs leaders have a unique and powerful role in supporting student advocacy. We often are the only people at the table mindful of the student voice and the concerns students have about various aspects of the campus community. Student affairs leaders must listen to student voices, support them as they express their concerns, and work with colleagues who are responsible for addressing those concerns. If you build strong relationships with students from the start, they will often include you in their plans to protest, demonstrate, or otherwise engage the campus community in hearing their concerns.

Of course, this is not always easy. Around the time that the University of Missouri was embroiled in controversy with student protests, issues related to race continued at TU as well. A group (known as #OccupyTowson) representing concerns of TU's Black students came forward to both the SGA and the university administration with a list of requests, such as increasing Black tenure track faculty, requiring all faculty and staff to take at least one cultural competency course every semester, and requiring a person of color on institutional committees as well as on each college's tenure and promotion committee. Based on our history of working closely with these students, student affairs staff members were able to coach the SGA leaders about effective ways to respond. As a result, they were calm, open, and receptive to the protests from #OccupyTowson leaders. Although there was no advance notice for the takeover of the president's office, the student affairs staff who were present supported the students while also assisting the president and their other colleagues to work through the process of agreeing on a list of the requests that TU was comfortable committing to moving forward.

Student affairs professionals can provide leadership with administration and be supportive of student initiatives by both challenging and supporting them. For example, when the SGA wanted to create a media campaign—#NotAtTU—to raise awareness about hate/bias incidents on campus, the administration fully supported the effort and readily assisted with the overall conceptualization. Because this was a student-led initiative, the administration remained in the background in a supportive role.

It is helpful to find and/or create opportunities to engage colleagues outside of student affairs with students so they also have an opportunity to build authentic relationships. This can be accomplished by inviting those colleagues to be a part of student events, introducing them to key student leaders, and encouraging them to connect with each other. For example, TU's SGA has a student director of academic affairs; the provost meets with this student leader regularly. The Division of Student Affairs invited all institutional vice presidents in welcoming students to campus during student orientation. A vice president provides a brief welcome during our summer program, and most vice presidents assist in distributing flavored ice during student move-in. There are many ways to connect senior staff to students, and most are very interested in building these relationships.

## Continuously Review, Revise, and Improve Policies and Procedures

TU has so many policies it is overwhelming. In fact, the university has an entire webpage just to keep track of them: faculty policies, academic affairs policies, research policies, student affairs policies, general administration policies, human resources policies, fiscal and business affairs policies, external relations policies, information technology policies, and even a category labeled "other policies." TU has a process on how to create policies. At TU, policies undergo four phases: development, coordination, approval and comments, and dissemination. Various stakeholders (e.g., administration, faculty, staff, students, campus police, general counsel) are involved throughout the policy development and implementation process. Although developing and navigating so many policies can feel tedious and perhaps even inefficient, having exceptional policies (and procedures) is important because they provide a lifeline both for students and the administration. We rely on them to inform our best practices and the ways in which we respond, in particular during emergencies and challenging times.

In 2016, TU experienced a series of incidents involving racist and disruptive behavior. For example, in celebration of Black History Month, a group of students, with their resident assistant's permission, posted information about influential Black historical figures on their floor. Some of the posters were taken down without permission. Two Black students on the floor noticed the missing posters and concluded this was done intentionally by other floor residents. The Black students took offense and reported the action as a bias incident. These two students were then invited to meet with housing staff to discuss the incident and were assured it would be investigated. In the meantime, as a way to address the issue, additional images of Black historical figures were posted on the floor. Residents also had an opportunity to write affirming comments on a bulletin board. Unfortunately, some of the reposted images also went missing and several written comments were disparaging, thereby escalating the situation. Ultimately, the incident was not resolved to the students' satisfaction. In response, the administration organized a Unity Rally to bring the campus together. What the administration did not anticipate was the raw emotions expressed by some Black students. The students were explicit in describing the psychological trauma they experienced inside and outside of the classroom. Overall, the sentiment was that the university was unresponsive to hate/bias incidents affecting students of color.

For the university president, the growing concerns related to the hate/bias reporting process became a top priority. In a campuswide e-mail, the president stated, "In my short time here, several individuals and university groups have widely criticized the hate/bias reporting process. It has been described as confusing, ineffective and non-responsive." The president asked Santiago, in his role as an associate vice president, to lead a full review of the hate/bias incident structure in order to create a more transparent, effective, and responsive hate/bias incident process. Santiago assembled a Hate/Bias Work Group (including the Office of the General Counsel, University Marketing and Communications, Office of Diversity and Equal Opportunity, Office of the Provost, University Police, Housing and Residence Life, Student Conduct and Civility Education, Counseling Center, Center for Student Diversity, TU Social Justice Collective, and SGA) to review and revitalize the existing reporting structure. The Hate/Bias Work Group met monthly to provide a coordinated multidisciplinary university response to hate crimes and/or bias incidents. It brought forward specific suggestions to improve the transparency, effectiveness, and responsiveness of the university's hate/bias process:

- Timely response to hate/bias incidents
- Central coordination of hate/bias response efforts
- Communication with hate/bias victim(s)

- Publicizing of hate/bias procedures to the entire campus community
- Increased transparency related to crime log reporting
- Clarification of purpose of crime alerts

This experience of creating a more transparent, effective, and responsive hate/bias incident process during a campus crisis confirmed for us that nothing is more frustrating than dealing with outdated policies and procedures, or trying to update them during a crisis. Instead, leadership must be proactive and identify key staff to lead and participate in committees to review, revise, and improve policies and procedures periodically.

In an ongoing effort to improve the transparency, effectiveness, and responsiveness of the university as a whole, the president also asked Santiago to assemble and co-chair a Large Event Procedures Planning Committee to balance student safety and risk management with clarity, fairness, and consistency. This committee (including Campus Life, Event and Conference Services, Campus Police, and the Center for Student Diversity) developed criteria and guidelines to determine levels of safety and risk management for all events and locations on campus. Part of this work involved testing TU policies and procedures in hypothetical scenarios. Student leaders helped to review policies and procedures while considering questions such as the following: Are the policies clear, fair, and consistent? Are they readily accessible and easy to understand? Are they relevant to particular issues and concerns on campus? Do they address/meet campus programming needs?

When you make it common practice to involve students in providing input and recommendations, they become your biggest advocates, helping explain and promote new policies and procedures to their peers. When students challenge your policies and procedures, be prepared and willing to open the lines of communication. Invite them to share their concerns and offer alternative ideas and perspectives. Student activists can also be very helpful and engaging them in dialogue before situations escalate is important.

## A Call to Action

The Retreat for Social Justice (RSJ) is an annual weekend retreat sponsored by the Center for Student Diversity (CSD). It gives attendees an opportunity to explore their cultural identities and interact with people from diverse backgrounds and helps students (a) explore and understand their identities and how those identities influence their attitudes, beliefs, and behaviors; (b) create dialogue with their peers from different backgrounds, perspectives, and experiences; (c) learn ways they can interrupt prejudice and advocate for social equity and justice; and (d) develop ways to create an inclusive and welcoming environment on campus and in their communities. During the spring semester, RSJ participants collaborate on projects, presentations, exhibits, performances, activities, and other initiatives that highlight specific campus and community issues, providing tangible opportunities for students to make a difference. Termed Social Justice Days of Action, this program series is intended to build a more equitable and inclusive campus community.

Each semester, TU's Division of Student Affairs brings culturally relevant speakers, educators, activists, and entertainers to campus, giving students, faculty, staff, and the surrounding community access to some of the most influential minds of our time. In spring 2018, actress and advocate Laverne Cox was the featured Diversity Speaker. Santiago opened the program by offering some introductory remarks:

As global citizens, I urge you to consider: What is your personal role and responsibility in creating a more just society? While many of you are allies, I would encourage you to become accomplices. Yes, you can retweet and reshare, but also consider that you can always do more.

An ally can engage in activism in solidarity with a marginalized individual or group. An accomplice will focus on dismantling oppressive structures. In other words, 'ally work' focuses on supporting and uplifting, but 'accomplice work' focuses on actively doing the work to change policies, practices, and structures.

Tonight, in this space together, let's reflect on how we can support and uplift marginalized people and groups, but also, let's think about and reimagine how structures and systems might be more inclusive, socially just, and community oriented.

I challenge you to: (1) Do one thing to make our campus more inclusive and welcoming, (2) be actively involved in your classrooms and learn from different perspectives, (3) challenge stereotypes and toxic language wherever you go—in dining halls, residence halls, student org meetings, locker rooms, athletic fields, and in the stands—and (4) get involved in the community to serve and address inequities. (S. Solis, personal communication, March 13, 2018)

As student affairs professionals, we are dedicated to supporting students' growth and development, and value and enjoy empowering students to make a difference on campus and beyond. We have a deep, vested interest in developing compassionate student leaders who understand and appreciate equity and social justice. We teach students the importance of community service and civic engagement. We challenge students to think critically about historical, social, cultural, political, and economic contexts and issues. We want students to consider alternative perspectives. We want students to improve society. So, when students use these skills to challenge policies and procedures, we must be ready, not to resist and push back, but to engage in dialogue and consensus. Typically, students do not just complain for the sake of complaining. Student activists, in particular, are deeply invested in improving their campus. Perhaps they are responding to the challenge to "do one thing to make our campus more inclusive and welcoming." Generally, students want to remove real or perceived obstacles—barriers they consider unfair or unjust—and student affairs professionals must be ready and willing to include them in difficult conversations about developing clear, fair, and consistent policies and procedures.

## Ongoing Professional Development

As many campuses continue to diversify by recruiting and employing staff from different backgrounds and with varying identities, providing ongoing, culturally relevant professional development opportunities can be challenging. How do you create a foundational understanding around activism, protest, and campus unrest for all team members? This general understanding can be developed only through intentional and continuous education and dialogue. To this end, it is essential to provide staff development opportunities throughout the year, particularly during winter break and summer. Ongoing professional development is necessary to educate staff. For example, in order to gain a better understanding of activism, protest, and campus unrest, it was important for TU's Division of Student Affairs to deepen staff understanding of terms like *social justice*, including how politicized language is used with students. Shared readings are an inexpensive way to introduce staff to new terminology and build a common language. The following are helpful resources we have used to introduce staff to new concepts and help them engage in productive conversations:

- *And Campus for All: Diversity, Inclusion, and Freedom of Speech at U.S. Universities* (PEN America, 2016)
- "It Matters Who Leads Them: Connecting Leadership in Multicultural Affairs to Student Learning and Development" (Stewart, 2016)
- *The Alt-Right on Campus: What Students Need to Know* (Southern Poverty Law Center, 2017a)
- "The Contours of Free Expression on Campus: Free Speech, Academic Freedom, and Civility" (Lawrence, 2017)
- "Taming the Madvocate Within: Social Justice Meets Social Compassion" (Viray & Nash, 2014)
- *Ten Ways to Fight Hate: A Community Resource Guide* (Southern Poverty Law Center, 2017b)

We used *Ten Ways to Fight Hate*, for example, to discuss helpful tips such as how to deal with the media, steps to build a healthy community, and how to fight for systemic change. The great thing about shared readings is that each reader can engage with an article from their own perspective. It is important to create respectful spaces—whether you call them "safe spaces" or "brave spaces"—for readers to feel that they can share their opinions freely. Publications more specific to your region can also be extremely helpful to better understand local issues and politics. Because of our proximity to Baltimore, we used *The Racial Wealth Divide in Baltimore* (Corporation for Enterprise Development, 2017) to explore the ways in which racial economic inequality impacts some of our students from Baltimore and other students of color from low socioeconomic communities.

As the term *social justice* has emerged in higher education in recent years, many colleges and universities have incorporated the term into their mission, vision, goals, and programs. Like many colleges and universities, TU strongly believes in human/civil rights and equity. We want all students to feel included, to know their voices matter, and to become an integral part of the campus community. In TU's quest to be diverse, inclusive, and welcoming, instead of simply adding the term *social justice* to an already long list of "well-meaning" and "nice-sounding" terminology, staff from the Center for Student Diversity (CSD) coordinated focused conversations about *why* and *how* we wanted to use this new term. What made TU a socially just campus? Were its programs truly grounded in social justice? What message was TU ready to convey socially and politically? Most important, how would social justice inform TU's work with students in teaching and encouraging them to be strong leaders on campus, and beyond?

In addition to shared readings, local community organizations and leaders can also be great resources to help develop staff professionally and personally across race, class, and/or gender continuums. In 2016, we hired a local activist and community organizer from Baltimore to work with some of our student leaders (including leaders from the SGA and Black Student Union, among others) to interview them and conduct focus groups. We wanted candid feedback directly from our students on how to improve the campus climate. TU has grown tremendously over the past decade, and the percentage of students of color has doubled. In the past three years, each incoming fall class has become more racially diverse. We felt we could, and should, do more to strengthen our ability to successfully interact with and support students from diverse racial, ethnic, and cultural backgrounds. What was TU missing and what could it do better to become a truly inclusive and welcoming campus for all students? How could we heighten our understanding and insight related to inclusion, equity, and social justice? The feedback from participating students was not complimentary: Nearly all students perceived a lack of safety at some level; communication across campus was viewed as strained from the top to the bottom (i.e., the administration to student groups); administration appeared to be reactive to student concerns, rather than proactive; and race was a major issue for students, who expressed concerns of insufficient engagement on all levels of the institution to address Black student issues. Our challenge was to receive this feedback, take time to critically reflect, and then create necessary conversations about it during staff development.

To examine the existing conditions at TU closely and constructively, we decided to utilize campus expertise by asking staff from the CSD to lead conversations based on current research and best practices. To shift the existing campus culture and build campus-wide momentum, we felt it necessary to have everyone at all levels of the Division of Student Affairs participate in the dialogue. We dedicated half of our Divisional Staff Development Day to examining how the Baltimore uprising impacted and connected with our work in student affairs. We wanted our student affairs professionals to critically explore structural oppression that creates barriers to student success based on socioeconomic class, race, and police violence. The goals for this particular conversation were to (a) examine our current personal and professional relationships with Baltimore City; (b) understand the historical, social, and political context of the challenges the city faces; and (c) explore how as a division we could be more intentional in connecting our work, our students, and ourselves (individually) to Baltimore City.

To achieve these goals, the CSD used the HBO Original Documentary *Baltimore Rising* (Sohn, 2017), which follows the Freddie Gray Jr. case, to dig into the complex ways that the TU campus and its students are both directly and indirectly affected by social injustice. The CSD staff facilitators started by giving all staff members an opportunity to reflect on their own personal relationship with Baltimore City. They also asked staff members to think about the ways in which that relationship with Baltimore manifested in their work with students. The facilitators then provided a brief overview of the current state of Baltimore City Public Schools (BCPS), which historically underperform, producing few graduates adequately prepared for college. The facilitators asked staff members to discuss how TU typically interfaces with BCPS in terms of outreach and recruitment. If few Baltimore City high school students are adequately prepared for college, then what is TU's institutional role and responsibility, as the second largest public university in Maryland, in addressing this issue? Ultimately, this conversation helped bring critical awareness to broader issues resulting from institutional oppression and systemic racism.

If facilitated properly, staff will respond positively to difficult and uncomfortable conversations. The key is to involve them in establishing ground rules about privacy; a commitment to learn from each other; actively listening to understand one another; responding with empathy, humility, and respect; challenging the idea and not the person; speaking truth to power; sharing honestly; and maintaining a "safe" or "brave" environment.

## ATTEND TO YOUR STAFF MEMBERS' EMOTIONS AND NEEDS

One of the lessons we learned when dealing with student activism and responding to student protests is the importance of taking care of staff—particularly professionals who have recently entered the field. During a protest or rally, emotions tend to run high and colleagues must process their own thoughts and feelings as they work to remain somewhat objective when working with students. Familiarizing yourself with campus (and off-campus) resources is important. The counseling center, for example, might offer or create specific, tailored services to support and advise staff when dealing with students in distress, and more generally assist with personal mental health care. If a staff member is directly impacted by a campus issue, rally, or protest, the following are some helpful tips:

- Allow space for staff members to remove themselves from specific programs and conversations, or from providing direct support to impacted students (perhaps the staff member is experiencing anxiety because they don't know how to support students, especially those directly impacted).
- Encourage staff to use the counseling center (and other campus resources) and check in with a mental health professional to process their feelings and emotions.
- Facilitate conversations about appropriate ways to support students. Take time to model for staff and/or practice with them how to respond to difficult, sensitive questions.
- Encourage staff members to form peer support/discussion groups to hear from and share their experiences with colleagues.
- Provide timely, updated information in a transparent manner to alleviate angst, confusion, fear, and panic.

Staff members may completely disagree, and even become angry, if a group of students is rallying or protesting in support of something they deem racist, sexist, Islamophobic, homophobic, or transphobic. For example, when the YWC was created, staff members did not understand why the university allowed such a hateful group to form. They were deeply offended and felt personally targeted. For some staff members, leading conversations with students about the

First Amendment and free speech was challenging. They disagreed that the university should protect YWC's freedom of speech and assembly because they strongly believed the group's ideology and premise for organizing were offensive, repugnant, dangerous, and antithetical to TU's core values. In such instances, creating "safe spaces" or "courageous spaces" for staff to reflect, process, discuss, and find community is important. In order to engage with students emotionally to provide support, comfort, and a listening ear, staff will need to check in with colleagues to make sense of what is happening; to ask questions about how the university will respond; to share their confusion, discomfort, apprehension, angst, anger, and fear; to educate themselves and others about the issue at hand; and to gain reassurance that the situation is under control. Although creating these spaces is necessary and important when dealing with a campus rally or protest, these spaces are also significant following a critical local, national, or global event.

Staff members of color working in student affairs at a predominantly White institution tend to advise multicultural student organizations and therefore develop formal or informal mentoring relationships with students of color. Often, they are expected to maintain a pulse on the campus climate, get a "feel" for what students of color think about any given issue, and report back to the administration. Because staff members of color are constantly asked and/or expected to intervene and problem-solve incidents involving students of color, they may feel overworked, overwhelmed, manipulated, and even exploited. Staff members of color may start to believe their most valued asset is their race or ethnicity instead of their qualifications and skills. Asking staff members of color to leverage relationships they have built with students is unfair because they assume all the risk. If relationships with students are damaged, they have to spend the time and effort mending them.

Student affairs professionals pride ourselves in developing good relationships with students. We connect them to resources, advise their organizations, develop their leadership skills, support them through difficult times, teach them self-advocacy, and even train them to become effective change agents and social justice warriors. Because staff invest so much time and energy into students' well-being and success, when students organize a rally or protest, staff members sometimes want to support them beyond the scope of their professional role. Clear guidelines should be provided for the staff in these scenarios: What are the overall expectations? Can staff members work alongside students, or take a leadership role, to plan a rally or protest? Are staff members expected to remain neutral? If so, what does that look like? Can a staff member attend a rally or protest in a supportive capacity as long as they are not vocal? Can they wear t-shirts with specific slogans (e.g., Black Lives Matter, I Stand With Dreamers) in solidarity with students to support a particular cause? Can staff members sign and/or help circulate petitions? Can they talk to the media? What about the campus newspaper? Do expectations differ depending on a particular staff member's title (e.g., someone hired to develop programs around diversity, inclusion, equity, or social justice)?

Depending on staff members' personal identities, political affiliation, or religious beliefs, they might sympathize or empathize with a group of students organizing a specific rally or protest (e.g., in support of installing a pride flag or declaring the university as a sanctuary campus). Individual staff members might disagree with the university's position to not install a pride flag or to not proclaim themselves a sanctuary campus. They may question their allegiance to the university, they may threaten to leave the institution, or they may distrust the administration's commitment to inclusion, equity, and social justice.

As a student affairs professional who holds multiple marginalized identities, Santiago values working closely with his staff to make sure there is transparent, timely, and honest communication. He notes it is important to have conversations on the record and off the record so staff are aware of behind-the-scenes politics and positional dynamics. He often reminds his staff that he leads from a values-based approach and that their input is paramount to the work they do together. Santiago wants his staff to know that they are appreciated, valued, heard, and affirmed—regardless of disagreements—because at the end of the day, they must provide support and resources for students. Any disagreements should be in the spirit of upholding the shared TU mission: to foster "intellectual inquiry and critical thinking to prepare graduates who will serve as effective, ethical leaders and engaged citizens" (Towson University, 2018, para. 1).

## Conclusion

Students' lived experiences are neither stagnant nor monolithic. As generations emerge and evolve, it is important to be aware of the influences that shape students. Student affairs professionals need to be the experts on current and incoming students and create opportunities to share our knowledge with a broad range of colleagues across the campus. To this end, we, the authors, have used generational data along with TU's shifting demographics data to talk with faculty and staff about the students who make up our student body. It is always surprising how little many professional staff members know about our students beyond a general sense of overall enrollment numbers. To counter that, we have been able to shift campus attitudes and stereotypes about our students by sharing data on where students live, how much they work or plan to work while in school, and a more granular breakdown of demographics including race, gender, and status as a full-time or part-time student.

Even though it is often complex and very challenging, student affairs work is very rewarding. As conversations related to racial justice and equity in higher education continue to dominate the national landscape, the work of higher education professionals, and in particular student affairs staff, will need to remain unapologetically student-centered. In order for our institutions to be successful, relevant, competitive, and inclusive, we must develop our resources and capacity to reflect our commitment to equity and inclusion. It is also critical to develop networks both locally and nationally through professional associations and to have colleagues outside of our institution to lean on for advice and support. These relationships and networks will be invaluable as we enter into new phases of student activism and the emergence of new issues presented to us by new generations of students.

## References

Corporation for Enterprise Development. (2017). *The racial wealth divide in Baltimore*. Washington, DC: Author.

Dionisopoulos, T. (2011, June 27). Youth for Western Civilization hosts first annual conference. *Campus Reform*. Retrieved from https://www.campusreform.org/?ID=2853

Lawrence, F. M. (2017). The contours of free expression on campus: Free speech, academic freedom, and civility. *Liberal Education, 103*(2), 14–21.

PEN America. (2016). *And campus for all: Diversity, inclusion, and freedom of speech at U.S. universities*. New York, NY: Author.

Sohn, S. (Director & Producer). (2017). *Baltimore rising* [Motion picture]. United States: HBO Films.

Southern Poverty Law Center. (2017a). *The alt-right on campus: What students need to know* (2nd ed.). Montgomery, AL: Author.

Southern Poverty Law Center. (2017b). *Ten ways to fight hate: A community resource guide* (5th ed.). Montgomery, AL: Author.

Stewart, D. L. (2016). It matters who leads them: Connecting leadership in multicultural affairs to student learning and development. *About Campus, 21*(1), 21–28. doi:10.1002/abc.21227

Towson University. (2018). Mission & strategic plan. Retrieved from https://www.towson.edu/about/mission

Viray, S., & Nash, R. J. (2014). Taming the madvocate within: Social justice meets social compassion. *About Campus, 19*(5), 20–27. doi:10.1002/abc.21170

# 7

# Critical Relationships During Stormy Times

## Greg Sharer

Speak with colleagues who have worked through crises on their campuses, and you will likely hear a clear theme: Relationships are essential. This chapter focuses on the relationships of the vice president for student affairs (VPSA) with three key partners: the institution's president, public relations, and legal counsel. It will consider each partner's potential shared and conflicting professional interests and considerations when facing a crisis.

## Mayhem Comes to Town

November 15, 2013, was the date of the 55th annual Cortaca Jug football game, pitting Ithaca College against The State University of New York (SUNY) College at Cortland. The game was played at Ithaca College, and as is the tradition in this rivalry, I attended in my role as the visiting team's VPSA along with a number of staff and students. The game was exhilarating, with SUNY Cortland pulling off a last-second win on an abnormally balmy, beautiful mid-November day.

I was riding home from the game with the SUNY Cortland's chief of police, the assistant vice president for student affairs, the acting director of student conduct, and the student government president when we heard a call over the police radio band requesting law enforcement support from all surrounding jurisdictions. The 911 dispatcher called in law enforcement from nearby counties to address a street party that had grown beyond control. At that point, I knew it would be a long night, followed by many more.

As we arrived in Cortland, we witnessed large groups of people wandering through the streets. We drove through the eye of the storm: Clayton Avenue. By the time we arrived, much of the crowd, estimated at as high as 10,000, had disbursed. What remained was a street covered in the detritus from the day's events—beer cans, cardboard, shopping carts, liquor bottles, red cups, and other flotsam and jetsam left in the wake. Of course, cell phones captured much of the action, which was posted to a variety of social media platforms, quickly becoming viral.

The chief of police, assistant vice president, and I went to the city's incident command center to get an update on the mayhem. I also called to our college president to brief him on the situation: 80 people had been arrested; 19 of them were our students (SUNY Cortland, 2014).

Between the emergency call over the police band and the viral videos, news outlets—first local and then national and even international—quickly picked up the event. News stations aired live reports describing what had transpired and interviews with students and community members, who had very different views of what occurred. News outlets covered the incident with headlines such as "More Than 30 Students Arrested at Football Game 'Riot'" (Attebury, 2013), "SUNY Cortland Students Were Out of Control at Cortaca 2013" (Kingkade, 2013), and "College President Apologizes After Student Football Celebrations Bring Chaos to Small Town" (Daily Mail Reporter, 2013).

Fortunately, there were no serious injuries and the property damage, though not inconsequential, was not severe. Nevertheless, we had a lot of work ahead of us to rebuild trust with the community, change the blow out party culture of the weekend, and address the behavior of those students involved in the "riot."

The college president issued an apology on behalf of the campus and emphasized that the college would work with the community to ensure that such behavior would never happen again. The president and the mayor established the College and Community Joint Commission on Cortaca (Cortaca Commission), bringing together leaders from the community and the college. The commission was charged to "Develop recommendations to the city and college with a comprehensive approach to policies, procedures, programming, services, rules, and assessment with respect to student behavior, safety and related concerns during the weekend of the Cortland-Ithaca football game" (SUNY Cortland, 2014, p. 20). The Cortaca Commission met throughout the spring semester, holding open forums with many stakeholders to determine the causes of what had occurred. The result of the multitude of meetings and discussions was a final report that outlined recommendations to prevent such future incidents.

Although what occurred that weekend may be a normal football event in some college towns, Cortaca 2013 was a crisis for our college and the city. It provides the primary backdrop for the theme of this chapter—exploring opportunities for working with the institution's president, building a relationship with legal counsel and college public relations, and balancing conflicting professional interests related to student crises and disasters. Because relationships are not one-way interactions, I discussed with my college president, legal counsel, and director of public relations how to work in times of crises, and specifically their relationship with the VPSA, and have weaved their perspectives into the narrative.

As with all sustained relationships, understanding the needs, priorities, goals, pressures, values, and frustrations of the other person in the relationship is important. We engage in this give and take each day with our spouses, partners, children, siblings, colleagues, and other people whose relationships we value. Developing an understanding of others does not always lead to agreement, but we hope it builds trust.

## Working With the Institution's President

To work effectively with the president, the VPSA must be able to advocate for the student affairs division's priorities while also recognizing that the president faces competing interests from internal and external stakeholders. The VPSA must understand how the president desires to work with stakeholders. Successful college presidents need timely, accurate information and to hear diverse perspectives. Building trusting relationships with others across the campus is critical in order for the president to gain a broad and deep understanding of the institution. This ability to build trust and relationships is especially critical during a crisis, as the president must balance a myriad of institutional priorities. Of course, presidents bring their own personalities and experiences to the position. The time to learn what expectations the president has of the VPSA, and vice versa, is before disaster strikes.

I am fortunate to work with a president who is open to discussion and supportive of the work of student affairs. It is common for us to spend some time in our weekly one-on-one meetings discussing our personal stories, because sharing our stories is how we build our empathy and understanding of each other. For this chapter, I invited him to articulate his expectations of the VPSA related to crisis, his priorities at a time of crisis, what goes through his mind during times of crisis, and how he balances conflicting professional interests during a crisis.

## The VPSA Must Be Aware of Threats and Vulnerabilities

It is important for the VPSA to be aware of potential threats and perceived vulnerabilities. In our preparation for Cortaca 2013, because we anticipated the potential for an influx of guests to the campus, we instituted stringent residence hall guest policies. Policies included registration of guests, limiting the number of guests in each room, requiring registered guests to wear wristbands with the name of the student host, and prohibiting guests from entering a residence hall without their host. Because of these actions, although other parts of the community were feeling overrun by partiers, the residence halls remained relatively calm. We also convened meetings with local law enforcement and the city mayor during the weeks leading up to the event to discuss communication strategies and safety and security plans.

We were confident that we had a sound plan for the weekend. What we did not anticipate was the volume of guests arriving in the city for the weekend. The influx of an unprecedented number of people coming to the community, many with no affiliation to the college, overwhelmed the plans that were in place in the city.

We continually scan our environment to stay current and attentive to what is happening locally, regionally, and globally in higher education and the lives of our students. The president looks to me to be the expert on college students. For that, I must rely on my staff members' expertise as well as my own ongoing professional development.

## *The VPSA Must Be Prepared to Deal With Crises*

The president expects the VPSA to be prepared to deal with crises. To prepare, the VPSA must work with departments from across campus to ensure they take the necessary steps to respond to crisis. I communicate regularly with the departments (e.g., university police, city police, counseling, residence life, county sheriff) that are on the front lines of crisis response to develop strong relationships. A key to addressing the crowd control issue during the 2013 crisis was quick communication with college and local law enforcement. Though the preparation did not prevent the mass gathering, it did prevent issues from moving onto the campus and prevent more serious harm to the community.

## *The VPSA Must Take Action Both During and After a Crisis*

The president expects the VPSA to help during and after a crisis to ensure that the college's leadership is asking the right questions and taking appropriate steps. For example, on the evening of the Cortaca incident, the president, director of public relations, and I discussed what message to send to the campus and community about what had transpired. I encouraged the college to send a clear statement that the behavior demonstrated by some on that day was not acceptable and that the college, working with the city, would take steps to prevent it from happening again. Because the story and images were already appearing on local television as well as trending on social media, we recognized that waiting even a few hours to make a statement would be seen as tacit consent of the behavior by the college leadership. The director of public relations quickly sent the message to the campus and media outlets.

## The VPSA Must Identify Practical Steps to Mitigate a Future Crisis

The president looks to the VPSA to identify practical steps to mitigate a future crisis. On the Monday morning after the 2013 incident, the president's cabinet met with city officials to lay out a plan to address the short- and long-term needs to prevent a reoccurrence. In addition to sending a clear message via college e-mail and local media outlets that the behavior that occurred was not acceptable and that steps would be taken to prevent it from reoccurring, the president and mayor created a joint task force that met throughout the fall and spring to identify the causes of the incident and develop action steps to prevent another one like it from occurring.

The president outlined seven priorities during times of crisis. These are not necessarily sequential, and actually, will often overlap:

- **Safety and health stand above all else.** This is consistent with my priority as the VPSA. Preventing the injury or death of a member of the college or community overrides all other considerations. During Cortaca, the safety of students and members of the community was paramount.
- **Look for solutions.** What immediate steps need to be taken to recover from a crisis? What are the longer-term solutions? During the Cortaca incident, we recognized the need to

stop the behavior, communicate quickly, and then begin to immediately repair the harm and prevent such a crisis from reoccurring. The events of Cortaca 2013 harmed the college's reputation. The physical damage to the community, use of police resources from the surrounding areas, and images of the mass gathering damaged the college's reputation well beyond just the immediate community. The college received calls and e-mails from numerous news outlets, parents, alumni, and other concerned individuals. Most expressed outrage over what they saw in the media and demanded that the college take action. They were anxiously watching to see how the college addressed the crisis.

- **Ensure continuity of operations.** The president wants to make sure the college can return to normal functioning as soon as possible. There was no question that classes would be held Monday morning while we mobilized to address the issues from the weekend.
- **Communicate a clear and consistent message to all constituents.** This includes students, faculty, staff, families, alumni, community members, board members, lawmakers, and the media. Selecting appropriate communication mediums is also critical. The public relations staff is essential to ensuring that the college speaks with one voice and keeps everyone informed. At my institution, the president often wants to be the spokesperson for the college during times of crisis. In today's era of multiple media platforms, it is nearly impossible to control information, highlighting the importance for the college to speak with a unified voice.
- **Determine the need for outside, ongoing assistance.** My institution is fortunate to have the support of local first responders and law enforcement as well as the support of a university

system. Does the college have access to the resources needed to support sustained efforts to adequately address problems?
- **Implement a recovery plan, assess it, and modify it as needed.** The creation of the Cortaca Commission was both part of the immediate recovery, as it gave internal and external stakeholders the opportunity to express their concerns and offer solutions, and a road map for long-term recovery through the recommendation of action steps.

When developing a relationship with the president, gaining an understanding of how the president thinks about crises, processes information, and prioritizes actions offers insight into how best to work together when a crisis hits. In times of crisis it is important to stay calm in order to think clearly and act rationally. My president thinks in terms of sequential action steps. Understanding this helps me frame my information and recommendations accordingly. He also values receiving continual information from his team and seeks to "pick the brain" of and gather information from many sources. It is important that I provide a student affairs context to the discussion. This highlights the necessity to remain current in the field's best practices and regularly communicate them with colleagues.

Understanding how the president balances potential conflicts of interests is perhaps the most critical element to the development of a working relationship, as this provides the insight into the president's decision making. My president has identified an overriding principle and two subprinciples that he follows when presented with a crisis situation: The college must come first. This principle comprises two subprinciples: the importance of the safety and well-being of the community and the desire to always be open, honest, and transparent. The first subprinciple underscores the value of each individual and the second the necessity to maintain integrity in decision making.

Integrity is also critical to the VPSA's relationship with the president. Open, honest, and transparent communication is necessary at all times, but especially during a disaster. If either party loses trust in the other due to assigning blame, acting on ulterior motives, and so on, recovering trust is difficult.

## Relationship With the Director of Public Relations

During a crisis, being able to see the larger picture while also working through the immediate needs of staff, students, and the community can be challenging. Information is often incomplete and the desire to act on the situation before checking facts can end up making a situation worse. Do not charge into the fire without knowing what is on the other side of the door. Others at the college also should not act without thoughtful consideration of the impact of their actions. However, colleges also face mounting pressure to respond quickly to events or face the accusation of indifference or, worse, malfeasance.

These competing demands are much easier to negotiate when you have a strong and trusting working relationship with your college's communications or public relations office. As with a student affairs administrator's relationship with the president, this relationship should be cultivated long before a crisis occurs and be based on a mutual understanding and respect of the other's responsibilities and priorities.

We live in a time when word of a crisis—whether factual or fictional, or a combination of the two—can develop and spread like a wildfire. Information travels much faster through social media than through an official college press release. This is a particular concern in times of crisis because social media posters often share images without context, place blame, spread inaccurate information, or incite others to act.

Social media spread news of Cortaca 2013 widely and almost instantly. According to the SUNY Cortland (2014) *College and Community Joint Commission Final Report*, social media was cited as one of the contributing factors to the "outlandish and dangerous behavior" (p. 6). Social media served to normalize the extreme behavior, inform others of the locations of parties, and immortalize some of the more outrageous actions. A picture of a person jumping from a roof into a crowd of partiers continues to appear online.

The use of social media presents an unavoidable concern when addressing any crisis. The director of public relations has an interest in managing the college's message by providing timely, accurate information while also respecting the privacy of those affected. This is a challenging balance, as delaying the sharing of information can result in the proliferation of rumors. During fall break in 2012, our college experienced a very different kind of crisis—a tragic suicide in a residence hall. Because it was fall break, only about 20 students were in the hall, but the presence of police, the coroner, and other emergency responders quickly drew the students' attention. Attempts to contact the victim's family through normal channels proved difficult. As the anxiety of the students in the building rose, it was clear that they needed information and reassurance. I was concerned that students would share information through social media that would reach the family before I could reach them. I cannot imagine the trauma of a parent learning about the death of their child through a Facebook post.

I met with the students in the building and shared what had happened. I asked them not to share information and explained my reasons for this concern. They were wonderfully supportive of one another and respectful of the concern about sharing the information. We were eventually able to share the information with the family members that night, about five hours after the discovery.

Timely and accurate communication about potential crises is a key expectation that our public relations officer has of the VPSA. By immediately collaborating with the public relations officer, who is professionally obligated to focus on a crisis and quickly assess its potential impact beyond the campus and the moment, the student affairs professional can focus on the immediate needs of the students. When an incident occurs, however, these pieces do not just naturally click into place unless a trusting relationship has previously been established.

Our public relations director knows that I will contact him right away if I sense that something has the potential to attract media attention or affect the college's reputation. He assesses that potential and acts—or does not act—accordingly. I was the one who alerted him to the 2013 Cortaca disturbance. That quick notification allowed us to work immediately with the president to craft an effective message and get it out to our community and the public while the news media were still reporting on the event.

In times of crisis, our public relations director approaches things in three phases: journalist mode, crisis manager mode, and public relations mode. As soon as he is made aware of an emergency, he slips into journalist mode and begins collecting facts and separating out what is and is not immediately relevant. By supplying the best answers to the questions of who, what, when, where, why, and how, student affairs can play a critical role in this effort. During Cortaca, by making certain that we communicated an accurate picture of the facts, we established SUNY Cortland as a source for credible information at a time when rumor, exaggeration, and misinformation was running rampant.

The VPSA is also an indispensable partner in crafting the messaging involved in the crisis management phase of the college's communications efforts. Once the facts have been established, student affairs is part of the team that decides on an immediate course of action and develops the message that is sent to the campus community to keep students, staff, and faculty safe. The public relations director trusts the student affairs' assessment of what students are facing, what they need, and how they are responding. In essence, the director helps craft the message to make it simple and effective, and to get it to the community as fast as possible. Moreover, a well-crafted message allows the college to talk with the community in a single, official voice, reducing confusion during times when multiple messages would be counterproductive, if not dangerous.

Once any immediate, on-campus communication needs are satisfied, the college's public relations director then turns his attention to the outside world. Although this is more the director's priority than student affairs staff, we realize its importance and work with him to ensure the messaging to the public—which includes parents and future students as well as community members and news reporters—is consistent with internal messaging. It is in all of our interests to protect and enhance SUNY Cortland's reputation, and we provide whatever information or insight we can to help with that effort.

The importance of relationships during crises was made clear during Cortaca 2013. Because the key players were talking together immediately, and because we already had strong working relationships and an understanding of the president's personality and preferred method of handling things, he was able to go beyond what most presidents would do in similar situations. Our president did not just promise to do everything he could to prevent another event like the Cortaca disturbance from happening; he promised that such an incident would never happen again. At the time, a stronger than expected statement was needed, and the open communication and trust established among the president, student affairs, and public relations gave us the confidence to make it.

That promise highlights an important aspect of relationships during a crisis: They are important for reaching long-term goals as well as for short-term crisis management. The public relations director played an active role in the work of the Cortaca Commission, ensuring parents, the public, and the news media were aware of the steps we were taking. Because our president had pledged there would never be a repeat of Cortaca 2013, we knew that failure was not an option. We had to develop and implement a multifaceted plan that would actually work.

The college remained focused on this and ultimately succeeded partly because the president, student affairs, public relations, and the other offices involved shared the same priority: the safety and health of our students. Although it is an obvious priority for student affairs and the president, it is also the top priority for college communications officers. After all, there is no greater public relations crisis than the death or serious injury of a student.

Although student affairs and public relations professionals who communicate regularly and understand each other's needs and responsibilities are generally in sync, especially in times of emergency, competing interests occasionally need to be managed. At times, for example, public relations' desire to offer as much disclosure and information as possible conflicts with student affairs' need to protect student privacy. The communications director may want to give the media more information than what the college is legally required to provide, which may be more than we are comfortable with from a student affairs perspective.

## Relationship With College Legal Counsel

I am an attorney by training; however, to paraphrase the old saying, I would be a fool to provide my own legal advice. For that, I rely on my college legal counsel. While legal counsel must have positive relationships with a number of professionals on campus, the relationship with the VPSA is unique. The risk of a mistake and actual harm must always be on the attorney's mind, well above other institutional risks. It is one thing to *say* that student safety is our foremost priority; actually practicing that pledge takes a lot of hard work, research into the current state of law and practice (law often has not yet caught up to current issues in student affairs), and a great deal of trust between attorney and client.

As with the president and public relations leadership, crisis communication with counsel is best forged at times of calm. Attorneys are well known as liking to go to lunch, and a VPSA's time spent with the attorney during these casual discussions is time well spent. In the best relationships, we develop a shorthand to refer quickly to concepts and requirements, which can save precious time during an emergency. What is the counsel's role during a crisis? Counsel should endeavor to take up the least amount of the client's time as possible, be clear about the risks and options, identify what steps are legally required, but save as much time as possible for the policy makers to communicate among themselves and with external actors, and to act. Shorthand developed in calmer times can assist in quickly getting information to the client and then letting them off the phone to address the crisis.

The VPSA and counsel should be in regular communication about issues large and small. My legal counsel shares his cell phone number with the VPSA on each of his campuses, and he has theirs because, unlike other administrative crises, student affairs emergencies rarely break during business hours.

As important as it is to have trust in your legal counsel, it is also critical to understand what it means to be the counsel's client and the privilege that attaches by virtue of that relationship. Although counsel and client should communicate often, it is important for the attorney to remember that they are not the decision maker; they are counsel to the decision maker, and it is their job to provide the decision maker advice in making sound legal judgments. The line between law and policy can be a thin one, and it is important that both client and counsel are clear about what is "must," what is "may," and who the decision maker is.

An in-depth discussion of the attorney–client privilege is outside the scope of this chapter; however, understanding what communication is privileged and how to maintain that privilege is essential. The purpose of the attorney–client privilege is to encourage full and frank communication between the attorney and client without concern that the communication will be found through discovery or admissible at trial (Kaplan and Lee, 1997). As a doctor–patient communication is privileged to encourage the candid discussion of the patient's health care, so is attorney–client communication privileged to ensure the candid discussion of the client's legal situation.

The question of who is the client is not always clear. Ultimately, the attorneys serve the institution, so their legal duty is to the college. In that sense, as an officer of the college, I am the attorney's client, but the attorney's primary duty is to the college. For example, if an officer of the college engages in illegal activity and that information is shared with the legal counsel, counsel has the responsibility to protect the interests of the institution, which would likely conflict with the officer's interest.

Discuss with your legal counsel how to maintain attorney–client privilege before sharing communication with other individuals or groups in any form. This legal privilege allows the VPSA to converse openly with the legal counsel without concern that the communication will be subject to discovery. If the communication is shared beyond the counsel and VPSA the protection of the privilege may be lost.

My legal counsel often points out the distinction of "may" versus "must" language in regulations. For instance, when may we share student information under the Family Educational Rights and

Privacy Act (FERPA) versus when must we share information and with whom? Similarly, it is important to distinguish legal questions and obligations, which require a knowledge of the law, from policy questions and issues, which require a balancing of priorities. Frequently, questions presented to legal counsel cross into both law and policy. Legal counsel can provide advice about what the law requires the institution to do (must) and what the law leaves for the institution to decide (may). For instance, on our campus we have examined our procedures for reviewing on-campus housing accommodations under the Americans with Disabilities Act and the Fair Housing Act. The issues raised by this review include questions of policy (what department initially reviews the documentation) and law (what the institution's compliance requirements are under the acts). Although one issue is a policy/procedure matter and the other legal, our legal counsel is able to assist in sorting through the issues to help identify practices that will help ensure compliance.

I had numerous discussions with my legal counsel following the 2013 Cortaca situation. Because the incident was very public and high profile, I wanted to ensure that confidential communication would not later become public through a Freedom of Information Act request or subpoena. In other words, I needed to know how we could maintain the privilege of the attorney–client communication while also being as transparent with our community members as possible. There was a great deal of interest from our community in knowing that the college was addressing the behavior of our students, while also recognizing the privacy rights of our students. Sharing information with the community and being transparent in the follow-up action was balanced with our obligations to protect students' privacy. As with most matters, there were also gray areas. It is in those areas that I find the advice or our legal counsel to be most helpful. What should we do when the law appears to allow for disclosure under some circumstances but leaves some ambiguity? Counsel lays out the various options and potential consequences for each option. Although counsel may prefer one option, the decision maker may choose a different path, understanding the potential risks posed by each one.

The legal counsel offers advice based on knowledge and experience. However, as the VPSA, I must decide how to use the advice in making a decision.

## Conclusion

Institutions regularly face issues that require cooperation among the president, VPSA, legal counsel, and public relations. Fortunately, most do not garner widespread notoriety or infamy, such as we experienced in Cortaca 2013. They often arrive in the form of an anonymous report or phone call. For example, recently my college received information from a person who wished to remain anonymous that an underground, non-recognized organization was allegedly engaging in illegal activity at an off-campus location.

We were faced with the issue of wanting to inform the campus community of the concern in the hopes of keeping students from harm while not revealing too much information, as this could place the reporting individual at risk and discourage further reporting. Should the college send a notice based on anonymous uncorroborated information? If a notice is sent to the college and community, what information should be shared with enough specificity so that people could take action to avoid harm while also being general enough to protect the anonymity of the reporting individual? In addition, any announcement to the college community raises questions from both the college constituents and the local media and community. Were we prepared to respond to media inquiries?

Would not sending a notice or sending a nonspecific notice be perceived as a lack of transparency and raise the question of the college leadership's integrity?

For VPSAs, such discussions and decisions are part of a day's work. Having trusted colleagues who appreciate various roles and perspectives allows VPSAs to reach informed decisions during a crisis.

### References

Attebury, E. (2013, November 19). More than 30 students arrested at football game "riot." *USA Today*. Retrieved from https://www.usatoday.com/story/news/nation/2013/11/19/cortaca-riots-2013/3639471

Daily Mail Reporter. (2013, November 18). College president apologizes after student football celebrations bring chaos to small town. *Daily Mail*. Retrieved from: https://www.dailymail.co.uk/news/article-2509699/SUNY-president-apologizes-Cortaca-football-riot-bring-chaos-small-town.html

Kaplan, W., & Lee, B. A. (1997). *A legal guide for student affairs professionals*. San Francisco, CA: Jossey-Bass.

Kingkade, T. (2013, November 19). SUNY Cortland students were out of control at Cortaca 2013. *Huffington Post*. Retrieved from https://www.huffingtonpost.com/2013/11/18/suny-cortland-cortaca-2013-riot_n_4297105.html

SUNY Cortland. (2014, June 1). *College and Community Joint Commission final report*. Cortland, NY: College and Community Joint Commission.

# 8

# Team Stewardship

## Care for the Caregiver

### Jeffrey C. Jordan

When a critical incident occurs on a college or university campus, employees are often affected as much as students. Staff and faculty may have been directly involved in the incident or know someone who was. On most college campuses, conversations about "community" are often heard. So, even when a faculty or staff member is not directly involved in an incident, there is often a felt sense that the campus community has been disrupted by the crisis. Care for employees is necessary for operations to continue inside and outside of the classroom.

Student affairs leaders know that our work with students is driven by and delivered through our staff members. We rely heavily on personnel in order to serve and educate students. Even in "normal" circumstances, there can be significant stress in this field. When a crisis occurs, that level of stress will increase exponentially—often affecting the quality and quantity of work. Attending to the physical, emotional, and spiritual needs of student affairs staff before, during, and after a crisis is critical to care for our colleagues and maintain our ability to work effectively with students.

Often, we think of caring for staff only during a crisis or just after. However, caring for staff members should start before an event occurs and continue well afterward. Many student affairs professionals have expectations outlined in job descriptions related to responding to campus incidents (Jablonski, McClellan, & Zdziarski, 2008). Additionally, many campus emergency response plans rely on these staff members and others during critical incidents. Taking time to train and prepare staff for these kinds of events is important. Training efforts provide details about how to respond. However, maybe just as important, these interactions provide insights about the suitability of a staff member to respond to critical incidents. As Collins (2001) purported, it is important to have "the right people in the right seats on the bus" (p. 41). I would add "at the right time," as crisis response preparation, training, and implementation are dynamic and continually evolving.[1]

## HAVE YOU HEARD? THE EMOTION OF THE MOMENT

When a crisis occurs at a college or university, immediate attention is necessary to ascertain the safety and stability of staff members. First, it is important to allow staff to contact family and loved ones

---

[1] The main focus of this chapter is student affairs staff. However, it is important to note that faculty often play important roles in responding to crises, and much of what this chapter addresses can also be applied to faculty.

to communicate their own well-being and ensure their family is safe. Allowing staff to make these contacts as quickly as is feasible will allow them to reengage and focus on their efforts to address the crisis. Also, as many have experienced, connecting quickly is important because phone systems (internal and external) can be quickly overloaded or damaged.

Many student affairs leaders are familiar with Maslow's (1943) Hierarchy of Needs; this model can be utilized to assess staff capability to perform during a crisis event. It is important to ascertain if staff members are physically and psychologically capable to engage and assist with the issues at hand, and to assess their availability. Knowing quickly who can assist during a crisis allows for swift deployment of services. Often, having a roll call of who is available is a critical first step.

External issues (e.g., family responsibilities, transportation) may affect staff members' ability to provide assistance when a crisis occurs. They may not be able to make other family arrangements and may need to leave. However, they may be the very ones who provide later relief for those who are able to stay on campus for the initial response.

Reassessing staff is important as more information becomes available, campus leadership responds, and individual staff members continue to process what has happened. Don't assume that a staff member's well-being is constant. Ongoing evaluation of staff is vitally important to ensure their well-being and their ability to respond to the institution's needs.

Confusion and lack of information can cause anxiety for all in a crisis event. It is better to overcommunicate with staff during these events. This communication may include messages that state no new information is available, but that administration and others are monitoring the situation or in contact with local authorities.

Having scheduled time for updates can reduce the anxiety of staff (and others), as knowing when an update will be forthcoming may provide some relief.

During the initial moments of a crisis, assigning small, specific tasks to staff members is helpful. Tasks may be as simple as monitoring a news station, taking attendance, or gathering some supplies. Having something to do that is helpful in the moment provides a sense of valued engagement and diverts one's attention away from the unknown or confusion, toward a focused effort.

The simple act of gathering staff together (if safety allows) provides a bond and reassurance that one is not alone. These interactions and collaborations deepen and expand working relationships. And, in responding to crisis, trusting in and relying on coworkers is necessary.

## Details, Details, Details

Once the crisis incident is better understood, it is important to know how the institution will need to respond. The scope of the crisis will help dictate the need for staff response, as well as how best to care for a staff member and their needs.

Too often, those who are deeply involved in responding to a crisis are not thinking about basic needs like water and food. If the incident is relegated to the campus and is not a local or regional crisis, external options are usually available to access these supplies. Having a variety of items brought to staff is important in caring for them.

Communication is extremely important. Many of us understand the adage that "knowledge is power." In crisis situations, it might be that "knowledge is comfort." Although campus leadership may not know all the facts or be able to release all the details of an incident, providing regular updates and/or messages about the efforts is helpful for the campus community at large. The specificity of details will assist in the specific response by some departments. It will also provide staff the opportunity to process the impact from the incident and make choices about their own self-care.

## 24-72 Hours: Managing Through the Pain and Preparing for a Marathon

With any crisis incident, the adrenaline rush of responding to the incident fades, and the reality of what happened and the impact on the campus is realized. At this time, campus leaders often need to shift from attending to immediate needs to begin addressing the impact for the time ahead. Although not all crises extend for lengthy times, many do—some reverberate for months and even years for some segments of the campus community.

After working through all the initial aspects of an incident, the next few days are important, as the reality of the incident sets in. For some, the awareness of tragedy and loss becomes more intense. This may be when it becomes evident that staff responders are emotionally affected by what happened. During this period, staff should have time to distance themselves from the campus and the incident. Often staff members are emotionally and physically exhausted. They need time to sleep, be with loved ones, and engage in other activities to take care of themselves.

If a staff member is significantly affected by the crisis ordeal, referring them to an off-campus provider may be necessary. Often, human resource departments can connect the staff member with an employee assistance program or other community resources.

After a crisis, campus leaders are pressed to keep the campus response moving forward. In the first few days after an incident, campus leaders are still pushing hard to manage logistics, press releases, legal issues, insurance and liability concerns, and operational decisions. Student affairs staff will typically have been working directly with affected students and their families, handling their emotional responses to the crisis. It is not unusual to have some conflict between campus leadership and student affairs staff, because each group (and many other campus constituencies) is working on very different aspects of the situation. No one person sees the entirety of the situation; only together can all responders have the full description. Unfortunately, during crisis moments, interactions can be tense. We need to do our best to recognize and understand these dynamics and have as much grace in our interactions as possible, knowing that decisions need to be made and tasks need to be accomplished. Student affairs leaders often serve as a bridge between their staff and campus leadership. It is important to navigate difficult and often emotionally charged interactions. Prioritizing and communicating as clearly as possible is an important aspect of staff care.

It is important that expectations for staff response be as clearly delineated as possible. For many institutions, this will mean rotating times on campus and may mean some departments shift their work from their typical routines in order to relieve other departments. For example, the career development staff may organize and host campus debriefing sessions so that the counseling center staff can focus on direct care and interactions.

In many cases, a campus can be inundated with outside offers to help care for students and others. Although this may be a good option, vetting individuals and organizations (prior to a crisis incident, if possible) is critical. Often, local services can reduce the load of or supplement campus services, so that staff can focus on other priorities and/or get a well-deserved break from the demands of the campus response.

For example, after one crisis incident during which a student died, my institution had a dozen calls from local churches, agencies, and individuals offering counseling services for students. We hardly had time to respond to the calls let alone vet them for credentials and methodologies. Because our counseling center utilized interns and externs, we were able to quickly partner with external service providers. We contracted with an expert in crisis response to formally train and prepare staff. She provided guidance and recommendations for campus leaders and staff responding to the incident. Additionally, we had set up a mutual agreement with area colleges and universities to share personnel and resources for brief counseling sessions. In considering these resources, student affairs leaders should work with legal counsel or risk management regarding any formal arrangements.

## When Things Have Changed, but No One Knows How to Talk About It

At some point, a campus starts to recalibrate to a "new normal." The amount of time this takes depends on the crisis incident. Regardless of the timing, it is important for campus and student affairs leaders to be intentional about this important transition.

The work of leading an organization and caring for staff is a delicate balance. Often there are pressures to get the institution and operations back to a fully functioning status as quickly as possible. Most of our institutions cannot afford to be closed for extended periods of time as there are short-term and long-term implications for students and others.

Campus and student affairs leaders should be intentional about sending messages to staff members. Being clear about expectations as staff members return and continue in the workplace, expressing gratitude for their contributions during and after the incident, and recognizing individual methods of processing a crisis are important.

Getting back into a routine that is familiar can be an important aspect of staff care. Depending on the degree of upheaval related to the crisis, staff will typically want and need their workplace to reflect stable and familiar patterns of how work is "supposed to be." Reestablishing work patterns should not be disingenuous or trite. For some staff members, stability may be related to their work schedule and holding meetings at a time or place that is familiar or predictable. For others, it may be the physical configuration of an office, or communication methods or messages. These seemingly mundane aspects of the work culture can be significant as staff return to a new normal.

Ongoing attention to staff is important. If staff members are struggling in ways that significantly affect departmental work, it is important to address those concerns as judiciously and quickly as possible. Student affairs leaders must be able to identify indications that a staff member is having a problem. Lower work performance, absenteeism, inability to focus on or complete assignments, and inappropriate interactions with other staff are some key signals that indicate significant concerns that should be addressed. Many helpful resources provide specific information and descriptions about staff well-being to assist in this stage of the recovery process. Of note, the Psychological First Aid mobile app provides easily accessible data, indicators, and suggested responses (National Child Traumatic Stress Network and National Center for PTSD, 2018). Additionally, it may be wise to seek guidance from human resources and/or legal counsel in these instances.

A more informal way of assisting is utilizing staff members as conduits for information to ascertain the well-being of other staff members. A word of caution is that one must be careful in interpreting the comments made by one staff member about another. However, there are typically select trusted staff members who can provide valuable and balanced information—even if it may be difficult to hear—that can lead to caring responses.

Having staff participate in restorative and restful efforts often provides the necessary distance and rejuvenation that will help sustain the person and, in turn, the program and organization. Therefore, it is extremely important to pay attention to cues about how staff members are doing as the campus reestablishes operations. Some research indicates that when staff perceive that the organization is supportive, there are lower rates of "vicarious trauma" (van Dernoot Lipsky & Burk, 2009, p. 21). Ideally, if staff perceive support from leadership then they work more diligently to assist the organization in restoring services and programs.

Sometimes it can be helpful to hold events to gather the staff and faculty who were and continue to be involved in the crisis response. For example, my institution held a gathering after an off-campus accident that took the life of a student. It was a time to hear more details from campus and civic officials and listen to their comments that clarified the circumstances surrounding the incident and the campus and community responses. It was a time to be together and recognize that we all had a part in the response for the good of the institution. The comments that day indicated appreciation for all who were involved in the response—whether directly or indirectly. After the gathering, staff members told us that they needed to be together. They appreciated the words shared by the president and the chaplain. They knew that campus leaders didn't have all the answers, but, they valued being together and being reminded that they are part of the community.

## Adjusting to a New Routine

Every leader on a college campus knows that the safety of the campus community is a major focus. Much effort is put into taking precautions so that crises don't occur, and into training regarding how best to respond if a crisis does occur. All agree that it is necessary and essential to continue to refine best practices for prevention and response. However, it is not unusual for staff who have experienced a traumatic event to be significantly affected by participating in these ongoing efforts after a crisis incident. Fire drills, lock-down procedures, and campus simulations can often lead to an emotional response by a staff member. Campus leaders need to consider what is best in both attending to the need for safety training and understanding the impact it will have on some individuals.

For example, campus leaders at my institution held a heated debate about holding active shooter evacuation and lockdown drills a few months after a shooting at the institution. Some felt that because the incident had happened so recently, people would "freak out." Others thought this was the best time to have a drill because people would pay particular attention. The debate went back and forth, and the points were valid from all sides, in making this difficult, but important, decision about policy implementation and balancing the readiness of the campus community with the emotional well-being of students, staff, and faculty.

Many colleges and universities have symbols (e.g., religious images, iconic building features, representations of a community or learning experiences) that uniquely relate to the institution's mission and identity. Organizational seals, phrases, mascots, and specific buildings are intended to message important values or themes to various constituencies. During and after a crisis, these same symbols (and others) are often utilized in campus responses. These symbols can evoke an emotional response for staff. At many campus memorial sites, messages are expressed in chalk on sidewalks. This medium is common for student clubs to announce programs and events. As most, if not all, institutions will continue to utilize these symbols for very good purposes, it is critical for student affairs leaders to understand the emotional response or impact this may have on students, staff, and faculty.

Crisis incidents that occur on a campus present a significant challenge related to the physical plant of an institution. The place where a tragedy occurred will evoke a myriad of responses from those who experienced the incident. These responses may affect a staff member to such a degree that they are unable to work in that space. Although much can be done to alter the space, such as changing the layout, there are often limits to the extent of the changes. For example, tragic incidents may occur in a place that has specialized equipment or historical significance for the institution. In these instances, it may be necessary for staff to move to other locations or have duties reassigned to reduce the lingering effect of the incident.

When traumatic events occur on campuses, it is common for temporary memorials to accumulate at the site of the incident. These symbolic expressions can also show up at different times of the year, such as a victim's birthday or the anniversary of the crisis. It is difficult to anticipate the timing and extent of the placement of memorial. Decisions need to be made regarding the length of time materials should be displayed, appropriateness of the expressions, location, and so forth. Student affairs staff are often involved in these difficult decisions.

## Accepting That Things Aren't the Same

The most critical time for caring for staff is during the first few weeks after a crisis. However, there are other times—which are somewhat predictable—when staff may be affected by a previous incident. Campus and student affairs leaders should understand and, when possible, be proactive in caring for staff when significant markers that relate to a previous crisis occur.

One of the most common dates that affect the well-being of staff members is the first anniversary of a tragic incident. If the incident affected a significant number of students (especially on a small campus), an organized campus recognition or reflection often is held. Student affairs staff are usually involved in the planning and implementation of such events. This means that staff are faced with remembering, and often reliving, the incident, while often being expected to provide services and support for others. Regardless of how well a staff member has processed the previous incident, these instances may result in them experiencing a significant emotional response. As the years go by, the campus may choose to recognize the anniversary date of the incident. Even if campus leaders choose to not recognize it, others in the campus community may organize an event that necessitates staff interaction or response.

There are other times in the rhythm of campus life when an event may be recognized, prompting staff intervention. The recognition may be related to a person who was killed. For instance, if the student was an art major, then the first show of the year at the campus art gallery may invoke some responses from members of the campus community. This may be the case with residence hall programs, traditions, and many other types of events held around campus. Student affairs leaders should try to anticipate these events and determine if there is a need to make specific support available.

Campus and student affairs leaders should pay particular attention to the year when a student victim was intended to graduate. Friends and family are typically interested in remembering the student's efforts on campus, subjects of interest, and dreams for life after graduation. For some institutions, it may be appropriate to formally recognize that student in a ceremonial fashion. Some examples have been honorary degrees, artwork permanently erected, endowed scholarships and/or research grants, and gifts that reflect the student's area of interest. These kinds of events, efforts, and recognitions may affect a staff member's well-being by bringing back images or memories of interactions that are extremely emotional.

Student affairs leaders are also often involved in discussions related to permanent memorials, especially those related to student tragedy. Just broaching the conversation can be a significant emotional moment. In these kinds of conversations, there are many opinions about what is appropriate for the campus as well as what best reflects a person's life. Often, these are difficult conversations laden with much emotion. Student affairs leaders need to participate in these conversations with great care and grace.

Too often a traumatic event is followed by some kind of legal proceeding in either civil or criminal court. The timelines of legal proceedings can be unpredictable—when they begin, how they proceed, and when they conclude. Campus and student affairs leaders must understand the emotional impact these events can have on staff. Media coverage can exacerbate the emotional impact with campus interviews and coverage. Additionally, staff members may be called to participate in the legal proceedings. When possible, preparing a staff member for such participation is advisable; preparation can be offered by the court system or by university legal representation. It is important to make sure staff have the appropriate support related to legal counsel and appropriate expert advocates for their well-being.

## Sneaker Waves: Surprised by the Unexpected

While there are many aspects of emotional response to traumatic events that are somewhat predictable, this is not always the case. Staff members who have experienced and assisted with trauma will often experience *emotional sneaker waves* (i.e., when unexpected waves of emotion take people by surprise). Often something unexpected initiates this kind of response. It may be a campus symbol that evokes an emotional response, as discussed above, or even a song, fragrance, sound, photo, or experience that produces a flood of emotions for a staff member.

Student affairs leaders can be caught off guard when something like this occurs. As most leaders understand, being flexible and having the ability to respond to unplanned events are prerequisites in leadership roles. Providing space for a staff member to process and/or compose themself in an unexpected emotional moment and following up with encouragement are important. Informing a staff member, especially one who isn't as experienced with traumatic events, that an emotional sneaker wave is not an unusual phenomenon can ease the anxiety and uncertainty that is often felt.

## Finding the Right Place: Assessing Staff Capabilities

As student affairs leaders know, it can be difficult to find time to reflect and consider how an organization can improve its crisis response strategies. Schedules can be full of meetings and other priorities that take our attention and time. Additionally, reflecting on an event that is traumatic adds the risk of bringing forth emotional responses and remembering difficult, traumatic events. However, it is important to align staff member characteristics and strengths with necessary organizational tasks and expectations to assess what is best for both staff and the campus.

Training alone can never fully prepare a staff member to emotionally deal with a crisis event and its aftereffects. After a crisis, student affairs leaders need to look back and evaluate how staff performed and what effect the incident had on each person. This assessment should inform training adjustments, staff assignments, and expectations.

Personal life events may change a staff member's ability to work in traumatic situations. The death of a loved one, the birth or adoption of a child, an accident, and so forth, may alter how a staff member perceives their work when engaging a campus crisis. The crisis may evoke strong emotional responses that relate to the recent personal event and make it difficult to respond to the incident. For example, in our People Response Team (a trained faculty and staff team that addresses the psychological, social, and spiritual needs of our community, thereby allowing campus life to return to a state of relative health and normalcy as quickly as possible after an incident) staff training, we are clear that a staff member can step out of the responsibility for responding to crisis events for any reason. We ask that the staff member communicate with their supervisor so that planning and expectations are clear. This opportunity to opt out of the work sends a clear message about care for the staff member. As training continues in future years, staff have the opportunity to rejoin the training, and often they do.

An important aspect of debriefing and assessing a crisis incident is to evaluate the training of staff. Keeping current with best practices and having regular training is important. Cross-departmental efforts on campus (e.g., student affairs, safety, university counsel, facilities) are necessary for the best responses. Ongoing, collaborative training builds partnerships and strength for a comprehensive campus response. It is often helpful to have staff access professional conferences related to this topic or have a third-party expert assist with evaluating response plans and training.

Student affairs leaders understand that our work is dynamic. That is, we have regular job expectations and responsibilities that can and will be interrupted by crises, issues of the day, and requests from others. Change is a constant, and we value learning from and with other professionals in higher education. Although it may be a challenge, finding a balance and being intentional with all the demands, including when a critical incident happens, is important.

## A New Normal for Ourselves and Our Work

Student affairs leaders face myriad challenges and stressors when confronted with a crisis on campus. One must balance many competing issues during and after an incident. Often, a leader may have more information about what happened, but not be able to share that information for a period of time—or ever. Being a leader means making decisions about how best to utilize resources and information. It may also mean having to push hard to get something accomplished. These decisions and facilitating this work can cause friction that is typically not a part of the normal work environment. Sometimes this will affect how one recalibrates back to a new normal. Due to the complexity and demands, student affairs leaders must take care of themselves. Accessing helpful supports on and off campus is important for a leader's well-being.

Crisis events can change a campus. They can be catalyst for changes in people, too. This is often the case for anyone involved in the event and in the response to it. Although student affairs leaders work in a field where development and formation of students is of high value, it is often difficult to understand and work through how a crisis may be developmental for staff and for themselves. It is important to understand and find the best new pathways for the organization and individuals following these kinds of events. Transitions can be difficult, but can lead to improvements, too.

It is obvious that one size does not fit all when it comes to crisis response. This holds true for how to care for staff during and after an event. Much will depend on the size, type, and resources of an institution. Location and access to external resources may also be critical factors.

All crisis events tend to knock an organization out of balance. A campus is like a bicycle wheel with many spokes. The crisis significantly alters the spokes so that the wheel is out of round. The bicycle may still operate and the wheel may still spin, but it is a bumpy ride. Campus and student affairs leaders must work to get the wheel back to a more balanced state. This may mean tightening, loosening, and even changing the spokes over a period of time. This work requires expertise and patience.

It is important to find grace and wisdom in our efforts with others and ourselves as we confront complex issues in student and staff development. Our work related to crisis events cannot be easily mapped or predicted. We need to continue to learn from each other throughout higher education and other fields. Our hope is that these events will be prevented and not occur at any time or place. However, until that day comes, we need to work together to prepare and care for all involved as we work and hope for resiliency and well-being—especially for our staff members in student affairs.

## References

Collins, J. C. (2001). *Good to great: Why some companies make the leap . . . and others don't.* New York, NY: HarperCollins.

Jablonski, M., McClellan, G., & Zdziarski, E. (Eds.). (2008). *In search of safer communities: Emerging practices for student affairs in addressing campus violence* (New Directions for Student Services, No. S1). San Francisco, CA: Jossey-Bass.

Maslow, A. H. (1943). A Theory of Human Motivation. *Psychological Review, 50*(4), 370–396.

National Child Traumatic Stress Network and National Center for PTSD. (2018). *Psychological first aid.* Retrieved from http://www.nctsn.org/content/psychological-first-aid

van Dernoot Lipsky, L., & Burk, C. (2009). *Trauma stewardship: An everyday guide to caring for self while caring for others.* San Francisco, CA: Berrett-Koehler.

# 9

# Student Affairs Administrators as Crisis Responders

## The Consequences of Care

THOMAS GRACE

It's the distinct biting smell of the acrid, smoky air that permeated Manhattan on September 11, 2001, that remains my most palpable recollection of that tragic event. It hung pungently over the city for days, irritating the nose and lungs of everyone who inhaled it and becoming—at least for me—the smell of death, destruction, and despair. All these years later, typically on the anniversary of the event—and especially when I catch a whiff of any slightly reminiscent odor—I am triggered back to the flood of sights and sounds that were imprinted on my mind that horrific day and in the weeks thereafter, all those many years ago. Not only am I flooded with memories of what I did in my role as an administrator at a university that was directly affected by the collapse of the World Trade Center Towers, but I re-experience some of the feelings that accompanied that fateful day.

Over the years, in speaking with student affairs colleagues whose roles have required them to deal with crises, I have come to find that my experience isn't unusual. The initial shock, stress, frustrations, doubts, and spillover between professional and personal lives that occur at the time of a crisis don't simply dissipate or become benign faded memories; rather, they can linger and be reactivated vividly in the present, at times even causing the person to relive—if only fleetingly—elements of the precipitating event. It seems that it need not be a high-profile incident—that is, one that affects the entire institutional community or attracts media attention—to leave a lasting imprint. Even a relatively small-scale or somewhat private event seems to have the potential to profoundly shape not only the professional but also the personal lives of those involved.

For example, one friend recalled how he, in his role as a residence hall director two decades prior, had been checking rooms to ensure that everyone had left for the winter break when he discovered the body of a student who had committed suicide. It is obvious that the shock of this event hasn't entirely dissipated: Today, whenever he hasn't heard from someone for a while, he becomes anxious. Another colleague was an administrator at a university where a student committed a mass shooting. When she speaks of it, there still is an unmistakable look of haunted disbelief—and perhaps a glimmer of self-inflicted responsibility—in her eyes. Whenever another colleague is working with an angry or frustrated student, he finds himself mentally transported back to a situation that took place years before: A student with unreasonable demands about a roommate conflict had become frustrated and stomped out of his office frustrated, only to take his own life a few hours later. That colleague still carries some degree of personal pain and a sense of responsibility for "failing" to have foreseen the tragic possibility. Today, this colleague tends to be hypervigilant in similar situations, often second-guessing himself and obsessing about the well-being of the student—long after the meetings and even into weekends at home.

## THE IMPACT OF CAMPUS CRISIS

Colleges and universities have a legal, ethical, and practical responsibility to care for the well-being of both their students and the institution. Accordingly, institutions have to respond to crises that jeopardize the safety and security of students and other members of their communities and/or that disrupt institutional operations. Each crisis, even a relatively small-scale tragedy, can sweep across the campus as a multilayered phenomenon—a psychological tsunami. There is a ripple effect as the impact waves extend out in a variety of directions from the focal point of the incident. Obviously and understandably, those directly involved in and affected by the precipitating incident are the first to experience the immediate effects.

But the impact waves emanating from a campus incident of violence or tragedy don't stop there. Certainly, they affect first responders such as residence hall staff, campus safety and security staff, and counselors who were on the scene and, ultimately, the senior-level leaders who are charged with crafting and coordinating the institutional response. These leaders experience the pressure of making high-stakes decisions, coping with political dynamics, and responding to the needs of various institutional and non-institutional constituencies. In these ways, senior-level leaders are exposed to the trauma sustained by those directly affected as well as the emotional turbulence of the response process.

## THE CONSEQUENCES OF CRISIS

To better understand the effects of crises on the student affairs administrators who deal with them, we may start by looking to the lessons learned by those who have similar roles in other contexts. Experts who work with people who have been affected by various types of crisis and disaster have identified reactions that fall into an almost predictable sequence. There is an initial shock of the event followed by euphoria at surviving and the passing of the initial incident. That excitement soon dissolves as the reality of the situation becomes apparent. The overwhelming nature of the event can precipitate depression and an accompanying sense of hopelessness that manifests in paralysis of action. Even when the recuperative process begins, it can be hampered by delayed psychological reactions which can emerge days, months, or even years later (Brozan, 1983).

This same sort of sequence is experienced by many first responders whose jobs entail going to the scene of an incident and being exposed to death, destruction, violence, graphic images, and the painful stories. An official at the scene of the 2016 Pulse Nightclub shooting in Orlando, Florida, reported what it was like for first responders:

> [Responders] went in and looked around, and all they could see were bodies lying all over the nightclub floor. They could see blood almost covering the entire floor, and [bullet] casing after casing after casing on that floor. When they first entered, they could still hear shots being fired. (Koman, 2016, para. 3)

But neither the night nor the incident is truly over when a first responder's shift ends. In fact, many of the first responders at Pulse said the ringing of the victims' cell phones was the singular thing they will remember and that will haunt them for the rest of their lives (Collins, 2016).

For other first responders, the sequence results from dealing with too many disasters and tragedies over too many years. Some mental health professionals characterize the cumulative effects of traumatic stress on first responders as a "wearing down of their psychological immune system" (Durbin, 2010, para. 6). The first 20 incidents to which they respond might not affect them; however, the 21$^{st}$ might elicit an unforeseen and disproportionate reaction.

What makes first responders particularly vulnerable to post-traumatic stress disorder (PTSD) is that they often work in professional settings that value being in control and remaining stoic; these individuals can fear ridicule for revealing emotions and other signs of distress. Thus, first responders frequently engage in avoidance behaviors, fail to seek support, and keep their emotions bottled up even while continuing to experience the effects of PTSD years after the precipitating event. According to a 2002 study of 181 first responders to the site of the bombing of the federal office building in Oklahoma City, 13% were diagnosed with PTSD symptoms within three years of the attack, 6% had panic disorders, and 24% developed a substance abuse disorder. Furthermore, there were almost 80 suicide interventions among firefighters in the years after the bombing, and the divorce rate among first responders was significantly higher than that of the general population (North et al., 2002).

Compassion satisfaction, compassion fatigue, direct trauma, and vicarious trauma are four constructs associated with first responders to crisis situations, and they are increasingly being recognized in the mental health field as important in understanding responders' reactions (Bercier & Maynard, 2015).

- *Compassion satisfaction* refers to the positive impact that someone may experience when they assist others during a crisis. By their nature, human service workers (including student affairs administrators) are caring individuals who empathize with the situations and pain of others. To some extent, these workers are energized and fulfilled by their profession, feeling engaged by the personal and the professional rewards inherent in the act of helping others, especially in times of need. Those who experience positive feelings and derive personal satisfaction from doing helping work are more likely to be engaged in their jobs and to remain in their chosen field (Anderson, 2000).
- *Compassion fatigue* refers to the emotional strain resulting from exposure to traumatic events—in other words, it is the cost of caring (Figley & Kleber, 1995). Dealing with a single demanding case or the cumulative effect of responding to one trauma after another takes a toll on the psyche and well-being of the helper. Compassion fatigue is manifest in the erosion of empathy, becoming numb to the suffering and the situation, and the emergence of detachment: "We have not been directly exposed to the trauma scene, but we hear the story told with such intensity, or we hear similar stories so often, or we have the gift and curse of extreme empathy and we suffer. We feel the feelings of our clients. We experience their fears. We dream their dreams. Eventually, we lose a certain spark of optimism, humor, and hope. We tire. We aren't sick, but we aren't ourselves" (Figley, 1995, p. 13). A form of secondary victimization, compassion fatigue, if left unaddressed, can progress to *burnout*, or emotional depletion, rendering the responder ineffective in his or her role.

- *Direct trauma*, according to the American Psychological Association, describes a response to being exposed to a sudden and typically tragic event, such as an accident, natural disaster, personal assault, rape, or other incident that involves violence, destruction, damage, and/or death or injury. Trauma is not the event itself; rather, it is someone's reactions to an event and can be manifest in strong emotional, psychological, and physical symptoms. While exposure to any distressing experience can induce some degree of emotions and shock, particularly overwhelming events can result in strong emotions. Some people who are exposed to tragic events are able to come to terms with their experience and the emotion dissipates, but those who are unable to do so can feel lingering effects in the form of PTSD that disrupt their daily lives.
- *Vicarious trauma* refers to an emotional/psychological response to a tragedy or disaster by someone who was not actually present at the event. While some experts contend that vicarious trauma can be induced in especially susceptible people through exposure to media reports, it is most often associated with individuals who are exposed to trauma and suffering through their work with direct victims and first responders.

## SECOND RESPONDERS: AN OVERLOOKED GROUP

Human services personnel who offer treatment, services, and support play a critical role in victims' recovery from a disaster, tragedy, or other catastrophic event. These providers not only may view the physical aftermath of the event—the destruction, the injuries, and/or the psychological distress—but also may become the ones to hear the "unspeakable" details of the trauma sustained by the victims, sometimes repeatedly. Thus, such workers themselves may be exposed to direct or vicarious trauma, and they can develop their own physical, psychological, cognitive, and emotional reactions that are not dissimilar to those experienced by the direct victims. For some workers, these reactions soon dissipate; for others, they develop into chronic symptoms that can have a profound and lasting impact on their professional and personal lives (Figley, 1995). For those suffering from pronounced vicarious trauma, even mundane events such as a triggering scene in a movie, a sound, or an anniversary date can reactivate the traumatic experience. Just as crisis responders in other settings, student affairs personnel are subject to what many have referred to as "cost of caring" (Melius, 2013, p. 2).

The American Counseling Association's (2011) acknowledgment that even those who were not present at a disaster or tragedy can experience vicarious trauma and PTSD certainly speaks to the experience of student affairs administrators. The finding that reactions tend to be exacerbated in persons who experience and demonstrate empathy for others—a common characteristic of student affairs administrators—is especially telling. A study of professionals who provided services to victims of Hurricane Katrina identified a direct relationship between the amount of exposure to victims and the negative psychological symptoms among those responders who were most empathic (Culver, McKinney, & Paradise, 2011).

Thankfully, very few administrators will encounter a national or regional crisis such as the 2001 World Trade Center attack or Hurricane Katrina, nor will most of them face the horrendous challenges of a campus-centered tragedy such as the 2007 shootings at Virginia Tech or the 1999 collapse of the bonfire tower at Texas A&M University. Perhaps only a few senior administrators will have to respond to relatively high-profile campuswide events, such as disruptive protests, data-security breaches, or athletic department scandals. However, we should not assume that administrators whose institutions do not experience a large-scale disaster or a violent tragedy are insulated from vicarious trauma. Over the course of their careers, most vice presidents for student affairs (VPSAs) and other administrators are repeatedly called on to deal with smaller-scale events, such as the death of a student, incidents of campus violence, sexual assaults, serious hazing, fires, or campus disruptions. The significance of these small-scale incidents can be overlooked because they typically don't involve the entire campus or large groups of students—there is little accompanying media attention, and they generally don't require senior administrators to drop everything in deference to the response and recovery efforts.

One exploration of the psychological impact of campus crises on administrators identified four interrelated overarching dimensions: immediate uncertainty and ongoing fear, heightened awareness about details of the tragedy, lasting personal impact, and incidental learning. That same study asserted VPSAs who have dealt with campus disasters and tragedies can self-impose enormous guilt over their inability to protect the community—particularly students—from harm (Treadwell, 2016). This self-blame occurs when VPSAs erroneously conclude that it was their responsibility to have anticipated and shielded the community from an event.

It also is important to remember that senior student affairs officers and other leaders do not have the luxury of abdicating all other responsibilities while managing the institutional response and recovery effort. They must continue with their regular duties while engaging in the often overwhelming task of coordinating the institution's crisis response system. Not only can the multiple responsibilities exponentially increase their workload and time commitment, adding to the pressure and stress they already are feeling from their relief efforts, but also the lingering effects of vicarious trauma can unconsciously be injected into other work dimensions. For instance, crisis management can become a preoccupying mindset and job focus—sometimes at the expense of other position responsibilities and areas of the institution.

College administrators involved in crisis management must "navigate a complex, unpredictable, and often chaotic institutional environment . . . in response to unprecedented campus tragedy" (Treadwell, 2015, p. 16). Indeed, the period that follows a campus crisis often requires an administrator to venture into uncharted ground, to discard those well-written protocols that were developed by task forces and committees, and to operate by instinct.

I remember how, in the days after September 11, 2001, my colleagues and I worked to transform a university gymnasium into a center for refugees who had been displaced from their residence halls and apartments by the wall of dust that had swept over the city when the towers collapsed. Few, if any, of us had experience dealing with an incident of such massive destruction and death, nor was there a written protocol or road map to follow in our crisis intervention booklets. No one had imagined or foreseen a disaster of that magnitude. We instinctively drew on our respective pasts, doing our best to apply what we'd learned from previous campus crises and tragedies to soothe fearful students, help friends locate one another, calm terrified parents, restore basic campus services, relocate students whose housing had been lost, and begin the recovery process.

For some administrators, such uncharted territory can evoke feelings of self-doubt and erode their sense of self-efficacy. It can hinder their effectiveness and decision making in terms of not only the immediate crisis but also later situations. One of the least discussed or explored aspects of being a crisis manager is the stress precipitated by organizational politics. Colleges and universities are imperfect organizations that sometimes produce dysfunctional dynamics (Roux-Dufort, 2007). The campus is a microcosm of a small community, with faculty, staff, students, alumni, and public all potentially assessing the actions—or inactions—of campus leaders in times of crisis. If stakeholders sense that a crisis was not handled well by leadership, they may feel their interests were not adequately addressed, feel excluded from decision making, or become highly critical of institutional leaders. That criticism, whether fair or not, can profoundly benchmark a leader's career. In some cases, leaders have been removed from their positions as a result of criticism about how they dealt with a crisis (Klann, 2003). One need only look to events at the University of Missouri or The Pennsylvania State University for evidence of this reality (Bataille, Billings, & Nellum, 2012). As the well-known psychologist Abraham Maslow contended, job security fears can cause an individual to become preoccupied with safety and security needs, affect decision making, and intrude into organizational relationships, thus compromising their efficacy (Bolman & Deal, 2013).

Among the organizational political dynamics that may be in operation during a crisis are the following:

- **Competition.** Various administrative units or administrators may look to preserve or advance their own interests by using the situation to jockey for power and resources.
- **Pressure.** VPSAs are under tremendous pressure to respond to press inquiries, rumors, and questions from institutional stakeholders—while protecting the privacy of the students, staff, or others who may have been involved. If perceived as not being forthcoming, an administrator can be accused of obfuscating or of "hiding something." If revealing too much, the administrator risks betraying the privacy of victims.

- **Criticism.** VPSAs may have to deal with attributions of blame (from both within and beyond the institution) for an incident, based on unrealistic assumptions about the institution's capacity to identify and intervene. In the aftermath of an incident, how often have we heard such questions as, "Why didn't someone see how disturbed this person was and do something about it?" Like leaders at other institutions marred by tragedy, Virginia Tech administrators faced seemingly endless scrutiny as they sought to help their campuses recover (Anderson, 2007).

Over time, the effect of crises can have a deeply personal influence on the physical and emotional health, personal and professional identity, faith perspective, and the personal and professional relationships of college administrators (Treadwell, 2016). Evidence suggests it leads to substance abuse, marital and other family problems, and discord at work (McEwen & Lasley, 2002). The consequences can also be physiological. When the stress response is active for a long period of time, such as over one's career, it can contribute to damage to the cardiovascular, immune, and nervous systems.

Renee Piquette Dowdy nicely summarized the consequences and frustration of living a "life of triage" in a 2013 NASPA blog:

What breaks you are the tiny fractures that start small and grow when not given time to heal, with the weight of one little thing after another creating more pressure, adding more weight. It can start with being asked to be at a useless meeting on an evening and adds up with each sharp e-mail; when you're talked to in a way that makes your role in a family, as a couple, as a single person, seem irrelevant; when your time is treated as expendable; when your efforts may feel, one day at a time, futile; when the most basic of requests or pursuits is met with resistance. Frankly, the basics of your work are met with exhaustion. (para. 6)

## COMMON REACTIONS TO TRAUMA

It is important to acknowledge that not every student affairs administrator who is directly or indirectly exposed to an especially shocking event will develop either direct or vicarious trauma, but it is not unreasonable to conclude that many such administrators will experience some degree of work-related trauma. The unique combination of factors involved means there is no universal reaction to a trauma that may manifest in the aftermath of an administrator–responder's involvement in a campus disaster or tragedy. Some administrators will escape relatively unscathed; some will temporarily feel the effects but recover quickly; some will develop minor or moderate symptoms that may complicate subsequent professional activities; and some may experience profound trauma that takes a toll on their careers and personal lives.

People who experience direct or vicarious trauma may engage in a variety of reactive behaviors—some seemingly contradictory. Crisis intervention can be exciting and energizing. Being called on to deal with a disaster or tragedy can fuel an administrator–responder's need to be needed and contribute to compassion satisfaction. Conversely, dealing with a particularly challenging and time-demanding event or especially having to deal repeatedly with too many crises over an extended period can leave the administrator emotionally exhausted and susceptible to compassion fatigue. If such fatigue is not effectively addressed, it can result in career-ending burnout. Without proper self-care and healing, student affairs administrators may find that what once fueled and energized their work often becomes a dull and onerous part of their professional life.

Some student affairs administrator–responders may seek self-preservation by engaging in psychological numbing, relying on objectivism, intellectualization, and self-anesthetization to suppress emotional pain. However, such attempts at stoicism often run counter to their very personalities, which possess concern and empathy for others—qualities that caused them to pursue a career as a helping professional in the first place. This internal contradiction can be perplexing to the administrator, and it can also inadvertently be communicated to students and colleagues as a lack of concern.

Even in normal times, student affairs administrators struggle to balance their professional and personal lives. For some, this involves a deliberate effort to disassociate painful events and/or to separate their professional and personal spheres to prevent negative experiences in one sphere from intruding into the other. Rarely, however, are such coping mechanisms entirely successful. In fact, the administrators employing this survival strategy may not even be cognizant of the fact that their professional responsibilities are affecting their private lives and families, or vice versa. An administrator's very efforts to preclude the consequences of their role as a crisis responder from impacting their families can lead to behaviors that may appear distancing rather than insulating.

Another common contradictory behavior that can be observed in times of stress, pressure, and trauma is the inconsistency between word and deed when it comes to seeking help. Most administrators tout the importance of seeking personal support and assistance in times of crisis and encourage their students and staff to do so. But they are often the last to recognize the same need in themselves or to heed their own advice. Such administrators may be driven by the desire to appear strong to support their staff and suppress their own reactions to avoid any sign of weakness. Unfortunately, their reluctance to seek help can be perceived as hypocritical, and it can send a message that devalues the importance of self-care.

Among my powerful recollections of 9/11 that occasionally flood back is what transpired when I finally could go home after spending three days at the campus crisis center. I had managed to catch a late afternoon train with other solemn-faced commuters. I immediately drove to the elementary school to pick up my 9-year-old son, whom I hadn't seen since I'd left for the university four days before. Since I had managed to get a message to my wife, I knew that he had been told I was fine and had been at the university working on the terrible situation he'd been hearing about from television newscasts and his teachers. When I arrived at the school, the students were parading out of the building. I still vividly recall walking across the school lawn to greet my son. When he saw me, he broke from the playground at full speed, evading the efforts of a teacher to catch him. With tears streaming down his face, he ran to embrace me as he'd never done before. Refusing to let go, he kept repeating, "You're home." It wasn't until that moment that I realized the extent to which my professional life could intrude on my personal one. I was just picking him up at school, but to him, it was something quite different. Admittedly, I'd never been all that good about compartmentalizing and separating these two spheres, but I don't believe I'd ever truly considered how my failure to do so could impact family members. After 9/11, all that changed.

Several researchers have sought to further explore the common coping strategies that responders employ to deal with vicarious trauma. Plutchik (1993) and Valent (2007) suggested that vicarious trauma activates a set of emotions that, in turn, tend to be operationalized in subsequent reactive survival behaviors—and these behaviors may or may not be positive in nature. It is not unusual for most responders to experience a period of acute disruption. Those who are more resilient are soon able to return to a relatively healthy level of functioning; however, those who are unable to come to terms with the psychological and physical challenges may carry with them the hampering consequence of chronic emotional unrest. The following are some common emotionally driven and counterproductive coping behaviors in which first and second responders may engage:

- **Flight.** Fear can prompt efforts to escape the pain by avoiding those whom we associate with the crisis, withdrawing from or reducing commitment, avoiding future crisis situations, or leaving a job entirely. Another common behavior is to immerse ourselves in other aspects of work, which has the benefits of keeping us physically and intellectually occupied—there's no time to contemplate the trauma when we're spending hours adding up timesheets.
- **Fight.** Anger can cause administrators to engage in antagonistic or counterproductive encounters with others in the organization, ignore the suggestions or contributions of their staff and colleagues, or get preoccupied in writing crisis protocols.
- **Rescue/caretaking.** Administrators who are driven by a need to care for and nurture others can feel that they personally must respond to every situation that arises. They can overburden themselves by taking on excessive responsibility.
- **Over-Attachment.** Student affairs administrators are often people who demonstrate great empathy for others, a quality that serves them well in their roles. However, an administrator coping with vicarious trauma may overreact to the losses associated with a traumatic event by engaging in excessive efforts at social bonding that can intrude into their work life. An example of this would be an administrator who becomes

too involved in the lives of the victims or staff members with whom that administrator is working.

- **Detachment.** As previously discussed, compassion satisfaction is a driver for many student affairs administrators. The loss of joy in one's work can lead to depression, loss of job fulfillment, and distance from the job and one's colleagues.
- **Venting.** An externalizing coping technique, venting is the outward expression of emotions, usually in the safe company of friends or family. In moderation, it can be healthy; however, over time, ruminating on the negative can lead to strained relationships.
- **Seeking understanding.** A coping technique often used to deal with overwhelming events is that of rationalization and/or intellectualization, a "flight into reason" that involves the effort to seek a logical cause for the event or the underlying dynamics. For many, what makes a trauma-inducing event particularly threatening or disturbing is its randomness—there is no way to foresee or forestall it. Seeking understanding of the causes and the dynamics of a crisis can alleviate anxiety by affording the victim some sense of control, even if the logic is illusory.

## Three Keys to Healing

There are many productive self-care strategies that student affairs administrator–responders may use to deal with the effects of vicarious trauma. Of course, there are the classic and obvious ones such as seeking professional assistance, participating in incident stress debriefings, sharing stories with colleagues and friends, seeking further training in crisis management, living a healthier lifestyle, taking time off, spending more time with family, setting personal and professional boundaries and balances, and even changing professions if that ultimately proves to be necessary.

But the key to success in trauma recovery appears to involve one's ability to make shifts in the conceptual paradigm; instead of thinking about how to avoid or cope with the trauma, one should acknowledge the trauma and view it as an opportunity for personal and professional awareness, growth, and change. In the days immediately following the deaths of 35 Syracuse University students in the bombing of Pan Am Flight 103, Geri Clark, a drama professor who knew several students on board, offered the following thought: "'The only way to move forward is to embrace the pain... If you try to avoid it, it just goes inside and destroys you" (Schmitt, 1988, para. 14).

A traumatic event can prompt administrators to look within themselves and to reach conclusions about what "really matters." For many whose identity is anchored in their careers, this shift in meaning may involve changes in the way they view themselves, how they prioritize their family and friendships, and how they balance time between their personal and professional lives. The administrator who can perform this sort of reframing—to find some sort of positive in what is otherwise a horrific occurrence—may come away from the traumatic event with a different outlook that leads to a renewal of family and other relationships and, ultimately, a more balanced and healthier lifestyle. Another positive shift in which an administrator might engage is to adjust their expectations. Too many—and I include myself in that group—may have entered the profession with grand ideas about making transformative differences in the lives of students and institutions. Perhaps we can be a bit irrational or overly optimistic about our ability to accomplish this goal. The truth is that we can neither protect our students from all harm nor should we want to do that, from a developmental point of view. We understand that personal growth occurs through exposure to ideas or issues that may conflict with our existing beliefs, assumptions, and experiences and that all adversity is not "bad." Administrators who feel a sense of frustration about being unable to alleviate their students' stress or to provide the answers their staff members seek may be condemning themselves to cognitive purgatory.

A more resilient approach to their work as a responder would be to view recovery as a developmental journey, which administrators might facilitate—but cannot take—for their students or their staff members. Perhaps our role as responders is best conceptualized as one where we help our students and staff heal the emotional and psychological fractures they have sustained, become stronger in the process, and place the event into perspective as being a part of their life journey. Despite our best wishes and intentions, we can never shield them from pain or restore them to a time before the disaster; we can only help them to move on (Pearlman & McKay, 2008).

Finally, just as administrators need to recognize the importance of helping their students and staff members come to terms with and grow from disasters and tragedies, they also must realize that such events also afford incredible potential for their own learning and leadership development (Treadwell, 2016). Being in a crisis response role brings VPSAs and other leaders closer to the students and staff members in the institutional community, helps them identify and forge relationships with key student leaders and staff members whom they might not otherwise have met, and enables them to make the campus more prepared and resilient should another crisis arise. *Collective efficacy* is a term used to describe what a group that is united in purpose and effort can accomplish. On 9/11 and the days thereafter, I was in the position to observe a phenomenon I'd never seen or thought possible: I watched from a front-row seat as a place as diverse and balkanized as New York City came together in an outpouring of concern for one another, found common meaning in being a "New Yorker," and—at least for a time—set aside the normal competitive rush that is emblematic of life in "the city." Simply put, people looked for ways to help one another. If that sense of collective efficacy can come out of a crisis such as 9/11, then it can certainly be created on a college campus.

## Conclusion

Although more research is needed to better understand the impact on student affairs administrators of being first and second responders to campus disasters and tragedies, both large and small, we can extrapolate from what has been derived from studies of responders in other contexts; thus, we conclude that these administrators are indeed at risk for direct and vicarious trauma. We also know that such trauma has consequences for administrators' professional and personal well-being. Some of the consequences are similar to those sustained by responders in other helping professions and some are unique to higher education. At the very least, it is essential that institutions—and administrators themselves—recognize the potential for trauma, implement prophylactic measures to reduce its propensity and onset, and offer services to support administrators who may be suffering unaware or in silence.

### References

American Counseling Association. (2011, October). *Vicarious trauma* (Fact sheet #9). Retrieved from https://www.counseling.org/docs/trauma-disaster/fact-sheet-9---vicarious-trauma.pdf

Anderson, D. G. (2000). Coping strategies and burnout among veteran child protection workers. *Child Abuse & Neglect, 24*(6), 839–848.

Anderson, L. (2007, April 1) Aftermath of a tragedy. *American City and County*. Retrieved from http://www.americancityandcounty.com/2007/04/01/aftermath-of-a-tragedy

Bataille, G., Billings, M., & Nellum, C. (2012). *Leadership in times of crisis: "Cool head, warm heart."* Washington, DC: American Council on Education.

Bercier, M. L., & Maynard, B. R. (2015). Interventions for secondary traumatic stress with mental health workers: A systematic review. *Research on Social Work Practice, 25*(1), 81–89.

Bolman, L. G., & Deal, T. E. (2013). *Reframing organizations: Artistry, choice, and leadership* (5th ed.). San Francisco, CA: Jossey-Bass.

Brozan, N. (1983, June 27). Emotional effects of natural disasters. *The New York Times.* Retrieved from https://www.nytimes.com/1983/06/27/style/emotional-effects-of-natural-disasters.html

Collins, K. (2016, June 14). This one thing will haunt Orlando first responders for the rest of their lives. *The Daily Caller.* Retrieved from http://dailycaller.com/2016/06/14/this-one-thing-will-haunt-orlando-first-responders-for-the-rest-of-their-lives/#ixzz4Z3fJNyFW

Culver, L., McKinney, B., & Paradise, L. (2011). Mental health professionals' experiences of vicarious traumatization in post-Hurricane Katrina New Orleans. *Journal of Loss and Trauma, 16*(1), 33–42.

Dowdy, R. (2013, November 13). What breaks you [Blog post]. Retrieved from https://www.naspa.org/constituent-groups/posts/what-breaks-you

Durbin, M. (2010, September 21). *The hidden dangers of being a first responder.* Retrieved from Wiland Associates website: http://www.wilandassociates.com/blog/detail.html?blogid=1

Figley, C. (1995). *Compassion fatigue: Coping with secondary traumatic stress disorder in those who treat the traumatized.* New York, NY: Taylor and Francis.

Figley, C. R., & Kleber, R. J. (1995). Beyond the "victim": Secondary traumatic stress. In R. Kleber, C. Figley, & P. Gersons (Eds.), *Beyond trauma: Cultural and societal dynamics* (pp. 75–98). New York, NY: Plenum Press.

Klann, G. (2003). *Crisis leadership: Using military lessons, organizational experiences, and the power of influence to lessen the impact of chaos on the people you lead.* Greensboro, NC: Center for Creative Leadership Press.

Koman, T. (2016, June 21). What the Orlando nightclub was like for first responders immediately after the massacre. *Cosmopolitan Magazine Online.* Retrieved from http://www.cosmopolitan.com/lifestyle/news/a60256/orlando-shooting-first-responders

McEwen, B., & Lasley, E. (2002). *The end of stress as we know it.* New York, NY: Dana Foundation.

Melius, A. (2013). *The lived experiences of vicarious trauma for providers: A narrative phenomenological study* (Doctoral dissertation). Retrieved from Digital Commons at Columbia College: http://digitalcommons.colum.edu/cgi/viewcontent.cgi?article=1042&context=theses_dmt

North, C. S., Tivis, L., McMillen, J. C., Pfefferbaum, B., Spitznagel, E. L., Cox, J., & Smith, E. M. (2002). Psychiatric disorders in rescue workers after the Oklahoma City bombing. *American Journal of Psychiatry, 159,* 857–859.

Pearlman, L. A., & McKay, L. (2008). *Understanding and addressing vicarious trauma.* Pasadena, CA: Headington Institute.

Plutchik, R. (1993). Emotions and their vicissitudes: Emotions and psychopathology. In M. Lewis & J. M. Haviland (Eds.), *Handbook of emotions* (pp. 53–66). New York, NY: Guildford Press.

Roux-Dufort, C. (2007). A passion for imperfections: Revisiting crisis management. In C. M. Pearson, C. Roux-Dufort, & J. A. Clair (Eds.), *International Handbook of Organizational Crisis Management* (pp. 251–252). Los Angeles, CA: Sage.

Schmitt, E. (1988, December 23). The crash of flight 103: At Syracuse, remembrance and prayers. *New York Times.* Retrieved from http://www.nytimes.com/1988/12/23/world/the-crash-of-flight-103-at-syracuse-remembrance-and-prayers.html

Treadwell, K. L. (2015). Compassionate complexity: Learning on the front lines of campus tragedy. *About Campus, 20*(5), 14–20.

Treadwell, K. L. (2016). Learning from tragedy: Student affairs leadership following college campus disasters. *Journal of Student Affairs Research and Practice, 54*(1), 42–54.

Valent, P. (2007). Eight survival strategies in traumatic stress. *Traumatology, 13,* 4–14.

# 10

# Faith in the Wake of Disaster

MARCELLA RUNELL HALL,
RACHEL ALLDIS, AND
TODD M. SMITH-BERGOLLO

"There was a time, not very long ago, when religion was all but invisible in the educational programming of most colleges and universities. That time is past; religion is no longer invisible" (Jacobsen & Jacobsen, 2012, p. vii). When disasters happen, it is important to help students think critically and to find ways to make meaning of their lives during complex and confusing times. Religion and spirituality can often be an important way to do this, and that is at the heart of this chapter.

The three of us, as coauthors, have had very different experiences with religion and spirituality in our own lives. Our childhood experiences, young adult identities, and how we see ourselves now in terms of spiritual identity is unique for each of us—as it is for many. Some see religion as an organization or institution, and spirituality as a personal identity. Jacobsen and Jacobsen (2012) defined *religion* as it relates to "'big questions,' (questions of meaning and purpose) and deep moral concerns whether these matters are expressed in explicitly religious language or not. Religion is about how people relate to God or the 'higher power(s)' of the universe, but it is also about how people relate to each other . . . And religion is about the values that we live by as individuals and groups" (pp. 4–5). According to Astin, Astin, and Lindholm (2011), *spirituality* "points to our inner subjective life. . . . It has to do with the values we hold most dear, our sense of who we are and where we come from, our beliefs about why we are here, and our sense of connectedness to one another and to the world around us" (p. 4).

We, the authors, all share a passion for students and for the field of student affairs more broadly. And we have spent much of our careers in higher education working in New York City at various types of institutions, which means that we have lived and served students through 9/11, Superstorm Sandy, and various other global and national disasters, and did so as we discovered our own leadership styles and competencies as student affairs practitioners attempting to create safe, inclusive, thriving communities on our campuses.

In the days and weeks following 9/11, many students in New York City needed something or someone to connect with as they, and the entire nation, grieved. Students, as well as faculty and staff, needed to find purpose and opportunities to help and heal. Those of us in student affairs needed to tend to serious logistical issues each day. In a crisis situation like 9/11, it is vital to connect students with resources that they find useful and life affirming. Having faith leaders to connect students with was as important then as it is now, because student affairs professionals can't always be there for students as we would like to be.

The role of *faith* in the wake of disaster is a poignant one. Many people struggle with issues of spirituality; they hold such a pervasive belief that this topic is so deeply personal and subjective, that it has become difficult for some to know how to navigate student questions and needs related to faith (DiLorenzo, 2015). How do we define *faith* and *spirituality*? What role do chaplains or other religious leaders serve on our campuses, and what roles do they occupy in the world of student affairs? And, perhaps more important, why is it often challenging to engage questions of religion and spirituality in student affairs work?

While it is true that higher education administrators are beginning to understand the full scope of religion and spirituality in higher education, as evidenced by seminal publications such as *Spirituality in Higher Education* (University of California, Los Angeles, 2010) and *Spirituality in College Students' Lives* (Rockenbush & Mayhew, 2012), it does not mean that the profession has resolved its questions and tension points. It is often difficult to balance extreme views of religiosity, fundamentalist beliefs, and exclusive practices with campuswide discrimination policies, or to regulate evangelizing that can bump against antiharassment policies and practices. Such issues have likely prohibited many student affairs practitioners from engaging in opportunities to work with faith leaders. The years since 9/11 seem to be a perpetual cyclical tragedy, and we need all the help we can get in supporting our students, our communities, and ourselves. But how do we successfully access that support? What is needed to make these partnerships effective and fulfilling?

Jacobsen and Jacobsen (2012) identified six sites of engagement where programs, services, policies, and practices in higher education can address issues of religion and spirituality. These include religious literacy, interfaith etiquette, framing knowledge, civic engagement, convictions, and character and vocation. These sites of engagement mirror many of the learning goals used in numerous student affairs departments, and even in matrices such as those developed by the Council for the Advancement of Standards in Higher Education (2015). As Jacobsen and Jacobsen (2012) observed, for many students today, "This means that, perhaps for the first time in American higher educational history, the push for talking about matters of religion and spirituality and answering questions about human purpose and meaning is coming from the bottom up, rather than from the top down" (p. 30). Students want to engage in larger questions of purpose and meaning and are looking for more resources on college campuses to do so.

Historically, religion was believed to be a relic in higher education, connected to the founding of colleges and universities at a time when Christianity dominated the landscape and the religious foundations of many institutions were nonnegotiable. However, as secularism spread in the 1960s and 1970s, many institutions of higher learning believed that as students became more educated, their desire for and connection to spiritual and religious identity would dwindle and eventually phase out (Jacobsen & Jacobsen, 2012). Colleges founded during that period through the early 2000s did not build new chapels or invest in new religious life staff. However, many variables, including changes to immigration policy and more diversity in the areas of national origin, race, ethnicity, and socioeconomic status in higher education, continued to shift the demographic landscape. Calls for additional support and acknowledgment of the saliency of these identities continued to be a variable, and the question of the privatization of religion as something that should only be discussed in personal spaces all came to a head in the early 2000s. Our own professional association, NASPA–Student Affairs Administrators in Higher Education, established a Spirituality and Religion in Higher Education Knowledge Community in 2002. Additionally, national crises such as 9/11 created unprecedented incidences of

Islamophobia aimed at Muslim and perceived Muslim communities, creating a greater need for religious literacy and understanding (Harper, 2008). Such tragedies also create an existential crisis across many identities, creating a need for spirituality as a way to make meaning from tragic events (Astin et al., 2011).

For the purposes of this chapter and the topic at hand, two key ideas must exist in relation to the role of faith in the wake of disaster: pastoral care/well-being and religious literacy/inclusivity. These two building blocks for student affairs practitioners are often disrupted in profound ways during times of crisis. Faith leaders are often uniquely equipped to support student affairs staff in cultivating these building blocks, because they can provide greater understanding and support regarding questions of spirituality.

Often, the faith leaders who are most successful in providing support on campuses are the ones who have been proactively included in the community before a crisis moment. For example, they have helped religious literacy training programs to build common language and relationships and have partnered with departments on campus focused on community building through residential life or diversity affairs. How well integrated chaplains are into the community prior to the crisis, and how supported and visible they are, sets the stage to successfully call on them in crisis moments in ways that feel authentic and useful. Programs like Faith Zone (Ennis, 2017) help to create models for teaching religious literacy on campus, space for people of faith to feel recognized and seen on campus, and intentional ways for people who identify as atheist or agnostic to exist on campus.

## Campus Resources and Structure

While preparing to write this chapter, the three of us realized that we could think of 20 different campuses off the top of our heads that each used a different model for religious and spiritual life. This seemed important to note, because the variation seemed to be indicative of the challenges related to balancing concerns against the opportunities for successful collaborations. We chose six examples to highlight and examined the variations in model/partnership between chaplains and student affairs practitioners. We acknowledge this is not necessarily a representative sample, and there are many types of institutions that we did not include. The examples are meant to illustrate the various models and to speculate how these models might serve students during times of crisis. We are especially interested in the history of how these relationships were negotiated, the proclivities for building proactive relationships between and among chaplains, and the structures in place to support this work. We are most interested in how the relationships are cultivated, maintained, and utilized to best support students. We are certainly aware of how chaplains are called on for bereavement purposes, global/national tragedies, pastoral counseling, vigils, campus celebrations of religious holidays, and services. It is our experience that the more that is done during routine operations, the smoother it is to incorporate faith leaders into the response to crisis events. The examples that follow present a variety of sample models gathered from student affairs professionals at each institution.

## *Institution One: Private Liberal Arts*

The vice president for student affairs (VPSA) has been supervising the Office of Religious and Spiritual Life for two years. The department transitioned from a dean of religious life to a director/college chaplain. The school eliminated chaplain positions about 10 years ago; it currently has a Jewish advisor and newly appointed Muslim and Catholic advisors (each working about 8–10 hours a week). The Jewish advisor is a rabbi who also performs several hours of pastoral care each week. The college has committed to funding these positions through the Division of Student Affairs.

The school's demographics have shifted from religious to spiritual, but in recent years it has had an increase in Muslim and Latinx/a/o Catholic communities that need additional support (the newly appointed Catholic and Muslim advisors were hired in response to that shift). These staff are committed to creating an inclusive environment on campus and to supporting the well-being of students. This model would be considered proactive and well integrated into the Division of Student Affairs. Because of this integration, the department has been able to provide substantial support in times of crisis.

## *Institution Two: Private Liberal Arts*

The VSPA has a long history of neglecting religious practice and faith on campus. This choice was made by former college administrators in the school's early years. One of those early senior leaders, who identified as salient Quaker by upbringing but detested religious "zeal," fought to guard the student body from what he believed to be the imposition of religious observances. As a result, until recently, religious practice was not cultivated and students' religious identities were not acknowledged institutionally. There is no chapel building, but now secular spaces are set apart for religious gatherings and meditation.

Religious groups and organizations have been on campus for at least a decade, but Jewish alumni from the 1970s and '80s report that Shabbat was not observed on campus when they attended. Relationships with local religious organizations and congregations have increased in the past 15 to 20 years, but they are not well developed because of a lack of institutional commitment. A rabbinical student and Catholic priest are assigned to work at the institution part time.

The institution also has some student organizations now, and it is giving this more attention to build a stronger program in the future.

The VPSA noted, "I would say that we have more 'practice' than 'expression.' By this I mean that students practice their faith in private or in small groups to have prayer, observances, or holidays, but that they do not have a 'presence' on campus in a public expression. We have some small interfaith dialogue programs that our assistant dean oversees and is developing. Baby steps."

Although the college does not have chaplains, it does have religious advisors with varied levels of time, commitment, and opportunities with students. The college does not employ any paid chaplains or religious advisors. The assistant dean (who works within the multicultural center) works to maintain connections with these outside individuals and has brought them together on occasion. Students find these advisors and local congregations through information on the student affairs website, referrals by deans and others, and on their own. The Jewish students and Christian students associated with Intervarsity Christian Fellowship, an international umbrella organization present on many college campuses, are receiving the most publicity, support, and resources in the current model. This campus has made a moderate effort to create space for religious and spiritual life within its other efforts to promote diversity, but it does not yet have a strong proactive commitment to the role of chaplains in campuswide well-being efforts. This model would be considered moderately proactive and somewhat integrated into the Division of Student Affairs, but it is unclear how the religious groups and student affairs professionals would partner in a time of crisis.

## *Institution Three: Private Liberal Arts*

For a long time, faith or faith groups of any kind had little visibility on this campus. Some students felt they had to hide their faith, particularly in the classroom. Faith groups also had no permanent staffing, instead relying on ad hoc advisors supported by endowment funding.

Over the past seven years, the school has worked hard to build a more robust Office of Religious and Spiritual Life, bring more visibility to this area, and encourage student engagement. The school now has a director of religious and spiritual life/Protestant advisor who is not considered a school employee because she is funded by an outside organization with endowment resources. But after she retires, the school plans to bring this position in house. This year, the school will have its first full-time Jewish student advisor; until now, the position has been half time. A half-time Muslim student advisor was hired about four years ago to support the growing Muslim student population.

The school has also had success with more visible programming and partnering around large religious holidays, including popular all-campus Eid and Passover celebrations and dinners. Visibility and collaboration will be enhanced when the new Intercultural Center opens, which will include office space for Intercultural Center staff, Religious and Spiritual Life staff, and International Student Services staff. These staff positions are funded by the college as part of the Division of Student Affairs budget.

These new campus groups were instrumental in assisting with recently emerged challenges that included, but were not limited to, swastika graffiti, concerns about lack of faculty understanding of religious holidays, kosher/halal food availability, and overall support/campus environment. When issues arise, the VPSA has typically been the institution's link, but they have also had student leaders from the religious groups approach them directly. The VPSA reported, "Like many concerns, we work to try to understand what all the issues are, then try to find productive solutions that help move us forward."

Overall, the VPSA has observed that students who identify as religious are likely to come forward with concerns. The school plans to build religious organizations into the fabric of other inclusivity efforts on campus, but because of the off-campus nature of the advisors (i.e., students must leave campus to access these resources), it is likely that the faculty, staff, and students will not see the spiritual support as part of the well-being efforts of the college. This model would be in a nascent stage of development and not well integrated into the Division of Student Affairs as it currently exists. The ability to work together in a crisis would likely depend on which groups were affected and who was called on, given the resource disparity.

## *Institution Four: Large Public*

This institution has a diverse range of faith groups, primarily represented through student organizations. The student affairs administrator reports that the campus culture is a mix of Christian, Muslim, and Jewish students, and more. There is no model or formal institutional partnership between these groups, their advisors, and student affairs. The student organizations and their advisors build relationships on an as-needed basis. Students, faculty, and staff look for chaplain referrals in the surrounding metropolitan area because they cannot access chaplains through the college. The only institutionally funded structure in place is an on-campus meditation space. This model would be considered to have a minimal commitment and unlikely to provide substantial support in times of crisis due to the lack of integration, training, and relationship building.

## *Institution Five: Large Public*

This school serves as a flagship institution for a state system and has a well-developed multicultural affairs department in student affairs, including several senior diversity affairs professionals.

However, despite its large and complex ecosystem hosting graduate and undergraduate students from all over the world, the departments responsible for supporting spiritual growth are decentralized, mostly standalone entities funded by their outside sending organizations. Examples include a Catholic Center, Chabad House, and several Protestant groups such as CRU (Campus Crusade for Christ) and Intervarsity Christian Fellowship. A handful of paid advisors work with Muslim and Hindu groups, but the overall model does not seem to leverage the religious diversity of the students or the broad array of chaplains who serve the community. The model also is not likely reflective of the student body's religious identities, given the high percentage of international students coming from South Asian countries. In moments of crisis, the chaplains are likely not being called on by the student affairs crisis team, and this is likely the byproduct of many years of separation of church and state and the belief in the privatization of religion in higher education.

## *Institution Six: Large Private*

This school has a robust support system for all students, from believers to those questioning to humanists. There are over 60 chaplains; some are financed through the institution, while others are financed through their sponsoring faith-based organizations. All chaplains are trained on college policies and practices, and they participate as trainers in a curriculum aimed at improving religious literacy and interfaith etiquette on campus. They also collaborate on programs, services, and pastoral counseling for students. This commitment is a well-resourced and well-integrated model for both inclusivity and well-being. The office that supports religious and spiritual life is part of the Division of Student Affairs and is well utilized in times of crisis, celebration, and remembrance—the chaplains are viewed as part of the emergency response team. This model appears to be high functioning, maximizing relationship building and civic engagement across religious denominations. Perhaps most notably, students and chaplains report that they can ask complex questions about the meaning of life, particularly in times of crisis. Chaplains can move beyond surface pastoral care and religious literacy to support the spiritual growth of students through meaningful engagement.

## Our Students

Students need to be able to talk through the bigger questions on their minds. Not just "How can I move on?" but "Why do 'bad things' happen?" and "How can I maintain my faith when it is challenged?" Students come to college with varying beliefs and exposure to religion and spirituality. Many use their college years as a time to grow in their faith, to look at other belief systems, or to step back from religion and spirituality altogether.

Clinical counselors can serve an important role in helping students heal, but some students are looking for ways to heal outside of a clinical setting. They may be looking for space to reflect, pray, or have a moment of silence. They likely want a place they can feel safe, cry, and express their emotions, and they may be looking to do this in a faith-focused space that is more familiar to them. They may want someone with them who shares their beliefs or at least validates them—a spiritual companion to walk by their side.

Unless you work in religious and spiritual life on your campus, it is likely that you have not received training or spent a lot of time learning how to have conversations about religious beliefs or spirituality with your students. How do you broach these conversations? How much do you share about your personal beliefs? When taking on the role of pseudo chaplain, what rules about confidentiality are you bound to? Wearing multiple hats as an administrator and as a spiritual leader can be a quagmire that most of us are happy to step out of and leave to the experts. However, when spiritual life professionals are not present, institutions need to define how they plan to provide support for students; when calling on staff to play this role, institutions need to offer appropriate training and direction.

A campus administrator can plan the vigil for students to gather and reflect on a campus, local, or national tragedy. They can set up the logistics for a memorial service, but managing the content for the service and the impact on student emotions is very different. Who is following the student who races away from the vigil in tears and just wants to understand why "their God" would let this happen? And what do you do when you find that student? What can you say?

We can listen to the student, but providing them with spiritual direction is a much harder needle to thread if you don't have the background and training. For the administrator without the training, knowing your resources is a good first step. Direct a student to nearby churches, synagogues, temples, or mosques, or know where you can quickly get such information. Having a basic understanding of different religious and spiritual practices is important as well. Encouraging someone to practice their faith by knowing what those rituals are can help students feel like you understand them better and allow for a sense of comfort. It also enhances your own professional competencies (Harward, 2016). Inform the student that you are not a spiritual advisor, but you are willing to listen, and you can help them find someone who can serve as their spiritual advisor. Know your colleagues and their background and abilities. If you are not an expert in a religion but know someone who is, connect the student with that person. As previously noted, if you do not have religious and spiritual resources on your campus, then establishing a network for staff members who are comfortable talking with students about religion and spirituality can be a good substitute.

One challenge many administrators face is knowing how much to share about their personal beliefs when talking with students, especially during a crisis. What role does your personal faith play in your work and interactions with students? This answer may look different in different places. If you work at a religiously affiliated institution, there may be some understanding that you would be open about your faith; other institutions may not want any personal beliefs being shared. Your campus culture and the relationship and connections that you have with students should dictate your response. When schools ask staff to play the dual role of administrator and spiritual advisor in times of crisis, they can and should provide guidance about sharing personal beliefs.

Sharing your personal beliefs can sometimes strengthen your relationship with a student and create a deeper connection, especially if you share similar beliefs. You can find that common ground and unite in your spiritual community. The opposite can be true as well. If you share your beliefs a student who has different or opposing beliefs, you can fracture that relationship and create distance with the student because they no longer see you as someone who they can trust or relate to. This is not always the case, and you should not feel that you can only share your faith with others with similar beliefs. We need to overcome these perceived obstacles. Many people unite in having different beliefs and debating the deeper questions of faith and religion. Knowing your students and getting a sense of who they are and how accepting they are will help guide how much you share, but it is important to consider all the possible outcomes of sharing your beliefs with someone else (Patel, 2012). You also need to consider the time and place. If you want to share your faith with other students, question your motivation and university guidance on this issue if it exists, and then determine if it is appropriate to do so. Often a crisis becomes the moment that we can or are forced to calculate these decisions and assess the opportunities for having such conversations, but try to be both reflective and proactive.

In times of crisis, students may simply want someone to listen. They are holding many feelings inside and they need an outlet. This might not be the ideal time to share your own faith. However, depending on the moment you are in, you may want to say a prayer together or just share a moment of silence. If they are looking for guidance on how to get through a tough time, sharing how you experience your faith, the things you do to bring you closer to whatever your higher power is, may be exactly what they need. Using your understanding of your students and your experience in reading and understanding student identity development is important. Well-honed intuition is ultimately the best guide for what to share and when to share it.

## Faith Leaders and Campus Resources

It is vital for student affairs practitioners to cultivate relationships with a variety of campus partners who can assist in times of need. Some campuses have faith leaders who serve as chaplains, religious life staff, advisors, fellows, or in other staff positions. When these professionals work on campus, they should be included in our circle of colleagues and partners on whom we can rely; when they do not exist on campus due to resource constraints, we need to create mechanisms for assessing their ability to serve students. Taking the time to build and strengthen these relationships on a professional, and sometimes personal, level can reap great rewards for us and for students (Love, 2001).

Pastoral care is a critical component in nearly all faith traditions, and there is a clear understanding of how spiritual leaders can play this role. However, their success is largely dependent on how well integrated they are into the fabric of the community in the first place. Have they been trained in the appropriate practices and policies and educated about inclusive nomenclature? Do they have access to student affairs practitioners to ask clarifying questions about additional on-campus resources, or what to do if a student discloses something that puts themselves or others at risk? These important issues should be clarified before faith leaders are called on in a crisis, in order for their involvement to be beneficial for all parties involved.

Astin et al.'s (2011) research shows that both students' psychological well-being and their religiosity decline during their college years; however, spirituality increases modestly, which is associated with greater "equanimity," meaning that students are learning skills that help them to deal with conflict, feel more peaceful, express gratitude, and have more optimism about the future. This equanimity has a positive impact on psychological well-being and shows growth potential in higher education (Astin et al., 2011). DiLorenzo (2016) also wrote about how religiosity declines for many college students, but during this time their desire to find and make meaning of the world, particularly in times of crisis, is stronger than ever. Faith leaders are uniquely positioned to assist student affairs practitioners in helping students develop through this phase of their lives.

Some campuses do not have these built-in colleagues and resources for students. In these cases, it can be up to us to seek out faith leaders in our local communities and find ways to build successful partnerships with them. Often, local humanist organizations, synagogues, mosques, and churches are open to providing resources to students for free or at a very low cost. These resources may include leading services on campus, forming relationships with faith-based student organizations, offering spiritual advisement or mentorship, or creating bridges to communities of faith off campus. These possibilities should be pursued, because many students look for spiritual guidance throughout their tenure on campus.

One proactive Office of Religious and Spiritual Life at a private nonsectarian liberal arts college found several benefits to having faith leaders available during the natural disasters that occurred in fall 2017. At this school, a Catholic Latina student was devastated to learn that an earthquake in Mexico had destroyed her extended family's home and that Hurricane Maria was on a path to hit Puerto Rico and possibly Mexico. She sought support from the dean of religious and spiritual life, a religious sister who also serves as the Catholic advisor. The student wanted to connect with others on the campus who were similarly affected by the violent path of the hurricane. The faith leader encouraged the student to reach out to others, and the student quickly formed a small group. The group decided to hold a vigil for those in Puerto Rico and Mexico. The campus community's positive response encouraged the group to launch a fundraising campaign for the victims of the natural disasters. The group invited the mayor of San Juan to come to the campus to educate the community, and she did. The group channeled the pain and anguish of being away from family during these crises into action that created lasting relationships and a path to healing.

In this case, the incorporation of faith leaders provided a natural personal connection for pastoral care that led to a community response for those who were grieving and ensured a visible expression of the solidarity and commitment to the college's values of diversity, equity, inclusion, and civic engagement (A. McDermott, personal communication, May 2, 2018).

When there are no such resources on campus, student affairs officers can start to build a network of faith leaders by simply asking community leaders if they would be willing to assist when needed during a crisis. Staying in touch with them periodically throughout the year, including having network meetings semiannually so that these relationships can continue to strengthen, is optimal. These connections can be useful for students looking for a religious service in their native language or a sect of a tradition that isn't represented on campus. These connections can help students find community.

While many of us subscribe to various wellness models that include spiritual wellness, we sometimes shy away from offering spiritual programming on campus for fear of accusations of exclusion or personal bias, fear of general disinterest from students, or our own discomfort (Anderson, 2016). But we should ensure that topics related to spirituality and religion are part of campus conversations that provide developmental opportunities for our students. We can do this in a variety of ways while being clear that our intentions are focused on inclusion, support, and student development. Consider including a faith leader on a panel discussion about political, service-related, global, or social issues. Incorporate faith and religion into your diversity programming by finding opportunities to bring students of different faiths together with their faith leaders to discuss their beliefs and practices, and offer training and workshops that educate and encourage participants to be more accepting of diverse religious beliefs (Ennis, 2017).

An important example of this is the Faith Zone module (Ennis, 2017). A general sentiment in higher education seemed to be that talking about religion and spirituality in the context of social justice and higher education was too messy, complicated, personal, and perhaps even anti-intellectual (Jacobsen & Jacobsen, 2012). The success and impact of Faith Zone is well documented in Ariel Ennis' book *Religious Literacy* (2017), and the model has been adapted at New York University.

There are many opportunities in which our faith leaders—either on or off campus—can be resources and partners with us. Those who are in the local community can get to know our students, our campus culture, and ourselves so that they can better serve our campus in times of need. Students may take these opportunities to build their own relationships with these faith leaders, which can help carry the load of meeting students' emotional and mental health needs. Additionally, without offering and engaging in this type of programming throughout the year, our inclusion of faith leaders only in a time of crisis can look disingenuous and hollow, and they may feel like strangers to our campus community when we need them the most.

We may be doing a disservice to our students by not expanding on the types of emergency situations in which we might include faith leaders. Many of us will immediately jump to include a faith leader if we are planning a memorial service for a member of our campus community. This can seem natural, and we will likely not second-guess this decision. However, there are many other crisis situations in which we should consider including faith leaders and/or faith communities where they might be able to create a "buffer zone," as Annette McDermott (personal communication, May 2, 2018) dean of religious and spiritual life at Mount Holyoke College, referred to it. McDermott reported that while cultural groups offer space between authorities, it is generally not space for "transcendence." It is the capacity to take what is hurting or burdening students and provide a way to channel the "big questions" into the spiritual sphere—to perhaps have a ritual through a song, a poem, a prayer, the burning of sage, deep breathing, or the reading of prayers, seeking relief through a higher power that differentiates the secular and creates the important "spiritual buffer zone." An example of this includes the days and weeks after the 2016 presidential election. On many campuses, students experienced a broad range of emotions, from fear and anxiety to excitement and enthusiasm. This was a moment in which many spiritual leaders cocreated gatherings of comfort and hope in an attempt to bring campuses and people back together in ways that may have been inaccessible or "off limits" to campus employees, considering the divisiveness of the election (A. McDermott, personal communication, May 2, 2018).

Communities of faith can be helpful partners in responding to many crises because they are uniquely positioned to be nimble and responsive. Local faith-based organizations are often the first to organize supply drives with which institutions of higher education can partner. They may also have already established connections with the affected communities, which creates natural points of entry for our students. If we are holding a vigil for a tragedy that has happened in our nation or globally, including faith leaders to speak or be present at the vigil to provide support and guidance to students can be greatly beneficial. When a disaster or crisis arises, many of our students turn to—or question—their own beliefs. Give them the opportunity to engage in conversations and engage with role models, and assist them in finding their way. If we think back on times when we have brought students together during a crisis, we may be able to identify instances in which we should have included faith leaders (Patel, 2012).

When we include faith leaders in our programming and outreach to students, we must set expectations and goals for their involvement. We need to be sure we are setting them up for success. We must take the time to share with them all aspects of the situation at hand, train them on our protocols, and help them understand our campus culture, our specific student needs, and our hopes for the program they are a part of. And we must decide the extent to which we want them involved after the program has concluded. If we are asking them to be part of something as intimate as a memorial service for a member of our community, we need to ensure they can connect with the friends and family of the deceased. We need to share with them the context of the event, the issue at hand, how students are feeling, and what we hope the program will accomplish. And after the crisis resolves, we need to reach out to those who assisted us, thank them, and review how our goals were or were not met and what our hopes would be for next time—all to continue to build our relationships with these important partners.

We also can't forget about offering ourselves as resources for students. We are quick to describe ourselves as role models and mentors to students in countless ways, but we need to be sure we are mentoring and supporting them in their religious identities as well. These conversations can provide opportunities for student development, inquiry, and mentorship. Engaging students in these conversations can help us provide important sources of support during times of crisis.

More and more, we are finding the need to communicate with students about the availability of counseling services on campus, particularly during crises. We let them know what the hours and programs are, how to access the counselors, and that we are all here to support them. If possible, we should be providing them with faith-based resources as well. This can help alleviate the extreme pressure on many understaffed and often underresourced counseling offices to be the primary source of emotional and mental health support for students. If we develop on-campus faith-based resources, we can easily include them in our list of supportive resources for students during times of crisis, even if it isn't our personal inclination.

## Our Collective Well-Being

Working through a campus crisis can be personally challenging and very draining for staff and faculty members. We must take time for ourselves and have personal time with our own faith or other self-care practices. If you work at an institution that has religious and spiritual staff on hand, explore how you can utilize these services for yourself, considering professional boundaries and reporting lines. Finding a moment with a chaplain to process your own experiences and emotions can renew your own strength and allow you to continue serving the community in the best possible way. If the college is coming together as a community to process a tragedy, thinking about how you are making the most of that time for self-reflection is important "oxygen mask–type work" (put your own on first, so you can help others do the same).

Thinking about what measures you can put in place to provide religious and spiritual support for staff and faculty members is also a helpful activity. While some of us have our own off-campus supports—our families and religious or spiritual leaders—we may not be able to utilize those support systems during a crisis because we are giving every moment we can to our campus community. Remembering to take care of ourselves and to seek out spiritual or wellness guidance can often give us the extra energy and strength we need to support our students.

## Self-Care

Incorporating your own personal spiritual or well-being practices into your everyday life on campus can become a lifeline when managing a crisis. Consider closing your office door for 5 to 10 minutes to meditate, pray, or sit in silence and reflect. Writing your thoughts in a journal, reading a passage that is meaningful to you, or listening to a song that helps you feel or express your emotions are all good strategies. You can take a walk, find a favorite place on campus to be alone, or find a colleague you can talk with for a few minutes to help you process and give you comfort. You can practice gratitude by reflecting on things you are thankful for, or you can write a note to someone to tell them why you are grateful they are in your life. Trying different things to see what helps you connect to your own spirituality—or simply quieting your mind to bring you a measure of peace—is important role modeling for our students.

Whatever practice is personally helpful for you, employ it during times of crisis to rejuvenate yourself. If you are a spiritual person, incorporate those practices into your wellness routine. If you are not, find other ways to administer self-care. Remember, even in crisis it is good to take a few minutes for yourself.

Questioning ourselves and the world as we understand it, especially in the aftermath of disaster, is critical for engaging broader ideas about faith. As student affairs professionals, we are constantly striving to assist students in thinking critically about themselves and the world. This is especially essential when tragedy strikes, and we seek to find creative and useful ways to explore how students make meaning in their lives. Spirituality is often an important way to do this, and it is our responsibility as student affairs professionals to support and/or create the relationships, structures, communities, and practices within higher education that allow spirituality to develop. Our students are depending on us.

## References

Anderson, D. S. (2016). *Wellness issues for higher education: A guide for student affairs and higher education professionals.* New York, NY: Routledge.

Astin, A. W., Astin, H. S., & Lindholm, J. A. (2011). *Cultivating the spirit: How college can enhance students' inner lives.* San Francisco, CA: Jossey-Bass.

Council for the Advancement of Standards in Higher Education. (2015). *Campus religious, secular, and spiritual programs.* Washington, DC: Author.

DiLorenzo, M. F. (2016). Spiritual development: Setting a place at the table for spirituality. In D. S. Anderson (Ed.), *Wellness issues for higher education: A guide for student affairs and higher education professionals* (pp. 223–238). New York, NY: Routledge.

Ennis, A. (2017). *Teaching religious literacy: A guide to spiritual diversity in higher education.* New York, NY: Routledge.

Harper, S. R. (2008). *Creating inclusive campus environments for cross-cultural learning and student engagement.* Washington, DC: NASPA–Student Affairs Administrators in Higher Education.

Harward, D. W. (2016). *Well-being and higher education: A strategy for change and the realization of educations greater purposes.* Washington, DC: Bringing Theory to Practice.

Jacobsen, D., & Jacobsen, R. H. (2012). *No longer invisible: Religion in university education.* Oxford, England: Oxford University Press.

Love, P. G. (2001). Spirituality and student development: Theoretical connections. In M. Jablonski (Ed.), *The implications of student spirituality for student affairs practice* (New Directions for Student Services, No. 95, pp. 7–16). San Francisco, CA: Jossey-Bass.

Rockenbush, A. B., & Mayhew, M. J. (2012). *Spirituality in college students' lives: Translating research into practice.* New York, NY: Routledge.

Patel, E. (2012). *Sacred ground: Pluralism, prejudice, and the promise of America.* Boston, MA: Beacon.

University of California, Los Angeles. (2010). Spirituality in higher education. Retrieved from http://spirituality.ucla.edu

# 11

# Learning From Tragedy

## Kimberly C. Thornbury

A career in higher education entails helping people and institutions in difficult situations, although no textbook or lecture could fully prepare us for the myriad challenges it's possible to encounter. When I originally enrolled in a graduate program for higher education specialists, I never imagined that one day my job in student affairs would force me to learn the details of state insurance for unplanned pregnancies, how to transform an entire hotel into a residence complex in just a week, or how to navigate complex laws involving the donation of corpses. Though I never expected to perform these difficult and diverse tasks, they made me more fully appreciate how proper crisis response is foundational to our work.

Crises of all scales can have a devastating impact on those who endure them. Throughout my time as a student affairs administrator, I have attended to the needs of students who have faced heartbreaking situations. How do you help a student who came home after midterms to find his beloved grandmother, who raised him and with whom he continued to live, deceased? She had unexpectedly passed away in the middle of the semester. There were no parents to help with the logistics of what to do next, so our student affairs team stepped in and walked the student through unfamiliar details: everything from working with the funeral home to contacting relatives and friends, to the much more complicated matters involved with navigating the closing of an estate. Such issues of care remind us that our institutions not only convey degrees and train students in various fields but also enable students to navigate some of the most difficult transitions in life.

This chapter explores the range of learning that occurs following crisis situations as well as how to create a mindset that allows you to navigate the complexity that results from encountering these unexpected events. Graduate programs in student affairs teach subjects including, but not limited to, the history of higher education, developmental theory, legal issues, and best practices; however, no curriculum can anticipate all the skills we need during an emergency.

## The Value of Case Studies

Higher education literature indicates that "colleges and universities were generally prepared only for those crises that they had already experienced" (Mitroff, Diamond, & Alpaslan, 2006, p. 65). This is hardly a desirable state of affairs in a rapidly changing world, so extensive scenario planning becomes a "must" for university administrators. By looking at a variety of case studies, leaders can have greater confidence in their ability to handle unexpected and diverse challenges. Feeling prepared is a way of being prepared. Much like how the act of taking standardized exams over and over can strengthen one's test taking capabilities, so, too, can reviewing sample crisis scenarios build one's confidence in responding to the unexpected.

Student affairs professionals, even when they have not studied how to handle a particular crisis, can learn to set the tone for effective problem solving. They can model resilience, working effectively across departmental lines and traditional skill sets for the good of the students, the university, and beyond. Just like a musician, the timbre and tone of how administrators deal with unexpected events and even disasters can make the biggest difference in how an institution looks and feels when it gets to the other side of a crisis.

My personal experience involves a case study of an F4 tornado hitting Union University, a faith-based college of just over 4,000 students, in west Tennessee. The tornado destroyed 75% of the residence complexes. I served as vice president of student services and dean of students at the time, and I saw my students' housing blown away in less than a minute. This event showed how student affairs professionals learned to handle a multitude of new tasks in the wake of unforeseen events. Having a good professional network and learning and developing characteristics such as creativity, flexibility within structure, positivity, and forgiveness toward oneself and others can enable one to endure both the professional and the personal toll of a crisis.

Similar case studies can encourage student affairs professionals to engage in "what if" thinking, a helpful exercise in anticipating needs and flexing creativity around a hypothetical problem. The challenges will often be professional and student-focused in nature, but at times they are more personal, like how a working mother will care for her family when she is called away to manage a crisis for days on end.

Sample tabletop exercises include such scenarios as an active shooter, a lice or bed bug outbreak (including how to protect a student when they are discovered as "person zero" in a lice epidemic), a student's death from meningitis, or an attempted kidnapping by an estranged parent. Perhaps a scenario involves how you might fill in for a key leader should they be called away for months due to an emergency. The school need not have to buy expensive tabletop exercise scenarios: Start by tackling a real, campus-based crisis you read about in the news. Recent examples include an athletics department bus that overturned coming home from a tournament, killing several students; protests that rapidly escalated in response to a controversial campus speaker; and persistent rumors that a prominent faculty member tied to major grant money was engaged in inappropriate behavior with an undergraduate student. Unfortunately, such examples can be found every week, many of which can stop an institution in its tracks. We need only take something from the headlines and apply it to our own campuses in order to engage in tabletop exercises that help move the needle on crisis preparation.

Conduct these exercises at least once a year. As you walk through the exercise, list operations protocols for residence life, food services, safety and security, and other departments. Crisis plans are often written by incident, but I have found that regardless of the crisis, or its size, many departments need to take similar actions no matter what the event.

Departments need to know who is in charge and, if that main leader is out, who exactly is the second and third leader in line. What do the departments need to have on hand or know before a crisis even happens? For example, is there a website that can quickly be put up that provides ongoing information and details? Does someone have media contacts ready? Are there extra cell phone batteries handy? Are there hard copies of emergency contact forms in case the server goes down, as was the case during our tornado crisis?

Look for gaps in your internal and external communications. Ensure that you have a message protocol and good sample scripts.

During a crisis, no matter the scale, people like to receive hourly updates. Early in the crisis, even if there is no new news, you should convey to people every hour that there is no new news, as this notification helps prevent them from filling in the gaps with false information and rumors. Learn how to control the message with short, clear facts, and plan for further training when your tabletop exercises reveal gaps.

The work of student affairs professionals is endless. Although we value crisis management, in reality, preparation can often fall into that "not urgent and not important" category when compared with the tyranny of immediate student needs. Everyday life and tasks (goal setting, assessment, relationship building, meetings, event planning and execution, qualitative and quantitative reports, budget management) can often take up 10 hours or more of our days.

Weather emergencies, fires, ethical breaches or crimes by leaders or students, cringe-worthy viral social media, technology flaws, lawsuits, pandemic flus or other outbreaks, active shooters, terrorism, student suicides and deaths, and transportation accidents—as well as the business interruption or revenue concerns that result from a crisis—are a good start to a possible list of case studies. Other examples may include the loss of key executives through sudden illness or a possible moral failure, or large-scale tragedies such as the 1999 Texas A&M bonfire collapse (see chapter 2). Even if a university has a 200-point checklist on what to do in each of these cases, we can never anticipate the amount of on-the-job learning that will occur.

## F4 Tornado

One of the largest crises I faced during my time as a vice president for student development at Union University happened when a tornado ripped through the heart of the campus in Jackson,

Tennessee. Striking on February 5, 2008, at 7:02 p.m., the tornado took just 38 seconds to inflict more than $47 million worth of damage. The storm destroyed or wrecked 31 of the 41 buildings on the main campus, including 75% of the residence complexes. The university was only five days into the spring semester. Students were bleeding and hurt: 51 students were seriously injured, with 13 of them trapped under building rubble or in a collapsed bathroom. All residential students needed housing not only for the night but for the entire spring semester. In the hours and weeks that followed the storm, my learning curve spiked.

Just before I heard the news that the tornado had touched down, I had placed my two daughters, ages 5 and 7, inside our home's downstairs bathtub, wrapped in blankets, which was the protocol for tornadoes. Sadly, this had become a routine for us. My husband, who was both a dean and vice president at Union University, was off campus at a meeting.

Within minutes, the local news weatherman explained that our university had experienced a direct hit. I was at home with two small children, knowing our campus was in desperate need and my husband was a few miles away. A close neighbor was out that night, and I had to call a neighbor I didn't know as well and ask if I could drop off my girls immediately. Student affairs professionals are often wired to get to know people, be friendly, and keep names and numbers. This habit helps in times of crisis when you need to rely on or build a village—fast.

I drove onto campus, broken glass crunching under my tires, hoping the wires strewn across the road were not live. Thankfully, one of the first students I saw on the side of the road was the student government president, who hopped into my car as we drove to my office. As I entered my office, the first thing I saw sitting on my desk was the yet-to-be signed contract for our new emergency text messaging system, which was supposed to be implemented and launched in three days. I tried to log in to the computer and discovered that our servers were down. We had a campus that was literally and figuratively in the dark.

I grabbed a bullhorn I had kept in my office since the last tornado and quickly realized that the batteries were dead. "The best laid plans of mice and men," I thought to myself. The student government president and a few other students who had found me were eager to help, and I instructed them to go across the campus and yell that all students should head to the main academic complex hallway. I did not have a clear idea of what to do next, but I knew that I needed to gather the campus quickly.

As students assembled I stood on a chair and loudly—but calmly—stated, "Everyone, I am glad you are here. You are going to be OK. You are going to have a warm bed tonight and a hot meal in the morning. You are going to be OK. And I want you to do two things. First, I want you to call your loved ones and tell them you are OK. Second, I want you to sign your name on this piece of paper so we know you are here and OK."

I didn't know how I was going to fulfill my promises to them that they would be safe. I am a person of faith and believe that God had put those words in my mouth. Students started signing the sheets. We never used the list, but I knew that people do better psychologically when they feel "seen and heard" and when they feel accounted for in moments of crisis.

I realize that at this point in the story, most readers will cringe, because crisis planning has come so far in the past decade and what we did back then feels unthinkable today. Student affairs professionals and campuses are always improving and learning, so, as with any profession, we hope our field in every area is better in 10 years than it is now. Crisis management is still a relatively new field, perhaps

25 years old, and continues to be refined (Mitroff, Diamond, & Alpaslan, 2006).

Located in the Bible Belt of Tennessee, the university has a great reputation and many friends within the community. Through our phone tree to churches and other contacts, we said, "If you have a bed, come pick our students up." We arranged for over 1,000 students to stay in homes that night. There was no process, and it could have been dangerous, but it worked. Once I knew the students were headed off campus into safe homes, I went down to the residence complexes. My work had only just begun.

The campus looked like a war zone. We knew two sets of students were trapped, and weather reports called for a second tornado to strike. The executive team, under the leadership of an amazing president, was faced with key questions: Were there any more pockets of trapped students? (We didn't know that all our students were safe until the dog sniffers, looking for dead bodies, went through each building. Police recorded a giant "0" in bright orange spray paint on each building when no bodies were found. We could not breathe during this process.) Would the injured students survive? How would we contact students' parents with our servers down and the hard-copy emergency contact numbers under 15 feet of rubble? Where would all these residential students sleep tonight, or this week, or this semester? How would we begin the technical assessment of a destroyed campus? Could we even continue the semester?

Over the next few weeks, everyone at the university simply had to learn new protocols and skills (e.g., learning how to help students submit insurance claims, the pros and cons of filing for Federal Emergency Management Agency (FEMA) help, how to obtain new contact lenses for students, how to store and record donated goods, how to remove tons of debris). Knowing we would need more communal space now that we were moving from a residential to a commuter campus for a time, we found a large underutilized billiards room and gathered the wellness director, student activities director, and a dozen entrepreneurial students and said to them, "You wanted a coffee shop on campus? Here is your space and the money [a ridiculously low number]. You figure everything else out." And they did.

Career services learned to create a database to photograph and record the hundreds of damaged cars on campus—some had been thrown on top of others. It was bitterly cold, and the parking lots were dangerous and full of broken glass, debris, and fallen trees. Health services learned how to replace contact lenses, glasses, retainers, and medicine. Greek life staff learned how to replace driver's licenses and passports. The tutoring staff helped wade through FEMA rules and the potential implications of students accepting cash from the organization.

Within three weeks, we converted a donated hotel into residence hall rooms complete with all new furniture. We secured alternate classroom sites and established 24/7 counseling for the entire spring semester. In the end, the university built 769 bedrooms within six months and 816 total bedrooms within nine months. Students moved into new complexes for the start of the fall semester.

## A Framework for Crisis

Reflecting on the tornado incident, I realized that the following five skills are a great framework for learning in crisis. They can be applied both personally and professionally:

- Build a peer and professional network.
- Be creative.
- Be flexible yet strategic.

- Be positive.
- Be forgiving.

While the tornado was the biggest crisis of my career, countless small ones provided opportunities to employ this exact framework—and it proved invaluable. I used this framework when a student refused to leave his residence hall and simply stacked jars of his own urine around the room. It structured my response when pet therapy dogs became a major disruption, when an estranged father broke into his daughter's residence complex to leave her cryptic notes, and when a group of students created a massive fire in their room while trying to deep-fry homemade donuts in their kitchenette. When a key member of my staff was suddenly left to raise three small children by himself, our team had to become creative with how to help this family and find innovative ways to continue the necessary work of the institution. Using the above framework, you can master new skills and learn in real time how to move forward in the right way.

## Build a Peer and Professional Network

In times of crisis, the student affairs professional should take a Wikipedia-like approach: there is no way you can know all the answers, so you have to tap into experts in the field. You often simply need to know someone who knows someone, who knows someone. I have always loved the story of John and Jacqueline Kennedy's desire to know a wide range of people. This kept state dinners interesting. During these state dinners, the Kennedys could call on each of their guests to help explain questions or update the rest of the group on recent trends in their field. They built a group of experts.

Without friends, you can't manage a crisis. And because you can't know everything, you must build strong relationships with trustees, local business owners, government officials, partner institutions, and other key influencers. A diverse pool of friendships will allow you to call on people with particular skills during a crisis. Remember names and store key phone numbers in your cell phone.

Always make goodwill deposits through the years, because one day you might need to rely on a full well of friendships. Columnist Peggy Noonan (2010) explained it best:

> In politics you must tend to the garden. The garden is the constituency. . . . No great endeavor is possible without its backing. In a modern presidency especially you have to know this, because there will be times when history throws you a crisis, and to address it you may have to do an unpopular thing. A president in those circumstances must use all the goodwill he's build up over the months and years to get through that moment and survive doing what he thinks is right. (para. 12)

Building goodwill with a wide network is the only way to manage today's complex crises. During the tornado, I not only had to rely on a friend of a friend (of a friend) for resources, skills, and knowledge but also for babysitting my small children and ensuring that my family was fed.

There will always be people in your inner circle you rely on. Children need to be taken to school, and bills need to be paid. The dishwasher needs to be emptied, and toothpaste needs to be purchased. Many will need to rely on a partner, family, and close friends to do many intimate tasks for them. During the tornado response, I was working 18-hour days on site at the university. My father, a former college president, visited from the Northeast to help as needed. My girls needed care and food, and my father bought them multiple new school uniforms because he had not quite mastered laundry.

But practical questions remained. Who among us knew someone who could make giant roadway signs within the hour to redirect traffic? Who knew how to negotiate turning a church-owned hotel complex into residence halls for students within weeks? Who has the best relationship with our furniture vendor to get hundreds of units delivered in a week? Who knew how to scour surrounding businesses to find alternative classroom space so we could begin classes in two weeks and salvage the spring semester? Who could create a rubric to most fairly divide the cash donations that came pouring in?

One practical habit student affairs professionals should practice is to keep everyone's contacts in your phone. You never know when you might need to reach someone. Student affairs heroes must always be charging their phones in their homes and cars, at work, and (probably) inside their purses. With phone in hand and the framework above, most crises can be managed.

## *Be Creative*

In some crises, you might actually have to use the proverbial duct tape to solve a problem. Think leaky tent on a resident advisor camping trip. Other times, your creativity will be stretched beyond usual limits. If classes need to begin in two weeks to save the semester, and you are now without dozens of classrooms because the building's roof came off, where can you hold classes? If a residence hall is destroyed, and space for 900 students is needed before the fall semester begins, how can you get design plans for a new residence hall from an architect by 8:00 a.m. the next day? Creativity doesn't mean wacky—it means considering all of the out-of-the-box solutions to your real problem.

One example of a helpful creative idea came from a junior residence hall director. She suggested hosting a dinner with students and their new host families to provide those families with specific advice on how to relate to the students suddenly living under their roof. Families who suddenly adopted students in need did not know about "roommate contracts," but our team did, and we used that model to help the families think about how they can approach subjects of food in the fridge, late-night hours, and socks on the floor with their new housemates. We wanted to offer learning and mediation tools before potential problems arose. We also provided advice to families on talking (and listening)—strategies to use with these students who needed months to process the trauma of almost becoming trapped in the rubble or of losing all their belongings, including journals, class notebooks, and family heirlooms. Establishing a culture of continual quality improvement and a culture of creativity on campus strengthens a muscle that is greatly needed during times of crisis.

## Be Flexible Yet Strategic

Have a plan, know where you are going, and be OK if things go off course. The president of our university said he made as many decisions in the first 100 hours after the tornado as he did in the 100 days before it. He slept 16 hours the first week. But within 14 hours of the devastation, he created a plan that would guide the decisions of the senior leadership team:

- Take care of students from Day 1.
- Lay out a 48-hour plan for immediate crisis response.
- Facilitate recovery (including salvaging the student's belongings).
- Restart the spring semester.
- Rebuild—look to the fall semester.

Within this framework was abundant room for discussion about how to move forward. But the president or senior leader should provide general steps—or at least a mantra and values that will guide all decisions. It cannot go without saying that student needs come first; the leader must articulate those words. They must be repeated and embedded in conversation to provide core guide rails to each decision.

## Be Positive

Model a Zappos, Nordstrom, or Southwest Airlines employee and say yes whenever possible (Solomon, 2017). Constantly support others, offer encouragement, and express gratitude. There will be times when you have to say no. There will be times when you have to prioritize, and there will be need for self-care. But modeling service to others when everyone is exhausted helps the team get through what must be done. This is especially important when you are asked to learn something new. During the tornado crisis, my team members had to take on countless new tasks, including following these instructions I gave them:

- "Find out the FEMA process, and be in charge of guiding students wisely through the process."
- "Be a resource for students to get new passports, retainers, contacts, eyeglasses, and medicine."
- "Obtain five furniture bids in three days, and create a simple report for senior leadership at the college to review."
- "Build a coffee house and space for students to gather now that almost all our students are now commuters."

I often tell my staff to "stay in their lane," meaning know what your strengths are and try to live within them. During a crisis, you probably will be asked to do things out of your lane and skill set. Positions and titles are often unimportant when caring for a community in crisis. Faculty and student affairs professionals had to work side by side for days to box up and sort students' belongings.

Only in recent years did I learn of the term *hangry*—the combination of hunger and anger. There is often little time for a leader to rest and eat during a crisis, but without such breaks, there are few reserves to problem solve in a gracious way. A leader and team must rest (even if that means only lying in bed in prayer or meditation, since sleep is elusive). Attempts at rest, eating, and time for personal devotion will decrease anxiety as the days and weeks prolong. Often the food provided is fast food, fried, or comfort casseroles. Volunteers often don't have the energy to be picky about limited food options. Trying to ensure, in due course, healthy eating options for staff will enable them to have longer staying power.

Keep spirits up by providing as clear direction as you can. Feed volunteers. Encourage them to rest. Have people "on the bench" ready to step up and help while one team goes to bed. You may need to create first-, second-, and third-shift teams. Tell your team that you appreciate them. Find ways to praise them to others.

Never underestimate the power of gifts and letters from other institutions. Residence life teams from across the country sent popcorn, movie tickets, chocolate, flowers, and serious and funny letters to our residence life staff. Other leaders at colleges facilitated letter writing campaigns of support—letters that we then taped on our main academic hallway to let our community and volunteers know they were not forgotten. Other vice presidents sent quick texts: "No need to respond. I am thinking about you. You can do this." Those words of encouragement were a balm for me and my team. I am ashamed to say this, but before this tornado, I rarely reached out to a partner school in crisis. I always assumed my words or gifts might be a distraction, that my colleagues were "too busy." Not so. Sending money (not used clothes) is one of the very best ways you can help an institution recover. Seeing donations pile in buoys volunteers and the staff. Personal notes and gifts mean the world when the days, weeks, and months of a crisis drag on. As leaders in higher education, we can guide our students or teams in showing care in this practical way.

## Be Forgiving

One must be forgiving, both personally and professionally, during times of crisis. Leaders can sometimes flirt with the temptation of pride and self-sufficiency when the organization and home life are well run, effective, and efficient; however, in times of crisis, one quickly realizes the utter insufficiency of self. Mistakes will be made. Decisions might be made on incomplete facts. Tempers can flare. But a spirit of forgiveness toward self and others is a key habit for persevering through a crisis.

Soon after the tornado, when I did not see my daughters for days, I am certain they wore the same uniform to school for days on end until my father arrived. I trust they changed their underwear. I know I certainly wasn't making sure their teeth were brushed.

People were so kind to bring the senior leadership team food during the crisis, as we often were on campus for 18 to 20 hours a day or more. However, people brought so much fast food and meat during the storm that my husband ultimately became a strict vegetarian following the crisis. He could not look at another hamburger without flashbacks.

My oldest daughter would not sleep anywhere without her green blanket for the seven years following the storm. The blanket was so large and heavy that it needed its own suitcase for overnight trips. I often wondered about the effects the storm had on her and the impact of her seeing me in crisis mode for weeks on end.

We need to be constantly ready to forgive others in times of crisis, but we also need to forgive ourselves. I needed to give myself forgiveness for not seeing my children for weeks, and for not being there to feed them something other than fast food and to tuck them in at night.

Then there were days, perhaps weeks, that went by before I could respond with a simple "thank you" text to my very best friends for their constant support. I felt exhausted and guilty. I needed the encouragement and was grateful for those who continued to care despite my lack of response.

When the time is right, you will assess the crisis, as all good student affairs professionals do. What do you wish you had done, or in which areas did you not respond as well? Are there things you missed? If you had done those things, would you have traded something you did do? Are there factors of the experience for which you need to forgive yourself or others? Assessing the crisis response through these questions may help you begin to reframe the situation and focus on the next phase of your professional experience.

## Conclusion

As former University of Florida Vice President for Student Affairs Arthur Sandeen (2006) noted, "An institution reveals its soul during a crisis" (p. 64). Sandeen (2006) argued that a person's soul (not just an institution's) is likewise revealed during a crisis, and often there are no checklists for exactly what to do on both a personal and a professional level.

Student affairs professionals are lifelong learners. Most are curious and eager to do something if they know it can improve outcomes. Many have generous spirits and will not only give you the shirt off their back but also try to ensure that it is the right color.

Through the crisis at Union, I did learn new skills. I now know how to recycle tons of cardboard from massive shipments of new furniture. I learned how to text (the crisis occurred in 2008, back when you had to hit the number 2 three times on your phone to get a "c" to appear on your screen). I learned the nuances of both post-traumatic stress and post-traumatic counseling and how each may look differently to different groups. I learned about business interruption insurance and the best stain removal products for blood and dirt.

In the more than 10 years since the event, I have used the crisis response framework to meet yet more unexpected challenges. I now serve at a university in Manhattan. We used the rubric to respond calmly when Westboro Baptist Church protested our school, which is located between Trinity Church and the New York Stock Exchange. We had a code of honor already established when an unfortunate student event went viral on social media. And, sadly, I used this plan as I dealt with my first student death to suicide—a tragedy I had never experienced in my 25 years in higher education.

Whether you work with students in a rural or urban setting, the framework remains the same. I learned how to build a network and how to be creative, flexible, positive, and forgiving. The next 50 years will bring challenges in higher education that no one has ever faced. But these principles of networking, creativity, flexibility, positivity, and forgiveness will stand the test of time.

## References

Mitroff, I. I., Diamond, M. A., & Alpaslan, M. C. (2006). How prepared are America's colleges and universities for major crises? Assessing the state of crisis management. *Change: The Magazine of Higher Learning, 38*(1), 61–67.

Noonan, P. (2010, January 7). The risk of catastrophic victory. *The Wall Street Journal*. Retrieved from http://www.wsj.com/articles/SB10001424052748704130904574644701673362182

Sandeen, A. (2006). Voice of the vice president. In K. S. Harper, B. G. Paterson, & E. L. Zdziarski (Eds.), *Crisis management: Responding from the heart* (pp. 64–67). Washington, DC: NASPA–Student Affairs Administrators in Higher Education.

Solomon, M. (2017, August 1). Three wow customer service stories from Zappos, Southwest Airlines and Nordstrom. *Forbes.com*. Retrieved from https://www.forbes.com/sites/micahsolomon/2017/08/01/three-wow-customer-service-stories-from-zappos-southwest-airlines-and-nordstrom/#4433d68c2aba

# 12

# A Deep Hurt and a Magnificent Hope

KATIE L. TREADWELL

The week before the manuscript for *Crisis, Compassion, and Resiliency in Student Affairs* was submitted to the publisher, I began a routine late-spring Friday only to learn a few hours later that 10 students had died in yet another school shooting, this time in Santa Fe, Texas. Days later, as I made final edits to the book, a gunman opened fire on a restaurant less than a mile from my family home. In recent months, student affairs professionals have helped students process the horrific Las Vegas shootings that killed 58, cautioned communities anew about terrorism after a driver plowed through tourists on a crowded New York City passageway, and mourned the unimaginable loss of 17 students in Parkland, Florida. Even as K–12 and postsecondary educators concluded another academic year and celebrated commencement festivities, we grappled with the understanding that during the spring semester, more American students had been killed in on-campus shootings than the number of individuals who died in military-related deaths in 2018 (Bump, 2018). The worst-case scenario has become increasingly routine.

In the years since the December 2012 shootings at Sandy Hook Elementary School, a gun has been fired on a school campus every week—389 school shootings in 318 weeks (Everytown for Gun Safety, 2019; Krishnakumar, 2018). To process the notion that, statistically, not one week of the previous five-and-a-half years has been free of campus shootings is to question the very nature of education. Many post–Sandy Hook shootings occurred at elementary, middle, or high schools, but over 40% occurred on a postsecondary campus (Everytown for Gun Safety, 2019). Students are arriving to our campuses and our care more traumatized than ever before. First-year students will bring residence hall decorations and academic advising questions, as well as post-traumatic stress disorder (PTSD) and the memory of barricading classroom doors or attending classmates' funerals. Some will experience the first anniversary of their school shooting on our campuses. Others will react to routine loud noises, campus drills, or tests of the emergency alert systems in visceral ways, instantly transported to the moment their world irreparably shifted. They are a generation in which "hope and fear are colliding" (Levine, Cureton, & Levine, 1998, p. 17). They are also a generation demanding great change, marching for our lives, and refusing to accept campus-based gun deaths as status quo.

Until it happens to you—your campus, your town, your child—you cannot possibly prepare for the emotions, the panic, and the lingering fear that will not subside. You won't understand how hearing nightly news of that day's active shooter situation will automatically retrieve the nightmares from the farthest corners of your subconscious and prevent sleep for days. Your supervisor certainly won't understand why the routine fire drill sends you into panic mode or the tornado siren leads to a full-blown anxiety attack, but your brain is incapable of separating one campus alert from the next—or a drill from reality. As student affairs professionals, we now serve campuses full of students (and other professionals) who one day went to school unaware that they would be the lucky ones who got to go home that evening.

I was one of the lucky ones.

## THE LUCKY ONES

As a child in Oklahoma City, campus bomb threats became routine occurrences after the 1995 Alfred P. Murrah Federal Building bombing that killed 168 and injured hundreds more. I was too naïve to realize the significance of the bombing or the subsequent school-based threats. I remember vividly my surprise that family members in central Texas called to ensure we were safe, and I will never forget not understanding why my father missed dinner that evening. Like others, he rushed to the building and spent that day triaging patients (including the 19 children) among the rubble and running from a suspected second bomb. I didn't understand, but I do now.

I slowly became obsessed with learning how communities recover from tragic events. I found myself glued to the television each time news broke of another school shooting or terrorism incident. Three weeks into my first year of college, I watched from an Introduction to Mass Communications class as the World Trade Center towers crumbled and later traveled to New York for a post–September 11 community service trip. Surrounded by my student affairs cohort, I sat in a master's-level Culture and Organization of Higher Education class watching the Virginia Tech tragedy unfold. These stories took hold of me, although I could not explain why. It was always something that happened to other people.

Fewer than two years into my student affairs career, I reported to campus one Friday morning excited about the rare ability to wear jeans to the office. A service–learning trip to the local food bank was on schedule for the day. The typical Friday restlessness increased with a not-unfamiliar fire alarm, providing welcome time to chat with a work friend outside while we waited for security to ensure that there was not, in fact, a fire. As my colleagues and I re-entered the building, I approached the office's front desk to clear the phone alert, confused by the active shooter message on display when I expected fire-related text. The following minutes and hours unfolded like a blur. We sheltered in place as a precaution, quickly reemerging to discuss the events in full Friday office-gossip fashion. Shouting broke our conversation. A large crowd of people approached. In the distance, I heard, "there's a gun." Seemingly as distant, I recall our director telling us to run. Life would never be the same.

In retrospect, we were the lucky ones. Our campus panic that Friday morning was the result of a false alarm, a near miss that could have ended so differently. A well-intentioned employee shared a routine, nationwide safety bulletin, causing each subsequent person to have a slightly more urgent version of the story. A campus safety officer accidentally discharged his weapon while investigating the report. Chaos ensued, and we sheltered under steel desks for 53 minutes. In the chaos, I began to understand more about the nature of higher education administration than I had learned through any formal education experience. I was a student affairs leader on a small campus, so I was quickly charged with representing student interests on a post-incident review committee. I didn't have words for my trauma. Since "nothing happened," I moved forward, but I dreamed every night for a year about an active shooter, always waking just before the gunman found me.

Nearly a decade later, I help students navigate crises (big and small) every day. Fortunately, few educators will face the horror of helping their students recover from an active shooter situation (although the number who will is increasing at staggering rates). But each of us will encounter students—and colleagues—in trauma. We will be unable to provide answers to their deepest questions, and we will at times fail to comfort them when their trauma becomes unbearable. Like countless student affairs colleagues, I have struggled to find words when a student approaches after class asking for guidance about their suicidal ideation because the campus counseling center couldn't offer an appointment for two months. Or when another student e-mails to acknowledge their absence from class, describing how their relative was killed in a shooting at a local religious community center. Or when a campus leader interrupts training to disclose their fear about the previous day's law enforcement shooting of an unarmed civilian. Or in response to widespread, immediate budget cuts that affect my colleagues' future employment. Or when a dear friend and student affairs colleague loses their battle with depression.

More often than not, our role in student affairs is to be all things to all people. We have specific titles, assignments, and silos in which to operate, but our job is to make learning possible. Often, that requires us to address food or housing insecurity, sexual violence response, mental health concerns, social injustice, family issues, and the routine stress associated with "the best years of a student's life." No one prepared me for the realities of this work. I learned about Chickering's vectors, but not about what to do when a student dies by suicide during orientation. I memorized the relevant adult development theories, but I was not prepared to select which of my colleagues were essential or nonessential when budget reductions demanded swift change. Our work is all-encompassing. I have rejoiced at my students' success, mourned for their grief, and spent more nights than I care to admit worrying about the toll it takes on my own health and family. As other authors throughout this book note, my vicarious trauma is very real. And yet, I go to work every day, immensely hopeful for the future and buoyed by my students' belief that their generation will enact great change. Most days, it feels as though my role is to manage trauma (big or small). But in the fleeting moments when it all makes sense, I am reminded that my job—and immense privilege—is to be the finder of joy and the keeper of hope.

## Growth Through Grief

As I neared the completion of my dissertation research on learning through high-profile tragedy, my friend and colleague Kevin Jackson shared his story of responding to the 1999 Texas A&M Bonfire collapse in which 12 students died and dozens more sustained injuries (Jackson shares his story in chapter 2). In reflecting on that heartbreaking time, Jackson reminded me that "we all have a deep hurt and a magnificent hope . . . the hope that we can make things better" (personal communication, April 4, 2014). His words perfectly capture the essence of our daily lives in student affairs. If you stay in the profession long enough—and you do the job well—you undoubtedly develop profound pain for all that you cannot erase. Even on the rare days when you leave the office on time, you spend the evening replaying concerning conversations or agonizing about how to best support a student in crisis. You lose sleep worrying about how you snapped at a loved one, the result of too much stress and not enough time to attend to your own wellness. You wake at 4:30 a.m. but, once again, forgo your morning workout to catch up on e-mail, aware of the anxiety that builds when you ignore your health for the sake of the work. For many of the authors who contributed to this text, the pain may be the result of a newsworthy campus tragedy. For most of us, it is the impact of one more day when we set aside the activities that make us whole to care for the students we deeply love, or simply to complete our assigned tasks in a meaningful manner. We may still be abundantly hopeful about the future, yet merely getting through our daily lives takes every ounce of energy. We care deeply about creating safe spaces for students, but many of us are depleted, exhausted, and barely hanging on. Which then becomes one more thing to worry about.

Following the 2007 Virginia Tech shootings that killed 32 students and faculty, faculty and staff reported experiencing PTSD as frequently as students, although it typically went undiagnosed in their efforts to support students' grief and healing (Sharma, Bershad, & LaBanc, 2010). Student affairs professionals are often the most visible campus leaders during tragedies, and we have a tremendous responsibility to help our communities find meaning when bad things happen. We need to provide meaningful opportunities for reflection and service while monitoring compassion fatigue and signs of PTSD among students, faculty, and staff at the center of crises (Brunson, Stang, & Dreessen, 2010; Sharma et al., 2010). Perhaps most important, as discussed in chapter 8, student affairs leaders must recognize the post-traumatic stress and emotional distress their employees may experience following stressful events (Brunson et al., 2010; Jones, Haley, & Hemphill, 2010; Paterson, 2006; Sandeen, 2006). And while catastrophic events certainly lead to campuswide trauma, student affairs leaders must be aware that the daily stressors of life on campus (e.g., psychological emergencies, conduct violations, student activism) can be just as painful for the individuals charged with response—the impact of a thousand paper cuts in the precise location to create maximum damage. Student affairs teams, as well as the faculty and student staff who support our work, should be given meaningful opportunities to support response and recovery efforts that may facilitate their own healing (Brunson et al., 2010; Sandeen, 2006; Wesener, Peska, & Trevino, 2010). We must allow for the restoration of campus operations, as well as intentional personal wellness time, to fully support community recovery and long-term growth.

In leading the campus community through substantial tragedies (or ones that have the potential to become major events), student affairs leaders are responsible for not just the survival of the campus community, but also the growth and potential learning of all involved individuals. Following the 2008 Valentine's Day shooting at Northern Illinois University, administrators utilized Boyer's Principles of Community to rebuild and move forward from the student deaths (Wesener et al., 2010). While developing a sense of community does not guarantee safety or the absence of tragedy, Boyer's descriptors of an effective collegiate community as purposeful, open, just, disciplined, caring, and celebrative hold great value to student affairs and institutional response teams navigating the heartbreaking task of leading their campus through the days, months, and years following an institution-redefining and life-changing tragedy (Bogue, 2002; Boyer, 1990; McDonald, 2002).

Colleges and universities may learn from previous crises, but the leaders' actual responses will vary based on their relationship with other administrators (both vertically and laterally on the organizational chart), the evolving institutional environment, and the expectations or needs of a range of campus constituents—making the challenge even more difficult to navigate. While as much as 25% of a campus community may experience ongoing PTSD in the wake of an event (Knowles & Dungy, 2010), student affairs leaders have the opportunity—and the responsibility—to guide their campus through a process of post-traumatic growth. As both a complementary and an opposite response to PTSD, post-traumatic growth results in positive and beneficial changes of feelings and general worldview (Bratkovich, 2010).

Post-traumatic growth is often confused with a simpler understanding of resilience, but instead the former "refers to what can happen when someone who has difficulty bouncing back experiences a traumatic event that challenges his or her core beliefs, endures psychological struggle (even a mental illness such as post-traumatic stress disorder), and then ultimately finds a sense of personal growth. It's a process that 'takes a lot of time, energy and struggle'" (Collier, 2016). Achieving post-traumatic growth is not easy, but in many ways it embodies our work as student affairs professionals. Tedeschi and Calhoun's (2004) five domains of post-traumatic growth include increases in appreciation of life, intimacy in relationships, personal strength, recognition of opportunities, and spiritual development (see also Bratkovich, 2010). In particular, individuals who are simply aware of the potential for post-traumatic growth are more likely to experience that growth, rather than feel caught in the fear of post-traumatic stress (Green, 2011; Seligman, 2011). As student affairs leaders, we have both an opportunity and an obligation to utilize models like Boyer's (1990) Principles of Community and Tedeschi and Calhoun's (2004) outcomes of post-traumatic growth to guide students, faculty, staff, parents, alumni, and other campus constituents through the difficult process of coping with tragedy, injury, death, or perhaps simply more subtle stress, in an environment previously assumed to be safe (Bratkovich, 2010; Ferraro, McHugh, & Dreessen, 2010; Wesener et al., 2010).

## COMPASSIONATE LEADERSHIP

While facilitating post-traumatic growth occasionally shows up through the national spotlight of heroic educators in worst-case scenarios, the vast majority of student affairs professionals do not serve in a vice president for student affairs role and will never have global media attention focused on their decisions. We work as residence hall directors, graduate assistants, student activities coordinators, health center providers, orientation directors, and academic advisors. We may supervise a team of undergraduate student leaders, but most of us are not yet leading entire divisions of student affairs. We complete our work to the best of our ability, often unable to provide broader context on the campuswide response or address the behind-the-scenes efforts underway within the division. Each day, we search for opportunities to move forward with grace, hold space for the trauma in the room, and honor our students' and colleagues' efforts to find a sense of peace for themselves and the community. Every day requires everything we have.

In my 15 years in the field, I have encountered one very public "near miss" active shooter nightmare and a daily barrage of individual student nightmares. On our first meeting, I held a young woman's hand during a sexual assault nurse examination. I responded to three suicidal ideation calls from one student in a three-day span. I prompted resident assistants to action when a campus alert announced a bomb threat on Columbia University's New York City campus, just hours after the Boston Marathon bombings. I served on a universitywide team to implement policies and communications related to the concealed carry of guns on campus. I postponed daily lesson plans to talk with students when bullet shell casings were found outside our classroom building. I, like so many others in student affairs, attempted to help students and colleagues make meaning of the 2016 presidential election and 2017 changes to immigration policies. And, as we do, I maintain the normal scope of my assigned responsibilities, few of which relate to the crises that emerge on a daily basis. Choosing this work day after day requires enormous compassion to navigate the unprecedented challenges we face—as well as the sensitivity to recognize our own compassion fatigue.

In the days following the September 11 terrorist attacks, questions about the tragedy's immense impact led to an even more meaningful truth. Researchers at the Compassion Lab recognized that "the managerial rule books fail us at times like these, when people are searching for meaning and a reason to hope for the future" (Dutton, Frost, Worline, Lilius, & Kanov, 2002, p. 1) and began to identify strategies for leading through traumatic circumstances. The Compassion Lab team discovered that "there is always grief somewhere in the room" (Dutton et al., 2002, p. 7) and outlined a framework for compassionate leadership, which seeks to help leaders and organizations support their constituents who are experiencing pain, whether it is the result of a medical diagnosis, the death of a loved one, a strained relationship, or a national tragedy. They identified leadership conditions to move beyond empathy toward action and to support organizational growth amid chaos. Leading through compassion creates conditions in which "people know they can bring their pain to the office, they no longer have to expend energy trying to ignore or suppress it, and they can more easily and effectively get back to work" (Dutton et al., 2002, p. 7). Through compassionate leadership, we create a context for meaning and a context for action, giving our students and teams space to process their experiences, contribute in meaningful ways, and grow as a result.

Compassion is, quite simply, the work of student affairs—the "intent to contribute to the happiness and well-being of others" (Hougaard, Carter, & Beck, 2018 para. 2). Institutions and leaders that demonstrate compassionate leadership "have better collaboration, lower turnover, and employees who are more trusting, more connected to each other, and more committed to the company" (Hougaard et al., 2018 para. 1). In the midst of trauma, tragedy, or simply unusually stressful situations, student affairs leaders demonstrate compassionate leadership through the scope, scale, speed, and specialization of the support they offer individuals (Cufaude, 2002). In the daily crises we encounter, compassionate leadership involves recognizing that our team members carry immense burdens as they serve students, creating conditions for trauma-informed approaches to student intervention (which Terry Martinez describes in chapter 5), and removing distractions that prevent us from personalizing efforts for the student or colleague in need of support. It may mean providing the student with options for their path forward or allowing a staff member to take time midday to exercise, meditate, or attend family events. In worst-case–scenario crises, compassionate leadership requires us to empower our teams to make these decisions, advocate for individual victims' needs, redirect staff efforts to serve as case managers, or support student leadership of campus vigils and memorials.

As the student affairs leaders in this book will attest, compassionate leadership is a multifaceted effort. While they cared for their campus community, triaged student needs, and worked to restore university operations, their colleagues, neighbors, and loved ones provided the compassion they needed to continue—school uniforms for their children, e-mails of gratitude from former students, warm meals after excruciating days, a safe bed during a citywide evacuation. And, as every student affairs professional knows and few of us consistently practice, compassionate leadership must begin with compassion for ourselves—sufficient sleep, nutrition, exercise, and time for activities that renew our souls and extend our capacity (Hougaard et al., 2018). Often, we demand this time for our staff but fail to practice compassion for ourselves, eventually subjecting our team to the unmanaged stress, exhaustion, and burnout that we can no longer control. If we are to truly create sustainable, compassionate environments where learning thrives, we must do better.

## Moving Forward

We are, as my incredible colleague Shane Lopez (2013) wrote, in the business of "making hope happen" (p. vii). Lopez (2013) believed deeply in four truths: "Hope matters, hope is a choice, hope can be learned, and hope can be shared with others" (p. 13). Often, our days in student affairs feel like never-ending triage. Who needs our help the most? Which fire do we extinguish first? If our days go as planned, we move from meeting to meeting, quickly eat a snack while running across campus for a program, make an appearance at two evening events, and return e-mails from home after everyone else has gone to bed. Even on the good days, we tend to ignore personal needs, recognizing that our lives will (at least in the short term) be easier if we just get the work done. Unexpected student or administrative crises derail our days and distract our vacations. The constant barrage begins to take a toll on our personal health and the quality of our work: "Leaders who are burned-out, fearful, or demoralized tend to shut down their own thinking. They struggle to solve old problems or deal with the crisis of the moment, leaving little energy for coming up with fresh ideas or flexible plans. With blinders on, they are more concerned with surviving the now than with preparing for the then" (Lopez, 2013, p. 183). When our lives are constant triage, we begin to lose the ability to respond strategically, demonstrate compassion, and remain fully engaged. If we are truly to create environments for learning and safe spaces for students, we must begin to redefine what it means to make hope happen.

Throughout my research on learning from tragedy, student affairs leaders told stories of unbearable pain and immense hope. Those who shared their stories experienced the darkest days in the history of our profession, and they emerged with a deep sense of hope that their experiences would help other campuses, student affairs leaders, and students find safer communities in the future. I had the immense privilege of sitting with them, sharing their pain, and learning more about the field of student affairs than any textbook ever provided. Just weeks after the 2013 Boston Marathon bombings, I listened as one student affairs leader described his message to students—and our ultimate charge as student affairs leaders: "Fear in an academic way is about ignorance . . . lack of curiosity . . . indifference . . . not having the constructs to deal with different perspectives. . . . All that's fear. That's highbrow fear. And hopefully we know that we can wrestle that with a deep understanding of what it means to be a human being who loves other human beings. . . . I'm firm that love is stronger than fear." When nightmares become reality, students expect us to provide meaning, safety, and a calm path to navigate the chaos. Our role is to guide them through the pain and uncertainty that come with social injustice, personal grief, and community tragedy.

Student affairs is, ultimately, the business of making hope happen. We may serve in residential life, counseling services, campus recreation, or the career center, or as the dean of students or vice president for student affairs. Our days rarely resemble our job descriptions. Regardless of title, we are charged with teaching our students—and ourselves—that "each time a man stands up for an ideal, or acts to improve the lot of others, or strikes out against injustice, he sends forth a tiny ripple of hope, and crossing each other from a million different centers of energy and daring, those ripples build a current which can sweep down the mightiest walls of oppression and resistance" (Kennedy, 1966, p. 4). This work is so very hard. There are days—most days—when it feels as though I will barely make it to the end of the day. The decisions are immense, time away from the office is too rare, and students' concerns are more complex than anything I experienced as an undergraduate. There are no easy solutions or quick answers for dismantling systems of oppression, protecting our students from harm, or restoring a sense of peace to learning. I do know that our work will only become more complex and that the coming years will bring challenges and turmoil for which we are currently unprepared. As student affairs leaders, we must begin to think differently about how we care for ourselves, model healthy lifestyles for our students, and expand our capacity to live such triaged lives. Only in doing so will we be able to show our campuses, our students, and—perhaps most important—ourselves that "tragedy is the author of hope" (Bolman & Deal, 2011, p. 37).

## References

Bogue, E. G. (2002). An agenda of common caring: The call for community in higher education. In W. M. McDonald (Ed.), *Creating campus community: In search of Ernest Boyer's legacy* (pp. 1–20). San Francisco, CA: Jossey-Bass.

Bolman, L. G., & Deal, T. E. (2011). *Leading with soul: An uncommon journey of spirit*. San Francisco, CA: Jossey-Bass.

Boyer, E. (1990). *Campus life: In search of community*. Princeton, NJ: Carnegie Foundation for the Advancement of Teaching.

Bratkovich, K. L. (2010). *The relationship of attachment and spirituality with posttraumatic growth following a death loss for college students* (Doctoral dissertation). Retrieved from ProQuest Digital Dissertations Database. (Publication No. 3422262)

Brunson, J. E. I., Stang, M., & Dreessen, A. (2010). Essential student affairs services in a campus crisis. In B. O. Hemphill & B. H. LaBanc (Eds.), *Enough is enough: A student affairs perspective on preparedness and response to a campus shooting* (pp. 107–114). Sterling, VA: Stylus.

Bump, P. (2018, May 18). 2018 has been deadlier for schoolchildren than for deployed service members. *The Washington Post*. Retrieved from https://www.washingtonpost.com/news/politics/wp/2018/05/18/2018-has-been-deadlier-for-schoolchildren-than-service-members/?noredirect=on&utm_term=.5585dc2019e6

Collier, L. (2016, November). Growth after trauma: Why are some people more resilient than others—and can it be taught? *Monitor on Psychology, 47*(10), 48.

Cufaude, J. B. (2002, April). Crisis leadership. *NACUBO Business Officer,* 51–56.

Dutton, J. E., Frost, P. J., Worline, M. C., Lilius, J. L., & Kanov, J. M. (2002). Leading in times of trauma. *Harvard Business Review, 1,* 54–61.

Everytown for Gun Safety. (2019, January 22). *Gunfire on school grounds in the United States*. Retrieved from https://everytownresearch.org/gunfire-in-school

Ferraro, R. J., McHugh, B., & Dreessen, A. (2010). Violence in the shadow of the ivory tower: Murder at the university. In B. O. Hemphill & B. H. LaBanc (Eds.), *Enough is enough: A student affairs perspective on preparedness and response to a campus shooting* (pp. 1–38). Sterling, VA: Stylus.

Green, S. (2011, March 3). Post-traumatic growth and building resilience. *Harvard Business Review*. Retrieved from https://hbr.org/2011/03/post-traumatic-growth-and-buil

Hougaard, R., Carter, J., and Beck, J. (2018, May 15). Assessment: Are you a compassionate leader? *Harvard Business Review*. Retrieved from https://hbr.org/2018/05/assessment-are-you-a-compassionate-leader

Jones, J. R. I., Haley, K. J., & Hemphill, B. O. (2010). Incorporating words of wisdom into the crisis management process. In B. O. Hemphill & B. H. LaBanc (Eds.), *Enough is enough: A student affairs perspective on preparedness and response to a campus shooting* (pp. 163–174). Sterling, VA: Stylus.

Kennedy, R. F. (1966, June 6). *Day of Affirmation speech*. Retrieved from http://www.rfksafilm.org/html/speeches/unicape.php

Knowles, C., & Dungy, G. J. (2010). The emotional health and violence connection: Prevention, intervention, and resiliency. In B. O. Hemphill & B. H. LaBanc (Eds.), *Enough is enough: A student affairs perspective on preparedness and response to a campus shooting* (pp. 39–52). Sterling, VA: Stylus.

Krishnakumar, P. (2018, May 18). Since Sandy Hook, a gun has been fired on school grounds nearly once a week. *Los Angeles Times*. Retrieved from http://www.latimes.com/projects/la-na-school-shootings-since-newtown

Levine, A., Cureton, J. S., & Levine, A. (1998). *When hope and fear collide: A portrait of today's college student*. San Francisco, CA: Jossey-Bass.

Lopez, S. J. (2013). *Making hope happen*. New York, NY: Atria Books.

McDonald, W. M. (2002). *Creating campus community: In search of Ernest Boyer's legacy*. San Francisco, CA: Jossey-Bass.

Paterson, B. G. (2006). Voice of the supervisor. In K. S. Harper, B. G. Paterson, & E. L. Zdziarski (Eds.), *Crisis management: Responding from the heart* (pp. 59–63). Washington, DC: NASPA–Student Affairs Administrators in Higher Education.

Sandeen, A. (2006). Voice of the vice president. In K. S. Harper, B. G. Paterson, & E. L. Zdziarski (Eds.), *Crisis management: Responding from the heart* (pp. 64–67). Washington, DC: NASPA–Student Affairs Administrators in Higher Education.

Seligman, M. E. P. (2011). Building resilience. *Harvard Business Review*, *89*(4), 100–106.

Sharma, M. M., Bershad, C., & LaBanc, D. (2010). Counseling during a campus-wide crisis. In B. O. Hemphill & B. H. LaBanc (Eds.), *Enough is enough: A student affairs perspective on preparedness and response to a campus shooting* (pp. 83–106). Sterling, VA: Stylus.

Tedeschi, R. G., & Calhoun. L. E. (2004). Posttraumatic growth: Conceptual foundations and empirical evidence. *Psychological Inquiry*, *15*(1), 1–18.

Wesener, K. S., Peska, S., & Trevino, M. (2010). Healing your community. In B. O. Hemphill & B. H. LaBanc (Eds.), *Enough is enough: A student affairs perspective on preparedness and response to a campus shooting* (pp. 115–134). Sterling, VA: Stylus

# The Editors

**Marijo Russell O'Grady** has been a student affairs leader and practitioner for more than 30 years, developing her professional identity at public, private, and religiously affiliated universities. She has been quoted in *Business Officer Magazine* and *The Chronicle of Higher Education*, and provided input on ECAR-EDUCAUSE Center for Applied Research Post-9/11 Emergency Response and Business Continuity at Pace University and New York University (ECAR Case Study 2007). She holds BS and MS degrees in art education with a concentration in art therapy from State University of New York College at Buffalo, and a PhD in higher education administration from New York University. Since 1998, Russell O'Grady has served as the associate vice president/dean for students at Pace University's New York City campus; she also owns www.innovativecollegesolutions.com, a consulting company.

**Katie L. Treadwell** researches and writes extensively about the aftermath of university crises and the subsequent experiences of campus first responders. Her work has appeared in *The Chronicle of Higher Education, Encyclopedia of Strategic Leadership and Management, Journal of Student Affairs Research and Practice, About Campus*, and other higher education publications. She has more than 15 years of experience in student affairs administration, including significant roles in crisis response, residential life, sexual assault prevention, suicide prevention and response, alcohol risk reduction, and mental health outreach. Treadwell currently leads student conduct and community standards at The University of Kansas. She holds undergraduate degrees in journalism and religion, a master's degree in higher education administration from Baylor University, and a doctoral degree in adult learning and leadership from Teachers College, Columbia University.

# The Authors

**Rachel Alldis** serves as the assistant dean of students and director of residential life at Mount Holyoke College. She earned her bachelor's degree in communications from Bradley University in Peoria, Illinois, and her master's degree in college student personnel at Miami University in Oxford, Ohio.

**Lee E. Bird** recently retired as the vice president for student affairs at Oklahoma State University (OSU)–Stillwater where she led numerous functional areas, including the student union, campus life, university counseling, university health services, career services, dining, residential life, and the department of wellness. She is also an adjunct professor in OSU's student development graduate program and serves as the chair of the OSU Behavioral Consultation Team. Bird received her PhD from the University of Arizona in 1991 and has worked in some aspect of student affairs for more than 40 years.

**Thomas Grace** is semiretired from a long career as an administrator and faculty member, most of which was spent at New York University. He continues to serve as a member of the faculty of the Counseling and Educational Leadership Program at Montclair State University, teaching graduate courses online. He holds a DEd from the Department of Counselor Education, Counseling Psychology, and Rehabilitation Services at The Pennsylvania State University; an MS in counseling from the University at Albany, State University of New York (SUNY); a BA in American history from SUNY Cortland; and an American Bar Association–certified diploma in paralegal studies from New York University.

**Marcella Runell Hall** serves as the vice president for student life and dean of students at Mount Holyoke College. She has a bachelor's degree in social work from Ramapo College of New Jersey, a master's degree in higher education administration from New York University, and a doctoral degree in social justice education from the University of Massachusetts, Amherst. Hall is the author of numerous publications; her most recent book project, co-edited with Kersha Smith, is titled *Uncommon Bonds: Women Reflect on Race and Friendship* (Peter Lang, 2018).

**Kevin P. Jackson** serves as the vice president for student life at Baylor University and has more than 30 years of higher education experience. He earned his doctorate in educational human resource development from Texas A&M University, his master's in higher education administration from the University of Denver, and his bachelor's in journalism and business from the University of North Texas.

**Jeffrey C. Jordan** is vice president for student life at Seattle Pacific University. He earned a bachelor's degree in sociology from Houghton College, a master's degree in education from the State University of New York College at Buffalo, and a doctorate in education with a focus on leadership succession from Seattle University.

**Terry Martinez** has served as a student affairs administrator for nearly 30 years. She arrived at Hamilton College in August 2017 and serves as the vice president and dean of students. A native New

Yorker, she holds a master's degree in applied psychology from New York University and a bachelor's degree in social work from the State University of New York College at Buffalo.

**Deb Moriarty** has served as the vice president for student affairs at Towson University since 2004. Since joining the university, she has received *The Daily Record's* "Maryland's Top 100 Women" Award, Maryland/DC Campus Compact's Institutional Leadership Award, and the Baltimore County Commission for Women's LaFrance Muldrow Woman Making a Difference Award. She earned a BS in recreation and leisure education from Southern Connecticut State College, an MS in college student personnel from Southern Illinois University, and a PhD in higher education from the University of California, Los Angeles.

**Greg Sharer** has worked in student affairs for over 30 years and has served as the vice president for student affairs at SUNY Cortland since June 2008. He holds both a Bachelor of Arts in social studies education and a Master of Science in educational administration and policy studies from the University at Albany. He earned his law degree from the Indiana University Robert H. McKinney School of Law and is a certified attorney mediator with the Indiana Bar.

**Todd M. Smith-Bergollo** serves as the assistant dean for students and director of student development and campus activities on the New York City campus of Pace University. He earned his undergraduate degree in mathematics and secondary education from SUNY Geneseo and his master's in higher education administration from New York University. He has been working in student affairs in New York City for over 20 years.

**Santiago Solis** joined Towson University in 2007 as associate vice president for student affairs. He completed his BA in history at the University of California, Berkeley; his MA in history at Brown University; and his EdD in curriculum and teaching at Teachers College, Columbia University. Solis serves on numerous boards and committees to improve the overall quality of programs and services for incoming and returning students.

**Kimberly C. Thornbury** serves as vice president at The King's College in New York City, overseeing enrollment, marketing, communications, financial aid, and strategic planning. She studies and writes about college student development and is working on a graphic novel with tips and advice for new professionals. Thornbury graduated from Messiah College and holds an MA in higher education administration from the University of Louisville and a PhD in higher education administration from Regent University.

**Laura Avitabile Wankel** is the senior advisor for strategic initiatives to the senior vice provost for educational innovation at Northeastern University. She has been on the editorial boards for the *Journal of Student Affairs Research and Practice* (formerly *NASPA Journal*), has served as a consultant and editor for a number of education-related projects and publications, and has presented on issues in higher education both nationally and internationally. She holds a BA in U.S. history from SUNY Oneonta, an MEd from the University of South Carolina, and an EdD in higher education administration from Teachers College, Columbia University.

# Index

## A

Active shooter scenarios, 6, 36, 166, 223, 238–240, 242–243, 248. *See also specific shootings*
Activism, 7, 111–136
    bias incidents and, 122–125
    communication and, 118–120
    diversity and, 111–114, 120, 122–123
    embracing student activism and, 120–121
    free speech and, 7, 112–114
    history of, 111
    knowledge of students and, 115–118
    leadership and, 119–120
    lessons of, 114
    media and, 118–120
    policy development and, 121–125
    professional development and, 127–131
    responses to, 112
    return of, 111–112, 113–114
    social justice and, 113, 125–127
    student affairs and, 7, 112, 113–114, 118, 120–121
    student leaders and, 113, 120–124
    at Towson University (TU), 112–135
    trauma and, 123
    VPSA and, 119–120
    well-being and, 131–135
Alldis, Rachel, 197
American Counseling Association (ACA), 182
American Psychological Association (APA), 181
Americans with Disabilities Act (ADA, 1990), 153
Amos, Wally, 69
Astin, A. W., 198, 212
Astin, H. S., 198, 212

## B

Barth, Sandy, 82
Bias incidents, 122–125, 205–206
Bird, Lee E., 67
Bolman, L. G., 15
Bonfire collapse at Texas A&M (1999), 20, 23, 26, 29–35, 38, 182, 225, 244
Boyer, E., 246–247
Branstetter, Olin, 77

Brown, Michael, 114
Budke, Kurt, 77
Burks, Suzanne, 70–71, 76–78
Burnout
    compassion and, 250
    definition of, 180
    leadership and, 108–110
    student affairs and, 8
    trauma and, 187, 245

## C

Calhoun, L. E., 247
Callahan, Steven, 12
Clark, Geri, 43, 192
Collective efficacy, 193–194
*College and Community Joint Commission Final Report* (2014), 147
Collins, J. C., 158
Collins, Taylor, 79, 87
Communication
    activism and, 118–120
    communication plans, 61
    crisis response and, 52, 56–57, 60–61, 147–148
    faith and, 217
    partnerships and, 151–153
    well-being and, 158–162
Compassion
    burnout and, 250
    compassion fatigue, 179–180, 187–188, 245, 249
    compassion satisfaction, 179–180, 187, 191
    crisis response and, 12, 13, 16, 31, 42
    leadership and, 38, 247–250
    self-care and, 250
    student affairs and, 249
    student leaders and, 126–127
    trauma and, 37
Compton, Dennis, 68–69
Cortaca 2013, 137, 139, 141–144, 147–150, 153–154
Council for the Advancement of Standards in Higher Education, 200
Cox, Laverne, 125
Crisis response, 5, 175–196

communication and, 52, 56–57, 60–61, 147–148
compassion and, 12, 13, 16, 31, 42
consequences of crises and, 178–181
counseling and, 56–58
emergency first responders and, 47
experience and, 47–48
fact-finding and, 46
failure and, 51
faith and, 51–52, 197–200, 208–210, 213–216
family and, 46
first responders and, 178–179, 194
frameworks for, 229–237
impact of crises and, 177–178
leadership and, 47, 51, 61, 177–178
learning from trauma and, 224–225
media and, 45–46, 52, 60
organizational politics and, 184–186
partnerships and, 13–16, 42, 56, 60–64, 137–140, 149–150
patterned reactions in, 178
peers and, 230–231
preparation and, 15, 41–42, 184
prevalence of, 67–68
priorities in, 143–145
responsibility and, 46–47, 51
second responders and, 181–187, 194
self-care and, 51
skills and, 49–50, 229–230
stress and, 16
student affairs and, 13–14, 43
trauma and, 177–179
volunteers and, 47
VPSA and, 142–146
well-being and, 50, 178–179

## D

Deal, T. E., 15
Death. *See also* Suicide
international students and, 82
regret and, 177
trauma and, 20, 25–26, 31–32, 176–177
Deferred Action for Childhood Arrivals (DACA), 7
DiLorenzo, M. F., 212
Diversity
activism and, 111–114, 120, 122–123
benefits of, 12
bias incidents and, 122–125, 205–206
faith and, 214
partnerships and, 140
race and, 114, 120, 129–130, 135, 200
student affairs and, 11–12
Dowdy, Renee Piquette, 17, 186–187
Doyle, Glennon, 8–9

## E

Ennis, Ariel: *Religious Literacy*, 214
Ethnicity. *See* Diversity

## F

Fair Housing Act (1968), 153
Faith, 197–220
bias incidents and, 205–206
case studies of, 202–208
communication and, 217
crisis response and, 51–52, 197–200, 208–210, 213–216
definition of, 198–199
diversity and, 214
importance of, 208–209, 219
increase of, 197, 199–200
leadership and, 211–217
learning from trauma and, 227
mentoring and, 217
models of, 201–208
partnerships and, 216–217
pastoral care and, 211–212
programs for, 199–201, 214
resources for, 201–208, 211–217
roles and, 198–200
self-care and, 218–219
sharing personal beliefs on, 210–211
spirituality and, 198
students and, 201–208, 219
trauma and, 201, 213
VPSA and, 202–204
well-being and, 201, 212, 217–218
Faith Zone, 201, 214
Family, 46, 69, 70–75, 79, 95–98, 102–103, 104, 158–159
FERPA (Family Educational Rights and Privacy Act), 7, 152–153
Fire at Seton Hall. *See* Seton Hall fire (2000)
Free speech and First Amendment, 7, 88, 112–114, 133

## G

Garner, Eric, 114
Good, Joshua, 58
Grace, Thomas, 175
Grey, Freddie, 114
Grief. *See* Trauma

## H

Hall, Marcella Runell, 197
Halligan, Jim, 70, 73, 74, 76
Hargis, Ann, 81–82
Healing, 27, 34, 51–52, 57, 73, 82–84, 191–194, 213
Hierarchy of Needs (Maslow), 159, 185

Homecoming tragedy. *See* OSU Homecoming tragedy (2015)
Hurricane Katrina, 182
Hurricane Sandy, 42, 44, 58–61, 198

# I

*In loco parentis*, 5
Islamophobia, 201

# J

Jackson, Kevin P., 19, 244
Jacobsen, D., 198–200
Jacobsen, R. H., 198–200
Jordan, Jeffrey C., 157

# K

Kerr, Clark, 43
Kilcrease, Mitch, 77

# L

Leadership
    activism and, 119–120
    burnout and, 108–110
    collaboration and, 62
    compassion and, 38, 247–250
    crisis response and, 16, 47, 51, 60–64, 177–178
    de-escalation and, 62
    faith and, 211–217
    position authority and, 61
    preparation and, 15, 62–63
    responsibility and, 62
    student affairs and, 119–120
    training and, 62
    volunteers and, 47
Learning from trauma, 221–238. *See also* Trauma-informed frameworks
    case studies and, 222–225
    creativity and, 232–233
    crisis response and, 224–225
    faith and, 227
    flexibility and, 233–234
    forgiveness and, 236–237
    forms of, 221–222
    framework for crisis and, 229–238
    natural disasters and, 225–229
    peers and, 230–232
    positivity and, 234–236
    strategy and, 233–234
Lee, B., 39
*Letters to a Young Poet* (Rilke), 17–18
Lindholm, J. A., 198, 212
Lopez, Shane, 251
Lucas, Nash, 80

# M

Mackin, Mary Beth, 88
Martin, Trayvon, 114
Martinez, Terry, 91
Maslow, Abraham, 159, 185
McDermott, Annette, 215
Media
    activism and, 118–120
    crisis response and, 45–46, 52, 60
    partnerships and, 146–149, 154–155
    social media, 116, 118, 138, 146–147
    trauma and, 31–32, 147
    VPSA and, 143, 148
    well-being and, 162, 169
Mentoring, 4, 108–109, 113, 115, 117, 133, 217
Moriarty, Deb, 111–112
Mothers Against Drunk Driving (MADD), 5

# N

Nakal, Nakita, 80, 82
Nance, Brian, 86–87
NASPA–Student Affairs Administrators in Higher Education, 200–201
National Transportation Safety Board (NTSB), 74–75
9/11 attacks. *See* September 11, 2001 terrorist attacks
Noonan, Peggy, 231

# O

O'Grady, Marijo Russell, 1, 5–6, 9, 14, 41–42, 53, 58, 60–61
Oklahoma City Bombing, 7, 68, 241
Oklahoma standard of care, 68–69, 72
Organizational politics in crisis response, 184–186
OSU Homecoming tragedy (2015), 77–87
    anniversary of, 85–87
    closure and, 83–85
    counseling and, 79, 83
    crisis response and, 77–79
    death and, 82
    early stages of, 78
    faith and, 83, 86
    family and, 79
    media and, 78
    memorials for, 82–85
    trauma and, 80–81
OSU plane crash (2001), 69–76
    background of, 69
    Colorado memorial for, 74–75
    counseling and, 73–74, 76
    crisis response and, 69–72
    early stages of, 69–70
    family and, 70–72, 74–75

Gallagher-Iba arena memorial, 74–75
*Kneeling Cowboy* statue and, 76
leadership and, 70–72
memorial service for, 72–74
mental health and, 73–74
partnerships and, 72
second crash (2012) and, 76–77
stress debriefing and, 73
trauma and, 70–72, 74

## P

*Pace Remembers 9/11* (film), 58
Pace University. *See* September 11, 2001 terrorist attacks
Partnerships, 137–155
    advocacy and, 140
    attorney-client privilege and, 152
    communication and, 151–153
    conflict of interest and, 146
    crisis response and, 13–16, 42, 56, 60–64, 137–140, 149–150
    diversity and, 140
    faith and, 216–217
    importance of, 137–140, 154–155
    integrity and, 146
    legal counsel and, 150–154
    media and, 146–149, 154–155
    presidents and, 140–146, 149
    public relation director and, 146–150
    student affairs and, 64
    trust and, 151–152
Peers, 160, 230–232
Pet therapy, 81–82
Plane crashes. *See* OSU plane crash (2001); September 11, 2001 terrorist attacks
Plutchik, R., 189
Post-traumatic stress disorder (PTSD), 35, 41, 179, 181–182, 238, 240, 245–247
Preparation
    continuity back-up plans, 56
    crisis response and, 15, 41–42, 184
    leadership and, 15, 62–63
    liability insurance and, 14
    student affairs and, 41–42
    thinking ahead and, 43
    trauma and, 41–42
Principles of Community, 246, 247
Professional development, 9, 33–34, 127–131
Pulse Nightclub shooting (2016), 178

## R

Race. *See* Diversity
Religion. *See* Faith
Reserve Officers' Training Corps (ROTC), 5
Resiliency
    student affairs and, 8–9, 16, 223
    trauma and, 19, 23, 37–38, 42–43, 247
Responsibility
    aspects of, 14
    crisis response and, 13–14, 46–47, 51
    leadership and, 62
    liability insurance and, 14
    mistakes and, 14
    responsibility charts, 13
    student affairs and, 1–3, 9, 15, 63–64
    trauma and, 21–22, 28, 183–184
Retreat for Social Justice (RSJ), 125
Roosevelt, Eleanor, 64

## S

Sandeen, Arthur, 237
Schmitz, Leo, 80
Schuster, Saunie, 88
Scott, Walter, 114
Self-care
    compassion and, 250
    crisis response and, 51
    faith and, 218–219
    student affairs and, 2–3, 9, 64
    trauma and, 35–39
September 11, 2001 terrorist attacks
    background to, 53
    collective efficacy and, 193–194
    communication and, 56–57
    continued importance of, 44, 47
    counseling and, 56–58
    crisis response and, 5–6, 42, 47, 54–56, 184
    early stages of, 53–54
    faith and, 198–200
    partnerships and, 56
    trauma and, 58, 175–176, 189, 249
Seton Hall fire (2000), 44–58
    common humanity and, 52
    context of, 45
    crisis response and, 45, 49–50
    early stages of, 44–45
    emergency first responders and, 47
    faith and, 45, 51–52
    leadership and, 47, 51
    media and, 45–46
    mental health and, 50
    outpouring of support after, 48
    responsibility and, 46–47
    self-care and, 51
    skills and, 49–50
    stratified approach to, 49
    student affairs and, 47–48
    volunteers and, 47
Shackleton, Ernest, 10–11
Sharer, Greg, 137
Smith-Bergollo, Todd M., 197

Social justice, 113, 125–129, 134, 214, 243, 252
Solis, Santiago, 111
*Spirituality in College Students' Lives* (Rockenbach & Mayhew), 199
*Spirituality in Higher Education* (UCLA), 199
Stone, Bonnie and Marvin, 82–83
Stress debriefing, 73, 191
Student affairs
    activism and, 7
    burnout and, 8
    compartmentalization in, 108
    competition in, 185
    crisis response and, 13–14, 43
    criticism in, 186
    de-escalation and, 15
    demands of, 8–9, 14–15, 41
    diversity and, 11–12
    entering field of, 4–7
    evolving nature of, 4–8
    experience and, 47–48
    faith and, 201, 219
    freedom of speech and, 7
    gender-based violence and, 7
    hope and, 251–253
    importance of, 24–25
    leadership and, 119–120
    lessons for, 11
    as lifestyle, 16
    limitations in, 4
    mentoring and, 4
    partnerships and, 64
    personality and, 14–15
    politics and, 7
    professional development and, 9
    redefining work of, 16–18
    resiliency and, 8–9, 16, 223
    responsibility and, 1–3, 9, 15, 63–64
    roles and, 14–15
    self-care and, 2–3, 9, 64
    skills and, 42
    stressfulness of, 9, 14, 157–158, 185–186
    student leaders and, 4–5
    substance use and, 7
    teamwork and team-building in, 12–13, 17
    trauma and, 41, 179, 243–244, 246–247
    as triage, 3–4, 10, 63–64, 253
    trust and, 64
    unpredictability of, 8–10, 91–92, 172
    well-being and, 7, 10
    work-life balance and, 16–17, 188
Student leaders
    activism and, 113, 120–124
    compassion and, 126–127
    student affairs and, 4–5
    trauma and, 24, 27
Suicide, 20, 147, 176, 179, 238

Sutton, Eddie, 70

## T

Texas A&M Bonfire collapse (1999), 20, 23, 26, 29–35, 38, 182, 225, 244
Thornbury, Kimberly C., 221
Title IX, 7
Towson University (TU), activism at, 112–135
Trauma, 19–41. *See also* Learning from trauma
    activism and, 123
    agency and, 21, 36
    anger and, 26
    aspects of, 37
    avoidance and, 22
    burnout and, 187, 245
    collapse and, 29–35
    common reactions to, 187–191
    community and, 246
    compassion and, 37
    continuum of potential negative impact of, 22, 22*f*, 36–38
    coping strategies for, 189–191
    counseling and, 34
    crisis response and, 177–179
    death and, 20, 25–26, 31–32, 176–177
    direct trauma, 181–182, 187, 194
    empowerment and, 38
    family and, 26
    "going there" emotionally and, 19, 34, 37–38
    grief and, 28, 31–32
    growth through, 244–247
    guilt and, 34, 37, 183
    healing and, 191–194
    increase in, 240
    lessons for, 89
    life-altering events and, 25–29
    media and, 31–32, 147
    memory and, 23–24
    motivation and, 34–35
    patterns in, 36
    persistence of, 176
    post-traumatic stress disorder (PTSD) and, 35, 41, 179, 181–182, 238, 240, 245–247
    professional development and, 33–34
    professional settings and, 179
    reason and, 35–37
    recovery as journey from, 193
    resiliency and, 19, 23, 37–38, 42–43, 247
    responsibility and, 21–22, 28, 183–184
    self-care and, 35–39
    stress over time and, 179, 186
    student affairs and, 41, 179, 243–244, 246–247
    student leaders and, 24, 27

trauma "because of me," 28–29, 36
trauma "through me," 28, 36
trauma "to me," 25, 28, 36
vicarious trauma, 165, 181–182, 194
VPSA and, 182–183
well-being and, 27–28, 187, 194, 245–246
Trauma-informed frameworks, 91–136. *See also*
    Learning from trauma
    application of, 106–107
    bullying and, 104–106
    burnout and, 108–110
    case studies using, 98–106
    compartmentalization and, 108
    counseling and, 95
    death and, 92–93
    family and, 95, 96–98, 102–103, 104
    holistic nature of, 95–97
    illness and, 96–98
    mentoring and, 108–109
    past situations and, 104–105
    peers and, 106
    as person-centered response, 94–95
    roles in, 93–95
    self-care and, 94, 109
    self-determination and, 102
    substance abuse and, 102
    suicide and, 92–93
    therapy, distinguished from, 107
    trauma and, 100
    usefulness of, 94–106
    well-being and, 94–95, 99–100, 108
Treadwell, Katie L., 1, 239
Triage
    learning to, 10–16
    life as, 1–18, 20, 22
    limitations in, 4
    living a triaged life, 8–9
    meaning of, 3–4
    medical triage, 3–4
    reflection in, 4
    skills and, 4
    student affairs as, 3–4, 10, 63–64, 252–253
    trauma and, 37

## V

Valent, P., 189
Vice President of Student Affairs (VPSA)
    activism and, 119–120
    awareness required of, 141–142
    blame and, 186
    collaboration and, 62–63
    conflicts of interest and, 145–146
    crisis response and, 142–146
    de-escalation and, 61–62
    faith and, 202–204

guilt and, 183
media and, 143, 148
mindset of, 62
multi-tasking by, 63
partnerships and. *See* Partnerships
roles and, 61–62, 138
students and, 119
trauma and, 182–183
volunteers and, 63
Virginia Polytechnic Institute shootings (2007), 182, 186, 245

## W

Wankel, Laura Avitabile, 41
Well-being, 9, 157–174
    acceptance and, 167–169
    activism and, 131–135
    adjusting to a new routine and, 165–167, 172–174
    anniversaries and, 168
    assessment of, 170–172
    commencement and, 168–169
    communication and, 158–162
    crisis response and, 50, 157–159, 160, 161–163, 166–167, 173, 178–179
    death and, 162–163, 168–169
    details and, 160–161
    emotion and, 158–160
    faith and, 201, 212, 217–218
    family and, 158–159
    hierarchy of needs and, 159
    importance of, 157–158, 167, 173
    leadership and, 161–162, 165
    media and, 162, 169
    memorials and, 167–168
    new normal and, 163–165
    planning and, 161–163
    professional development and, 170–172
    residential life and, 168
    resources for, 161–162, 164–165
    roles and, 158
    stability and, 164
    student affairs and, 7, 10
    student life and, 172–173
    surprises and, 169–170
    symbols and, 166–167, 170
    transition out of crisis and, 163–167
    trauma and, 27–28, 165, 169–170, 187, 194, 245–246
    variability in, 159

## Y

Youth for Western Civilization (YWC), 113–114, 119, 132